Alfred J. (Alfred John) Morris

The open secret : sermons dealing mostly with the heart of christ and christianity

Alfred J. (Alfred John) Morris

The open secret : sermons dealing mostly with the heart of christ and christianity

ISBN/EAN: 9783741172922

Manufactured in Europe, USA, Canada, Australia, Japa

Cover: Foto ©Andreas Hilbeck / pixelio.de

Manufactured and distributed by brebook publishing software (www.brebook.com)

Alfred J. (Alfred John) Morris

The open secret : sermons dealing mostly with the heart of christ and christianity

THE OPEN SECRET;

Sermons

DEALING MOSTLY WITH THE HEART OF CHRIST AND CHRISTIANITY.

BY THE LATE
REV. A. J. MORRIS,
FORMERLY OF HOLLOWAY.

LONDON:
ARTHUR MIALL, 18, BOUVERIE STREET, E.C.
1869.

CONTENTS.

—:o:—

		PAGE
I.	THE SECRET OUT; OR, THE UNCONSCIOUS CONFESSION	1
II.	FAITH IN THE CHAMBER AND FAITH IN THE WORLD	18
III.	CHRIST ALONE WITH HIS DISCIPLES; OR, THE PARABLE EXPOUNDED	33
IV.	THE TRANSFIGURATION OF CHRIST; OR, THE REDEEMING MAJESTY OF THE SON OF GOD	51
V.	THE FAMILY AT BETHANY; OR, NATURAL VARIETIES IN RELIGION	74
VI.	THE APPARENT NEGLECT OF SELF-DENYING LOVE	94
VII.	CHRIST AT A GRAVE	108
VIII.	CHRIST AT JACOB'S WELL; OR, THE TWO FOUNTAINS	127
IX.	CHRIST SEEKING AND SAVING THE LOST	142
X.	ENOCH; OR, THE EARTHLY WALK AND THE HEAVENLY HOME	162
XI.	AFFLICTION CONSIDERED AS PUNISHMENT	181
XII.	THE DIVINE REJECTED IN THE COMMON	198
XIII.	CHRIST LEFT SORROWFULLY	212
XIV.	THE LOVE OF GOD	229
XV.	REST AND PROSPERITY OF CHURCHES	248
XVI.	CHRISTIANITY, A VOICE TO THE PEOPLE	268
XVII.	THE DEVIL IN CHURCH	290

PREFACE.

—:o:—

IN presenting to the friends of the late Rev. A. J. Morris the following Sermons as a memorial of his ordinary preaching, the publisher deems it of importance to state that, beyond authorship, their author is responsible only for the title which the volume bears. The selection and correction of the Sermons for the press were made after his death, and it must ever remain doubtful whether he intended that they should assume the permanent form which is now given to them. In a little book for children, which Mr. Morris published at the close of last year, he promised to collect into a volume, under the title of "The Open Secret," fifteen Sermons. Want of health, and the demands which it made upon his time, prevented his doing more than write the advertisement, which was gladly welcomed by all who had known him. After his death, which occurred unexpectedly, and from home, the following Sermons were found among his papers, collected with others, into a parcel, and manifestly reserved for perusal and consideration. The first, bearing the title which had been announced for the volume, could leave no doubt that it was intended for publication. The selection of the remainder was a task of some difficulty, which, now it is made, leaves a fear lest it is not that which he would have approved. The selection was determined partly by the recollection of references he had occasionally made in conversation to subjects on which he had preached, and by the desire to present a memorial of his ordinary public ministry, which should convey to those who were unacquainted with him a just view of him as a religious teacher, and which should be to the many who knew him a means of preserving the image they so much desire to cherish.

It is to be feared that the critical reader will discover a few blemishes in the construction of some of the sentences, and some instances in which the thought is indistinctly or infelicitously expressed. It is believed that such inaccuracies will be forgiven, when it is known that nearly all of these Sermons were written for immediate delivery, and with the haste which is the condition under which the preacher labours. None of them were composed with a view to publication, and the revision which they have received has been chiefly confined to the correction of verbal errors. Those who have read a volume of sermons, entitled, " Words for the Heart and Life," published by Mr. Morris some years ago, will not need to be told that his style was singularly clear and beautiful. The present volume bears sufficient evidence of its author's high mental and spiritual endowments, so that, though an explanation may be due to the critic, no commendation is needed for the work.

BIOGRAPHICAL SKETCH.*

THE following sketch is an effort to reproduce and present within narrow compass, impressions, feelings, and reflections which a friendship extending over a period of twenty-five years has cherished with special tenderness. It has been undertaken on the suggestion of a friend whose wishes, expressed or understood, have almost the authority of a law with those who know him. The task thus imposed has been, however, a labour of love; for memory will ever hold among its richest treasures the materials it has had to use, and though a present sense of bereavement casts around them now the dark shadow of a great sorrow, they will ever bear with them a balm of healing and of solace, their abiding presence being not merely the relish of past joys, but the foretaste of future enjoyment.

The life of our deceased friend, Alfred John Morris, furnished but few incidents for narrative. With the particulars of his early history we have only a slight acquaintance. He was born in the spring of 1814, at Hampstead, in a house which was pleasantly situated for prospect, but scarcely had he entered on the more receptive years of childhood when his parents removed their residence to a village in Gloucestershire. The surrounding country was of a character well calculated to exercise an abiding influence on a susceptible mind, and being strongly tenacious of early impressions, his

* *Reprinted (with slight alterations) from the* CHRISTIAN SPECTATOR *for February*, 1869.

thoughts in after life reverted with feelings of tender attachment to the scenes where Nature taught him the first lessons of which he had any distinct recollection. There was the quiet of lovely valleys and the solitude of wooded hill sides and sunny slopes, with clear prospects far reaching towards the setting sun. The hum of prosperous trade mingled there with the music of running brooks and the sweet song of birds. A spirit of religiousness, moreover, pervaded the district where Whitefield had, within the memory of many then living, preached to countless numbers of eager inquirers, and had planted in sequestered spots his tabernacles for the worship of God. Amid such scenes there was everything to enrich the ear and the eye, and to feed the soul with thoughts that had a flavour of heaven about them. The dawning faculties of the youth opened up lovingly in response to influences so genial and formative, and while his childhood was blessed with the visitation not merely of playful fancies, but grave reflections, he acquired very early the powers of evolving thought out of the materials of self-consciousness, as well as the habit of self-communion in relation to the deep things of spiritual life.

Mr. Morris was not quite eighteen years of age when he made an engagement with a Mr. Edkins, of Nailsworth, to take charge of the junior classes in his school, in return for which he was to receive assistance in the pursuit of his own studies. Here his powers were certainly well taxed, for Mr. Edkins engrafted on his school work the more arduous work of regular preaching. This latter was to him, however, a congenial exercise, and to it he devoted himself with an eagerness, energy, and success which foreshadowed the career of the future preacher. In incessant labours of this nature, ten months were passed, but their action on a mind of such native resources was like that of the ploughshare on virgin soil; and evidences in manuscript still remain of the golden quality of the sheaves which he had even then garnered. While residing at Painswick, whither he had removed about this time, and while he was still undecided in the choice of a profession, the Independent Church at Warrington, whose pulpit happened to be then vacant, was induced by the representations of a friend, who had knowledge of Mr. Morris's capabilities, to request his services as a temporary supply. His visit resulted in an invitation to become the pastor, which the inherent modesty of his nature, and a deep sense of the responsibilities involved in its acceptance, would not allow him to entertain without considerable hesitation. Finally, however, he consented, and henceforth his undivided energies were consecrated to the work of the ministry. Transplanted thus into a new soil, his whole character and intellect underwent some important modifications in the course of their development. The quiet and seclusion of the lovely valleys and sunny hills of the more genial south were exchanged for the bustle, squalor, and general unattractiveness of a district which industry had selected as the scene of its busiest exertion and most diversified labours. He was thrown into intimate intercourse and relationship with men, some of them of his own age and of great natural intelligence, whose faculties, sharpened by the commercial pursuits in which they were engaged, were just then stimulated to still higher and more general activity by the political excitement generated in connection with the passing of the Reform Bill. Whatever the spiritual vitality of the Church was at that time, the powers of the young preacher must have been tested and exercised to the utmost in obtaining toleration and acceptance for truths and modes of their presentation, which, being the result of independent inquiry, conducted by a mind of singular freshness and originality of thought, could not but startle by their novelty of aspect a people whose creed had been cast in the strictest mould of a rigid Calvinism. But these larger demands, made on him in such new circumstances, served to deepen the hold in his own mind of convictions which had assumed greater definiteness and consistency, and to expand very considerably his capabilities for wider usefulness. His toil for five years was incessant, and even excessive; but the burden of it was lightened by being shared with one who, for the remainder of his life, in joy and in sorrow, in days of the darkest gloom and seasons of brightness, proved a steadfast helpmate and a loving wife: and now lives widowed to deplore her irreparable loss.

There is little to say of his settlement in Salford, whither he removed to become the pastor of Windsor Chapel, except that, under the pressure of circumstances while there he was induced to give to public and political matters an amount of attention which he was otherwise indisposed to bestow on them, through being almost totally absorbed in the work of the ministry. Throughout the whole of the manufacturing districts and the country at large the iniquitous corn-laws had just at this time produced wide-spread desolation and despair, and he felt, in common with his professional brethren generally, that in the interests of humanity he was bound to render the service of pen and speech to obtain their abolition. He attended the great conference of ministers held in Manchester in 1841 for the furtherance of that object, and delivered himself an able lecture on the subject, which was afterwards published. Several of his own friends connected with his Church and congregation were severe sufferers from the collapse and panic with which commercial enterprise had been thus disastrously smitten throughout the district; and this circumstance, together with the declining health of his family from the unsuitableness of the climate, determined him to seek in southern regions for another sphere of labour. He had lived now nine years in Lancashire—five of them in Warrington and four in Salford. They were an eventful period of our history. The mind of the country was in a state of continuous fermentation. It was prolific in thought, energetic in action, and generous in purpose. Mr. Morris was affected by the general movement; his powers rapidly expanded under its influence. Without the aid of academic instruction, he had been able to hold his own in circumstances of no ordinary difficulty, and in zealous devotion to his work to fix his faith, though oft perplexed by doubt. He was now a man of ripened faculties, abundant labours, and manifold experience. He was fit for any post.

The Congregational Church of Holloway was fortunate in being at this time in full possession of its prerogative of choice, and in having the grace to exercise it wisely by its selection of Mr. Morris. In 1842 he received and accepted the invitation to become its pastor. A. J. Morris, of Holloway, was henceforth the name by which, for the succeeding twenty years of his life, he was to be widely known, by which he was honourably associated with the sphere of his most efficient ministerial services, and by which now his friends will like most to distinguish him. Of the work he was enabled to accomplish during these years it would be wholly impossible to convey an adequate idea. The Church was certainly in no flourishing condition when he became acquainted with it. The chapel in which it worshipped was an erection entirely destitute of outward attractiveness; it was undistinguishable in its obscure situation from the private dwellings surrounding it, unless by an aspect of settled gloominess; and in its internal arrangements there was nothing of comfort or convenience to which the most austere religionist could take the slightest exception. It was indeed, as an abode for religion, altogether dreary and dismal; but with Alfred Morris a new spirit took possession of its inner sanctuary, and a new fire was kindled on its altar, so that the house of gloom soon wore an air of cheerfulness, and being enriched with the opulence of his thought and speech, became the centre of attraction to an appreciating audience. But not content with the work thus auspiciously begun, he very early inspired his people with the resolve to raise a fitting temple for the service of God, and under the guidance of him who had given a new beauty and value to worship, a chapel was erected on a site central and appropriate, in the best style of Gothic architecture, distinguished by its chaste and simple elegance, which was capable of affording ample accommodation to the increasing audience which he was rapidly gathering around him. But all this was not achieved without an occasional encounter with difficulties, which it required the utmost firmness and forbearance to surmount. Of the Church proper there were not a few inveterately wedded to old forms of doctrine and old modes of practice. Truth, in any other garb than the one in which they were accustomed to receive it, was apt to be looked on by them as a hobgoblin of heresy, and they had a preternatural power of scenting out the things which were marked down in the catalogues of the orthodox as common and unclean. It was scarcely possible that Mr. Morris should altogether escape the suspicions of this class. His antecedents were not of a character to win their confidence, and it was in their nature to be troublesome when they could not be satisfied. We have sometimes thought that the buzzing and biting of these ecclesiastical gnats gave our friend a disproportionate amount of annoyance: their attacks were never formidable, and in due time ceased to disturb him altogether.

It was very favourable, though not essential, to the success of Mr. Morris' ministry that he should have a large area from whence to draw the materials of his congregation. He was a man of marked powers and individuality, and could not be popular: still there was an adaptation in the spirit and range of his teaching to the requirements of persons of very different degrees of mental development, and of great diversity of religious character. Strong thought was in him pervaded and mellowed by the flavour of devotional feeling; weighty argumentation was lightened and enlivened by illustration and homely remark; quaint humour and quiet irony occasionally employed their implements of striking antithesis and happy alliteration with most effective force. Sobriety of judgment tempered, if it did not quite subdue his pre-disposition to the speculative. He was thus endowed with a power of attractiveness of a highly diversified character, and this power he cultivated assiduously. It was habitually exercised under the controlling influence of the idea he had formed of the proper functions of the preacher. The ordinance of preaching he held to have been divinely instituted with a view to provide for the sustenance and growth of our spiritual natures. It was designed to quicken in us a religious life by the action of saving and vital truth on the intellect and the heart. Instruction was the common need of all, and the truth had "to be shown and fitted to souls possessing every kind of inward characteristic and outward lot." The sympathies of the preacher require to be comprehensive in their range, quick to embrace all variety of moral and spiritual condition.

Mr. Morris was in no small degree able to realize his ideal. At the time we first knew him his congregation was composed of persons among whom there existed a great diversity of tastes, tendencies, and pursuits. It would be easy to enumerate men of the highest moral and intellectual order, of great literary attainment, and professional eminence, who were regular attendants on his ministry. With the students of the Dissenting colleges, as a class, he was a great favourite. They generally formed a portion of his audience, and he was ever mindful of the possible influence he might exercise on them in the direction of the rightful performance of the duties of the office to which they aspired. But while these, and all, however highly educated, were refreshed and strengthened by the bountiful provisions of his sanctified intellect, it was always with him a matter of primary concern that the souls of the humblest and lowest mental condition should find nourishment from his ministrations. This comprehensiveness of aim, however, valuable as it undoubtedly was, had its drawbacks; and to our mind the chief excellence of his preaching consisted in the deep impression which it produced of the thoroughness of his belief in what he taught. The Book was to him a living Book—emphatically the Book of Life; and the lessons he learned from it, he taught in the full conviction that they were essential to the growth in man of godliness and grace. The attacks of modern criticism were wholly ineffective to disturb a faith which in him was nourished at its lowest roots by the felt sufficiency of the Scriptures to satisfy the spiritual necessities of his own nature at its deepest need. The truths he learned there constituted for him the essential and vital elements of the Gospel, and his thorough belief of them was felt to be the real source of his power as a preacher. Exception might be taken occasionally to his method of dealing with Scripture. Much which he deduced from passages selected as topics of discourse may have been the product rather of the action of his own spiritual intuitions on them, than of careful exegesis. Still, all this by no means detracted from the impression that his highest aim as a teacher was to subordinate his own mind to the mind of God, as revealed in the Bible, and that he spake with authority, because he had himself seen and felt what he delivered. Very marked and memorable too was the relation which his preaching invariably bore to the business of every-day life. Of doctrines in their abstract form, or in the mutual and qualifying relation as parts of a system, he discoursed but little; but with facts, especially those which formed the material of the Evangelical narratives, and of which doctrines should be the development, he dealt as ever present living powers. The great passages of Christ's history he regarded as symbolical of His spiritual work and mission, having *now* a relation to the life of the Church and of the individual as real and immediate as when they were first enacted; their potential significance in such relation having been made abundantly manifest in the experience of our regenerated humanity in the ages past, while it has been reserved for the generations still to come, to reveal in yet fuller measure the life-giving power which dwells in them unexhausted and inexhaustible. Great stress he laid on the fact that the personal element had been employed so largely for the purposes of revelation; drawing from it the great practical inference that eminent spirituality was essential to the exercise of power over the hearts and minds of men, and that personal religion was an indispensable condition of the Church's growth and prosperity. Another quality which distinguished Mr. Morris' preaching in an eminent degree was that of suggestiveness. His sermons abounded with pungent sayings and pregnant aphorisms worthy of Fuller or Feltham. In no stinted measure did he dispense the best and largest results of his thinking, through the apprehension that in enriching others he was impoverishing himself. He was constantly putting his hearers into positions of advantage whence they might pursue for themselves subjects of inquiry independently of his help and guidance. The aim and effect of his preaching were to make men think—to remove the scales which hindered intellectual vision—to pour light into the inner chambers of the soul, and to awaken faculty into full vigour of action. We must make the remark, however, that in our judgment his discourses would have gained much in cumulative force, had he taken more pains to maintain in them a continuity of argument, and if he had not presented his thoughts in a somewhat fragmentary form, through too strict an adherence to the model traditionally prescribed for the construction of sermons.

One other feature of Mr. Morris' pulpit services deserves, we feel, special commendation and remark. There was a felt oneness about them which gave them a peculiar impressiveness. Each one seemed to be the product of one seminal thought, which, brought into full light by the sermon, was perceived to have pervaded the prayer with its spirit, and to have presided over the selection of the hymn, the anthem, and the Scripture lesson. Thus these, in virtue of the special functions pertaining to them, were made to afford mutual help in working out some one great spiritual result, and each truth thus variously expressed and presented found readier entrance into the inner chambers of heart and mind. We have been often led ourselves to anticipate the selection of the text by the tone and thought which ran through the introductory parts of the service. But the prayers always preserved their identity, and never assumed the quality of the sermon. They were the natural outflow and overflow of thoughts and feelings which grew out of and gathered round the subjects discussed, from their being felt to have vital relationship to man's eternal interests—thoughts and feelings fitting for devotion, free from all subtlety and entanglements, "refined, spirituous, pure;" "the bright consummate flower" which meditation grafted on the stock of truths whose roots were planted deep in our spiritual nature. Not unfrequently several services in succession were characterized by this unity—the prayer-meeting expressing the higher devotional temper and the finer practical issues to which the preacher and people had been alike wrought up and touched by the previous Sabbath exercises. Participation in such worship was a privilege which even now, after the lapse of years, it is a refreshment to think of as having been once an actual possession. It enabled one to realize, in a fulness of measure which may never be vouchsafed again, that strength and beauty did indeed dwell in the sanctuary of God. The "lively" oracles gave forth responses there which moved to virtuous resolves and high endeavour. The Sabbaths of those days were looked forward to with a keenness of anticipation which prepared the soul to appropriate their hoarded delights, and not a few of them abide in memory still, as seasons of golden opportunity, when, moved by the joy of elevated thought, the power of sympathy was quickened and expanded, and individual consciousness was absorbed in the communion of saints.

Our well-beloved friend was a man of beautiful presence: in the pulpit especially it was impressive and even commanding. An air of solemnity, softened by tenderness, surrounded him. His noble forehead, of three-storied dimensions, was built up on a brow which high intelligence had unmistakably made its favourite abode. His eye, bright and bountiful of love, looked pensively out on the phenomena of life surrounding him, as if striving to penetrate their wondrousness and their mystery. The lines of the delicately-moulded mouth and chin indicated firmness and refinement, with a subtle sense of the ludicrous; and his voice, whose tones throughout every variety of modulation sounded musically in our ears, was an organ fully adequate for the distinct and appropriate expression of the thoughts and feelings committed to its utterance. Such was A. J. Morris when we knew him in the prime of his manhood, and for the twenty years of his ministerial service in Holloway, such he was to his people, who loved and revered him as a pastor and a friend. Much occupied with his own musings, Mr. Morris was naturally disinclined to engage much in social intercourse; but he was a man of a really companionable nature, fitted for and keenly relishing the society of congenial minds. In his happier moods his conversational powers showed to advantage, as he abounded in the resources of anecdote, humour, ready reply and profound observation. But that special quality by which he touched most sensibly and deeply those with whom he was intimately associated was his marvellous power of sympathy. There was an outflow of tenderness in the expression of the eye, the tones of the voice, and the impressive grasp of the hand, which sufficed to soften the keenest anguish, and to inspire the fainting spirit with strengthening hope.

Our observations on the character of Mr. Morris's ministry have been protracted to such a length, that we have but little space left to do more than very briefly indicate his position relatively to matters and movements lying beyond the sphere of his immediate work. That position was determined by the predominant influence of two leading ideas. He held firmly that the full and free development of individual life was an essential condition of human progress in religion—in moral, intellectual, and political well-being. Also, with still firmer grasp, he held that Churches were spiritual institutions, organized exclusively for the promotion of spiritual ends and purposes. He could not help, therefore, being a Nonconformist, and he was so eminently and thoroughly in his teaching. But he was strongly averse to personal involvement in any political movement, lest the character of the Church as a purely spiritual institution should be in any measure compromised by his action; and his dread of undue interference with the liberty of the individual made him unfriendly to the multiplication and growth of all sorts of associations. It was as much as he could do to tolerate one which had for its distinct object the advocacy and dissemination of the very principles which he regarded as truths of primary importance. His Protestantism perhaps partook too strongly of an historical element to allow of an undeviating adherence to those principles on all occasions. Popery he regarded with intense detestation and dread, and though he could not vindicate, he would not condemn the employment of gentle force in dealing with an enemy of so subtle and dangerous a character.

On his merits as a writer we should like to descant, but must be content with furnishing two or three extracts as specimens of what may be found in his published volumes. The first is the opening paragraph of a noble sermon entitled, "Christ, the Spirit of Christianity;" it is a fair specimen of the elevation of style reached by Mr. Morris, when moved by the expansive power of a lofty thought.

"Most men accustomed to strenuous mental effort, especially if endowed with a high order of imagination, occasionally find themselves in a condition in which they are conscious of the presence of certain objects without being able clearly to discern them. The mind, like the body, may be in a scene which it cannot well see. It may be aware of the vicinity of glorious things, and yet have no distinct conception of their form and features. It may come into contact with a great idea, but, being in the dark, may know only that it is something, without knowing exactly what. A due sense of sublimity may be quickened in the soul, apart from the direct exercises of understanding, having more to do with sympathy than with sight, with love than with logic. So it seems to have been sometimes with the Apostle Paul. In reading his writings we occasionally meet with the marks of such an experience. The Spirit of God charged him with thoughts of surpassing majesty, and working them out with the fervour of a holy excitement, he was sometimes carried beyond the limits of a definite conception, and led to the use of expressions which reveal and convey rather sensations of the heart, than notions of the intellect. There are passages which exhibit the fruits, not of logical processes, but the friction of an inspired imagination. These are not to be dealt with by the criticism of words or systems. You might as well attempt to weigh the atmosphere in common scales, as estimate things so ethereal by the help of lexicons and grammars; and after the utmost application of the rules of literal interpretation, that man will most appreciate and most enjoy them, not whose memory is best stored with verbal learning, but whose heart is best filled with Paul's divine ideas, and he will be reverently gazing upon a glory, while others are irreverently looking out for a doctrine."

The trenchant vigour which marks the utterance of an unpalatable, though necessary truth, in the following passage is most striking:—

" There is no obligation anywhere to maintain an inefficient, and especially a spiritually inefficent, ministry. The ends of God are not answered in filling so many pulpits, and sustaining so many churches. Numbers have no mystic virtues here. Ministers are to be weighed, not counted. We are persuaded that the best policy, as well as the best principle, is to let the truth of things come out. To patch up institutions, to paint sepulchres, to cover a certain amount of surface, to uphold a certain amount of machinery, is worse than useless. Speaking literally, there are just as many ministers as there are right ministers—no more; speaking practically, there are not so many, if there be more. Men who are wanting in the sterling qualities of able ministers of the New Testament—who make no impression on the world— whose official position is kept up chiefly by successive expedients —who are more indebted for it to the backing of brethren than their own power—who are as often thinking of removing from, as remaining in, stations—men of this kind are doubtless of no value to any denomination. They may reckon in a manual or register, but they reckon not otherwise, ' true zeros, nothing in themselves, but much in sequence,' and something has to be deducted on their account from other men's labours, before the true worth and weight of a ministry can be appreciated. We say, then, that if the point were, which we do not believe it is. that if the ordinary kind of ministers are not received into our colleges and churches, there must be none received at all, there is nothing in the conclusion to alarm or distress us. Be this as it may, the question we put to the congregations of Nonconformists is this —Shall there be a ministry among us, having 'the spirit of power'?"

The following is a sketch of John Foster's character from Mr. Morris's little volume, called "Glimpses of Great Men," which an appreciative critic once gave as an admirable portrait of himself:—

"He could not build the 'house' of great conclusions on the 'sands' of common report and familiar faiths. He could not 'believe' simply because of the 'sayings' of others—he needed to hear for himself. Naturally gifted with the powers of profound reflectiveness, intensely interested in the gravest problems of humanity, and providence, and God, and, withal, too conscious of his own dignity and claims as a *man*, and as the man *John Foster*, to like or bear the thought of being made the victim of imposition and falsehood—thus endowed and thus prompted, his investigations were conducted with much care and nicety. He could not be content with shows and seemings, even of the clearest, fullest form—was not to be satisfied with the shells awarded to serious thinkers by the moral monkeys of the world. He weighed each portion of moral merchandize, rang each piece of mental coin, scrutinized each vote tendered for truth. A proposition uttered to him, the first effect was not belief, but inquiry; a fact stated, and he 'asked questions.' Prevailing opinions, received theories, common customs, were fair matters, he thought, for examination; many of them, alas, he found for *post-mortem* examination! And the things that were discovered to be true and genuine were not the goal of his investigations. They could not be received as ultimate realities. They were surfaces, counters, windows, locks, indicating, representing, revealing, opening truth, which was always to him the 'great deep,' 'the true riches,' 'the inner room,' 'the hid treasure.' The process was of course slow, but the results were blessed; and he might well 'like his mind for its necessity of seeking the abstraction upon every subject.' Such a man's life is to be estimated according to the number—not of his nights and days, his eatings and drinkings, his walkings and restings—but his thoughts and feelings, his ponderings and solicitudes, the 'visions of his head,' and 'the searchings of his heart.'"

Bright and beautiful were the last twelve months of the

life of which the preceding sketch is but a faint and feeble reflection. Dark clouds of despondency had for some few years mysteriously wrapped him round, obscuring the fair prospect which opened before him upon his removal to Bowdon: a place, perhaps, yielding only to a metropolitan pulpit in its capacities for furnishing material worthy of so gifted a worker. These were at length mercifully rolled away, though the dread disease which had occasioned them, and whose lurking presence was not detected till too late, was the cause of increasing physical suffering. His spirit shone out with a brightness and a tenderness which transcended all that we had known of him previously. We looked forward with hope and joy to his return to the labours in which his soul delighted, and were even favoured with an earnest of his resuscitated powers, refined, chastened, elevated by the trials through which he had passed. But this blessedness was not in store for us. The Master summoned him to higher service, and with a heavenly smile upon his lips he entered into rest.

The rehearsal of these reminiscences has had its pleasures, which have been subdued, however, by a deeper sadness. It was very sorrowful to reflect that almost all that was valuable in one who was loved so dearly abides with us now only among the treasures of memory. But it was a happiness to feel that we could, in some measure, still hold communion with the spirit of our friend as in the days that are gone, and that in taking leave of this sketch, which is offered as a tribute to his memory, we do not suffer the bitter pang of feeling that we are now bidding him a final farewell.

> " He is not dead, whose glorious mind,
>   Lifts thine on high;
>   To live in hearts we leave behind,
>   Is not to die."

Bowdon.   JOHN KINGSLEY.

THE SECRET OUT;

OR,

THE UNCONSCIOUS CONFESSION.

Gen. iii. 11.—"*And he said, Who told thee that thou wast naked?*"

THE celebrated George Canning is credited with the saying that "there is nothing so false as statistics, except facts;" and W. S. Landor observes that "fiction is always true." These paradoxes, like all such things, are but striking ways of expressing very simple and common sentiments; and their untruthfulness is the measure of their force. A dexterous and unusual use of words gives an appearance of originality and independence to thoughts familiar to all that think at all; and what at first sight seem almost philosophical discoveries, resolve themselves into the well-worn common-places that human testimony is often unreliable, and a great deal of truth may be set in an imaginary framework. It is the *representation* of facts that is so unfounded; it is, not the incidents of fiction, but the views of nature and society that are more or less correct.

Such modes of speech are useful in attracting attention to truths apt to be forgotten. Nowhere are people carried away more by words than in connection with fact and fiction. There are many who have a perfect horror of fiction, and an idolatrous reverence for facts. That is, their estimate of a story or a book is determined by the circumstance of the narrated incidents having actually occurred or not. It does not matter to them that there is no pretence of historic accuracy, that there is no violation of historic probability, that the things are not professed to have happened, and that there is no impossibility in supposing them to have happened; it is quite enough that they have not. And to such critics the plainest and barest of real events will possess an interest denied to the finest products of genius.

The worth of facts is chiefly in their being the forms and actual embodiments of ideas, and modes and orders of procedure: and these may be exhibited as well in fictitious as in real history. It is the truth which they express that makes them important, and their having literally taken place is only one true thing, and not necessarily of much account. If it be moral truth that is exhibited, what matters it whether the medium be something that has, or something that might have come to pass? If a man reach an eminence whence he can command a magnificent prospect, what does it signify whether he has attained it by artificial or natural means, or whether he has walked or ridden thither? There may be vastly more truth in a fiction than a history—more of the highest and worthiest truth—a fuller representation of the great laws that govern providence, and the great principles that actuate men, the methods and features of the moral government of God, and the varied phases and intricate workings of the human heart: the mystery of evil and of good. The fact may be but a tree—a real object—but in wintry bareness, with trunk and branches; the fiction may be that tree clothed in leafy loveliness, and laden with luscious fruit.

We may apply these thoughts to the study of the Bible. There are those who give a mythic and poetic character to the early records of our race, especially its paradisaic period; there are those who accept them as literal representations of actual occurrences. I am not about to discuss the question which is the true view, or whether both are not true in part. But this we may say, that the amount of truth, moral and religious truth, in the narrative is not dependent on the actual occurrence of the facts described. The value to us is not in the mode and circumstances of Adam's fall, but in the fact that he and all his race have fallen; not in the manner in which evil took form and voice, but in the fact that evil is always coming to us in guileful ways: not in the outward change effected in man's circumstances by sin, but in the fact that it has alienated him from God, made him ashamed of himself, and turned every garden of joy into a waste wilderness.

What a picture we have of the desolating, perverting, cursing consequences of sin! You have been sometimes rejoicing in a summer scene of brightness and beauty, and chirping merriment, when lo, in a brief space, all is changed; the sky is overcast, the song of the birds is hushed, a brisk breeze rattles through the trees, and a chilly gloom envelopes all. Thus was it with Paradise—every object was changed, "the morning was turned into the shadow of death." The bright and graceful creatures of God became objects of disgust and loathing; the blessed relations of life and love, without which even Eden lacked a "goad," became the occasions of censure and crimination; the fair form of man, the noblest material type and temple of the Deity, was associated with fear and sin; and the very voice of the Lord God, to which they had listened as to richest music, made them vainly seek a hiding-place among the trees of the wood; while the noblest spirit of man, "the image and glory of God," could only meet its Maker with a falsehood and absurdity. "And the Lord God called unto Adam, and said unto him, Where art thou? And he said, I heard thy voice in the garden, and I was afraid, because I was naked; and I hid myself. And he said, Who told thee that thou wast naked? Hast thou eaten of the tree whereof I commanded thee that thou shouldest not eat?" My subject is the fact that Adam's excuse was his condemnation; and the first effect of sin was to make him fool and knave.

I.

Adam's *haste to make excuse* proved that he had eaten of the forbidden tree.

The consciousness of evil leads to self-vindication: the consciousness of innocence is slow to suspect a charge. If you ask a man, how he is, and he answers, "I am sober," you are tempted to suppose that he may have indulged too freely: and, if inquiring what he is carrying, he replies that it is his own, you fancy it possible that he has made too free with his neighbour's goods. Why should a man deem it needful to defend himself, unless he is attacked? and if there is no attack from without, is it not likely that there is one from within, and conscience does the office of accuser? We say nothing against a disposition to self-defence. It is a "noble art," and not less so when used to protect the moral, than when used to protect the material, man: as worthy to guard the character as the carcase or the cash. A man ought to to be in readiness to meet a formal charge or virtual impeachment. He should err, if error be necessary, in the way of self-vindication. It is a sign of a mean, base nature to be pre-disposed to the concession of guilt, to hear coolly, and without passion, accusations of sin and wrong, and take no measures, or slow and insufficient ones, to resist and resent them. We ought to be "willing to justify" ourselves; we ought to be anxious to do it, when assailed, and only when it is impossible, should we resign the task, and then with bitter sorrow.

I say "when assailed," but, when not assailed, the eagerness of self-defence is symptomatic of guilt. "He that is first in his own cause seemeth just, but his neighbour cometh and searcheth him." The forward protester was the worst case; his very forwardness comes of a clear or dimmer sense of the unsoundness of his case. It is as it is with hypocrites. They proverbially overdo it. They who strain at, or strain out gnats, generally swallow camels. The consciousness of hollowness leads to extravagance of outward form, and they seek not to express, but to make up for the want of, inward reality. They act always on self-defence. More or less conscious of unworthiness, they feel as if they were always being accused, and the goodness of their defence depended on the measure of outward and visible religiousness.

Adam's eagerness showed his fall. God did not accuse him. He simply asked him where he was. He might have been among the trees innocently enough; he had probably been there before, and God asked where he was, not why he was there. It is a bad sign when such a question cannot be asked without giving the reasons for being there. It shows that the forbidden tree has been eaten.

II.

The excuse which Adam made proved that he had eaten of the tree. He was afraid, and hid himself.

It is useless for us to speculate what notions our first parents must have had of God. It does not look as if Adam was created the finished philosopher and theologian that some have supposed. It savours more of the infancy than the manhood of our race. It looks as if the Divine revelation was such as we are wont to make to children. God appeared in the likeness of flesh, and dealt with him, and spake to him as a man; and Adam thought that he could conceal himself from God among the thick trees, and that there might be some use in telling God lies. But whatever he knew not, he should have known that he had no right to be afraid of God. Fear was no feeling for "man new made." If a child dreads its parent, the child or parent must be wrong. He had not been afraid before. What had made the change? Only eating of the tree. Ah, that was it. He had committed "the offence." With abundance of all kinds, he had coveted the one reserved good: with almost unlimited freedom, he had trespassed on the one forbidden spot. He had broken a law, not which withheld all things but one, but which allowed all things but one; and for the gratification of a single sense in a single mode, he had despised the riches of God's goodness, and defied the terrors of his curse. And when he heard the voice of God (even though he had been insensible till then) it echoed through his guilty soul, and aroused his slumbering conscience, like a voice of doom, and he sought a vain shelter in what might have been a grateful shade. He was afraid of God, because he had sinned against God. It was not his unclothed body, but his naked soul, that frightened him. Whatever occasion of shame might have been furnished by his natural nudity, there was no shame until he made shame. He had not been ashamed until now, and would never have been so but for sin. If he connected any thoughts or feelings, except of honour and purity, with what God had created honourable and pure, he must have undergone a sad deterioration, must have admitted a perverting and polluting influence into his nature. God's work was perfect, and if man saw in it aught of dread or of disgrace, he must have lost his own perfection.

Adam's plea was thus his condemnation. He had

no natural right with the feelings he acknowledged, and urged as the excuse of his conduct. A child afraid of a perfectly good father, one who had made him in his own image, and prepared for him a garden of delights! A creature afraid of God for being in the state in which that God had made him! No better proof were needed of the " broken covenant," and commandment trampled under foot! It is so to-day. Men are still afraid of God. Go where you may, the dark traces of unfilial dread are upon the soul of man. The very religion of man is fear: and its temples are slaughter-houses, and its rites are bloody offerings, and its spirit is dread, dismay, and cowardice. It is the proof of sin, the standing demonstration of the fall, and the nearer he approaches to his Maker the clearer is the evidence of his estrangement and alienation. And all the superstitious dread with which he has invested God's glorious works, his "fear of the signs of heaven," his trembling notice of the occurrences of earth, all are, like Adam's unnatural blush, the sufficient proof that he has sinned against his God..

III.

This leads to a third thing, that guilt is indicated by *morbid moral sensitiveness*.

The worst kind of indelicacy is in being shocked at what is natural and proper, in being so far "better than God." For that indelicacy is in the person that is shocked, not the things that shock. This was Adam's. He was "naked and not ashamed" while innocent. He became, or professed to become, squeamish when he fell. And so it is always. I don't suppose he ever thought whether he was clothed or not till he fell. He needed no artificial protection, and other creatures had none; why then should the thought of garments enter his head? At any rate, we have here a suggestion of truth—that one of the most certain indications of evil is self-consciousness. The normal condition of things and beings is to work out the ends of their existence without attracting or giving attention to the process. The most perfect machine is the smoothest and most quiet in its movements; the measure of noise and friction is the measure of imperfection. The glory of health is to be absolutely unconscious of the animal organism, for brain and heart, liver and lungs, and all lesser and inferior parts, to fulfil their functions without compelling or inviting recognition of their work: for a man not to know that such things are, from their mere operations. A living writer has said, that "if Adam had remained in Paradise, there had been no anatomy, and no metaphysics." Like many sayings of the same great mind, it is an exaggerated expression of an important truth. Healthy activity is concerned with the objects of life, not its processes. The sickly heart may employ itself in self-inspection, but the heart strong in the love and pursuit of good and right has no taste nor time, it has no requirement and no liking for the task. I can imagine that Adam, especially in "the morn and liquid dew" of the world's "youth," was much too happy and too occupied with things without, to think of things within, too busy with the exercise of his senses and his soul to take cognizance of either, too full of delight to think of dissection, as the child somewhat wearies of his toy before he takes it to pieces to find out the secret of its cunning work.

But if the mere self-consciousness intimated something, the consciousness of something *amiss* indicated more. There was no harm in being as God made him; and God could not well be angry with him for that. If harm there was, it must have been imparted. He had no business to "know evil," and would not have done so unless he had become evil. There are ten thousand things in which there is naturally nothing to be ashamed of, but which we have made shameful, and which, by the laws of association, we cannot help awakening emotions of shame within our breast: to which the question might be applied, Whence got you to know that they were so? Take a man fresh from some dark *crime*, the breaking into a house, or the commission of a murder, and if not hardened by criminal habit, mark how his consciousness gives meaning to all that passes in company, and he is as in a room surrounded with mirrors, each one reflecting his own image; and there is something in every common remark, and something in every unconscious look, and something about *himself*. Take a man whose mind is saturated with *vice*, who is well versed with all its forms and terms, who has practised it in every excess, who has got it mixed up with all his modes of thought and feeling, with all times and scenes and companionship; why, the least thing will suffice to suggest vice to him. He is in a state of morbid moral susceptibility, and will take the infection both of the vicious idea and the vicious feeling vastly easier than another. The thoughts of evil, the memories of evil, the prospects of evil, are awakened in him by acts and words of the most natural and innocent nature : and the consequence is that from his very fulness of iniquity, he is more precise and proper in his carriage and his words than those who "are simple concerning evil." "Unto the pure all things are pure, but to them that are defiled and unbelieving is nothing pure, but even their mind and conscience is defiled." Time was when speech was much plainer and freer than it is with us, when grave divines, as well as unregenerate playwrights, talked in a style that would now expel from all respectable society, when they translated God's everlasting word in a way to scandalize all genteel souls ; but who shall say that we eschew their speech because we have improved upon their morals ? Who told us that there needed a clothing for some ideas and things ? Have we eaten of the tree ? " Very nice people," once wrote a dean, " have very nasty ideas:" they are so nice because they are so nasty : their nastiness spoils things good and pure, and then they are ashamed of the good and pure. Like Adam, we want, we have created a necessity for clothing by sinning : and to the wise of heart, what we deem the proof of our refinement and delicacy, is really the consequence of our *knowing too much*. Unsophisticated children are by no means so particular as worn-out debauchees, and pure-minded maidens are often quite a scandal to painfully proper prudes. Adam the sinner was disgusted with the ways of Adam the innocent.

We go further. We not only put evil with innocent things, and then blush for them, but our sinful consciousness makes us ashamed of *our own good.* "Few men have the courage to appear as good as they are," are words found in a book of wisdom. The fact is, that as I once heard one, not a fool, remark, when requested not to bestow his charity on an impostor, "We are all impostors;" or, as a Quaker once said in a public service, and it was all his service, "We do all cheat a little." Hypocrisy is the common property of men: it is only in the subjects and modes and objects of hypocrisy that they differ. Those who are fond of connecting hypocrisy with religion, as if they were inseparable, if not identical, are apt to forget that hypocrisy may be just as easily connected with irreligion. It is as possible for men to pretend to be worse than they are, as to pretend to be better than they are. It may not be as common, but it is in some connections and in some circumstances as natural and habitual. There are few men so bad as not to have some good in them, which they are anxious to conceal. The fact is, that herein lies the rationale of much that seems, to superficial observers, a sad indication of levity and profanity. There are two subjects on which men, and good men too, are very prone to speak in a somewhat light and jocular manner, and when in any but a light and jocular temper. They are the two greatest of all subjects, having most vitally to do with man's character and well-being. They have survived the fall, and indeed have received since the fall, and partly in consequence of it, a new importance and interest: *Love* and *Religion.* Except in set and formal discourse, the habit of man is to touch on these things in a way of humorous and bantering speech. And why? Not because the themes are felt to be vulgar or trifling, but for just the opposite reason. They are too grave for formal recognition and public presentation: too momentous to be introduced into common and familiar talk in a manner answerable to their sacredness and solemnity. The heart is half afraid to face them boldly, and must deal with them incidentally, and as if unawares, giving them the honour of acknowledgment, but not daring to trust itself to an expression of all it feels, feeling, indeed, more than it cares to expose to the eye of every chance beholder, or speak into the ear of every thoughtless listener. But whence this feeling? Why ashamed of our good? Have we eaten of the tree? It is in part the fruit of a *sinful fear;* and in part of the consciousness of our own inconsistency. We are awed by the presence of evil in others; and kept back by the sense of our own, and our good impulses are seized and held by our evil consciousness. This, I believe, is one reason why there is such a backwardness to speak on the most important subjects—I mean religious ones—to others; and why the difficulty is proportioned to our intimacy with them, and their consequent claims upon our care and love. Who has not observed, who has not felt, that it is easier to speak on spiritual themes to strangers than to friends and relatives, to casual acquaintances than to wives and children? At first sight you would say, it cannot be so, but so it is; and it has been a subject of lamentation to multitudes, who have mourned it as the fruitful source of neglect of duty, and to multitudes who have mourned it as the mainspring of unutterable loss. Why is it? They are ashamed of speaking:

and their shame comes from their consciousness of evil. They are so alive to the degree in which they themselves come short of all that they would profess or inculcate upon others—they see such a chasm between speech and practice—that they hold their peace. And the reason why the nearest and the dearest are harder to be addressed than strangers, is because it is felt, though, perhaps, not acknowledged always even to themselves, that they are most aware of the discrepancy of word and deed, of teaching and temper; and the most likely to think, if not to say, " Physician, heal thyself." The same kind of remark applies to the making of what is frequently, but unhappily, called " a profession of religion." There are vast numbers who do not, and never will, make such a profession, and yet they have that within them which would move them to do it, if it were alone. They have that which suggests and craves and would find strength and safety in some recognized position of discipleship. "The things of God" they feel to be the things that are most worthy of avowal before man, and, living as they are, they are dissatisfied with the unharmony and unfitness between their outward and inward life : Do they not love Christ ? The question is an insult to them. Do they not try to live so as to please Him ? They feel no other interest in living. Are they not at home in intercourse and sympathy with the highest themes of truth, and the noblest hopes of souls ? Their wonder is that men can find a home, a rest and joy, anywhere but there. And yet they are but " secret disciples." They keep in their deepest convictions, their strongest impulses, their purest aspirations. They would conceal them as Adam his noble symmetry of shape and form: and their truest, deepest self is a secret to many, and the "world knoweth them not," and their very best being is "the *hidden* man of the heart." Why is it? They have eaten the tree, and their very good has become evil; it is the secret sense of defect, of a sad difference between their actual and their ideal, a fear lest they dishonour the truth and disappoint its friends, that makes them ashamed of appearing as they are. They had not suspected the need of a garment to hide their good, but for the existence of evil. "Who told thee that thou wast naked?" It is no accession of purity that has opened thine eyes to the reality of the impure; it is thy sinfulness working with, and working under, thy goodness, that moves thee to keep thy goodness to thyself.

There are two or three reflections which arise out of the subject, to which I beg your serious heed. The first is that *sin cannot escape from God*. It tried, and it failed. It tries still, and it fails. Adam sought a spot where the eye of God could not penetrate, and found it not. You do the same in substance, and with the same result. Perhaps you deem him the very pattern and parent of absurdity for what he did; but you may be quite as, and even far more absurd. Folly is not according to acts, but to means; and your means of knowing God and His ways are very much beyond his. There are many "trees of the garden" where men still hide themselves, and the branches are very large, and the foliage is very thick, but there is the voice, "Where art thou?" which, in Hebrew idiom, will "walk," that is, become louder and louder, until they are forced to hear it; and vain will be the refuges of lies. We may go farther; with our knowledge of the most High, we say that the sinner not only cannot escape from God's presence, but cannot get out of *God himself.* God needs not to visit him, needs not to follow him, but actually surrounds him, " compasses his path and his lying down."

Sin cannot stand before God. When called to account, it must lie or be silent. It is its very essence to necessitate falsehood and perversion. It is wrong, and it has no proper place in a system of right. It is unnatural, and it cannot fit in with the natural. It is like a broken tooth, and a bone out of joint, and will make itself felt somehow or other. Its inconsistency and uncongeniality will not suffer concealment. Here or there, sooner or later, its dreadful enmity to all things and beings must come out; perhaps everywhere and for ever. It has nothing to say, and its very attempt to say anything makes its case worse. It cannot frame a vindication which is not a condemnation. When charged home to a man, there is nothing for it but confession or falsehood; nothing for it, really, but to throw the blame on God! Adam lied. Adam "charged God foolishly;" if not directly, yet by implication. It is the custom, the necessity of our fallen nature. "The foolishness of man perverteth his way, and his heart presseth against the Lord." It was so from the beginning. "The woman whom *thou* gavest to be with me;" "I was afraid, because I was naked," because I was as thou didst make me. The first human excuse was a virtual divine impeachment. And sin never can excuse itself without condemning

God, and "he that reproveth God, let him answer it!"

Sin may find compassion from God. It was Adam's own fault that he cared for, or knew of, his being naked: yet God took pity on his fault and its consequences. It was his own fault that he needed clothing, yet God "made coats of skins and clothed them." And God has mercy still on those who have "destroyed themselves," and "in him is their help;" help from their own evil, help from things which they have made evil, help from the feelings which their own evil has excited within their breasts. All salvation is of this kind; it is a saving from ourselves. There is no devil in hell from which we need to be saved half as much as from ourselves; and God does it. We have filled ourselves with all evil of guilt, and shame, and fear, and He must give us peace, and boldness, and trust. Blessed truth! we are taught to reason quite otherwise than Adam, and to act in a way exactly opposite to his. We are "afraid," and therefore do *not* hide ourselves; we are afraid, and therefore we seek His face; and our very misery and guilt are the pleas with which we address His mercy: "Pardon our iniquity, for it is great!" And He speaks peace to us, and takes compassion on our poor attempts to shield and hide our sins, and though he leaves us in the wilderness of this world's work and woe, solaces us with His presence and His promise, and, though we still have shame and fear, they are of quite another kind, and from very different sources; for we now "fear the Lord and His goodness," and are silent for "shame," because He is "pacified towards us."

FAITH IN THE CHAMBER,

AND

FAITH IN THE WORLD.

JOHN xvi. 29—32.—"*His disciples said unto Him, Lo, now speakest Thou plainly, and speakest no proverb. Now are we sure that Thou knowest all things, and needest not that any man should ask Thee: by this we believe that Thou camest forth from God. Jesus answered them, Do ye now believe? Behold, the hour cometh, yea, is now come, that ye shall be scattered, every man to his own, and shall leave me alone.*"

NEVER was there such a scene as that in the Paschal Chamber, where Christ partakes the last Passover with His disciples on earth—the Passover which "with desire He had desired to eat"—never was there so solemn an interest, such varied representation of moral nature, such "seeds of things," and seeds of souls. The incarnate Christ on the very threshold of His final agony, the incarnate devil within easy grasp of his final triumph; the human fathers of the future world wondering, questioning, now in doubt and now assured—now almost too full of sorrow for silence, and now lighted up with a gleam of hope; words of counsel and of comfort deeper, fuller of meaning and of sympathy, than this world's air has ever borne but then; and a prayer, which, could prayers be breathed in heaven, were fitter to be uttered there than here—all these things make that upper room and that evening hour the most significant of all.

It has been truly said by Mr. Binney, that "the valedictory addresses and the intercessory prayer of the Son of God are distinguished by extraordinary elevation of thought, by sublimity and pathos of expression. His mind, just before His departure, would seem to have imbibed, in a more than usual degree, the purity and the grandeur of the world into which He was about to pass. As He approaches the Cross, He approaches the Crown too;—as He advances towards the scene of His deepest degradation, He is also advancing towards the seat of His highest magnificence;—and the brightness and splendour of that divine abode appear, as it were, to fall upon His spirit, and to invest it with glory." In His pre-existent state, He "clothed Himself with light as with a garment;" in His transfiguration on the mount, "His countenance shone as the sun, and His raiment was white as the light;" and now, in His last interview with His disciples, though the "earthly tabernacle" puts on no new or luminous appearance, the spirit within, by the greatness and grandeur of its views, appears as if it were wrapped in the mantle which it wore before all worlds, and had resumed its position at the summit of the universe.

These farewell words of Jesus, like all His preaching and more than all His preaching, have a value which not only "speaks to the heart," but which transcends the value of other words. They are more precious than all the uninspired words ever spoken. Speaking of the Father and of Heaven, of love and fellowship, of inward life and victory over the world, and with the solemnity and authority of one who knew and realized and embodied them all, who was the living voice and personal manifestation of all, they are worth more than all the philosophies and theologies of men, the study of which is like hunting rainbows, or eating dead-sea fruit. Coming into that upper room, and listening to Him who was the light and bread of the world—the Leader and the Lamb—giving men His thoughts and Himself —and coming thither from the doubts and dogmatisms, the speculations and scepticisms of the world, is like coming upon a pool of water in a dry and thirsty land, or an outburst of sunshine through dark clouds, or the first sense of solid ground to the shipwrecked mariner struggling for the shore; and as the poor woman mentioned in the gospels, bankrupt in body and in purse, having spent her all on physicians, and being nothing better, but rather worse, found in the touch of Christ's garment more good than in all her doctors, so we, worried and mocked by human teachers, get some healing wisdom from the mere fragments of His speech.

I have chosen a subject from the latter part of this address, which records the impression produced by a portion of it on the Apostles' minds, and the prophetic admonition which their confession extorted from the lips of Jesus. May we be able to avow a better faith than theirs, and to profit by their mistaken estimate of its truthfulness and strength. May He who was in the Paschal Chamber to teach and comfort His followers by promises of His spiritual visitations, comfort and instruct us by their fulfilment.

I.

They professed to believe, but they did not know *why*.

Christ had reached the end of His discourse, which, to minds so clouded by carnal thoughts and hopes, was as in "proverbs" or figurative language, and He promises them a time near at hand when He would "show them plainly of the Father;" when they should pray in His name, and be able to approach the Father in the consciousness of His own free and spontaneous love. "I came forth from the Father, and am come into the world; again I leave the world, and go to the Father." Upon this their doubting minds are assured, and their sorrowful hearts are soothed, and they exclaim, "Lo, now speakest Thou plainly, and speakest no proverb; now are we sure that Thou knowest all things, and needest not that any man should ask Thee: by this we believe that Thou camest forth from God." The clue to their meaning is in the word, "ask," "Thou needest not that any man should ask Thee;" not, "that any man should tell Thee." There can be but one reference here. If they had said that Christ needed not to be *told* in order to know, the reference might be to anything; but as they said that He needed not to be *asked* in order to know, the reference can be but to one thing. The only thing told by asking is the mind of the inquirer, the thoughts and feelings, the doubts and desires, which may be solved and satisfied by the answer.

1. Now here was a great, though natural mistake. It was a vast conclusion to draw from Christ's knowing what was passing in their minds *now*, that He came from the Father, and knew all things. Surely they might have found another ground, and a better one, and one that might have dispensed with that. He might have known that, and yet not be divine in any sense. Any man present that evening might have known that. Why, they had shown their hearts as plainly as if they had worn them on their sleeves! They had *looked* and *whispered* their meaning. But a few moments before they had inquired, "What is this that He saith, A little while? We cannot tell what He saith." But so it is; simple and guileless men often know not what they say, and unconsciously reveal the things they think most secret; and we are all apt to exaggerate the knowledge that indicates acquaintance with our inner selves and private history. It was only two facts that made the woman of Samaria speak of Jesus as having "told her all things that ever she did."

They made another mistake. They thought that Christ spoke plainly now, and no proverb, about going to the Father, and therefore believed, when in fact He had (John xiv. 2, 12, 28; xv. 26; xvi. 20,) said the same thing before substantially and even verbally in this very address. Christ had spoken several times within the hour of going to the Father; and yet then it was a dark saying, and now it was a light one. And they do not profess to understand words now which were before obscure, but they contrast the plainness of His words now with the obscurity of His words before. "It is a strange instance of the dulness of the

Apostles," as Doddridge observes, " that they did not understand Him" before; it is as strange an instance that they imagined Him to have become more explicit in His statements afterwards. But we all know how easy 'tis to reflect ourselves upon the speaker, and, if we think we comprehend his meaning better than we did, to attribute it to his improved lucidity of exposition, which, of course, implies that our previous non-apprehension was occasioned by his defectiveness of statement.

But in thinking that they understood Him now, they were mistaken also. They never understood Him on this subject. It would be difficult, perhaps impossible, to discover the precise ideas they affixed to Christ's language. Perhaps they affixed none, perhaps different ideas at different times. But it is clear that till Christ's death they did not think of His dying at all; nor, till His resurrection, of His rising at all. These events, as predicted by Christ, were matters of wonder and surprise, of discussion and objection, but they never entered their minds distinctly as things that would come to pass, and were never expected by them. Christ's words on these subjects are clear enough to *us*, for we look at them through plain history; but they were anything but clear to those who looked at them through beliefs entirely incompatible with their occurrence. Statements respecting facts that have been may be easily understood, while similar statements respecting things beyond all possibility of taking place, are sore puzzles of the brain. Ignorance and prejudice can make any words obscure, and, in listening to Christ on these themes with minds full of Jewish traditions and fleshly expectations, the Apostles were like men beholding objects through coloured glasses, or hearing tidings in an unknown tongue; they received no impressions, or false ones. This was the reason of Peter's "satanic" objection, and cowardly profaneness; this was at the root of the abandonment of Christ by all, and the treachery to Christ by one even in the Paschal Chamber; with all there was to assist their understanding of His language, they understood it not; and in so far as their faith was founded on His language, it was founded on an error.

2. And yet *they did believe*. He had just admitted it:—" Ye have loved me, and believed that I came out from God." They believed more than they thought, and better. They could not fail of the solemn, softening influence of Christ's presence now. They did themselves injustice. They knew the Teacher, if not the lesson. While they were basing their faith on knowledge of His meaning, they had a faith already built on a surer foundation than that; and while they were rejoicing in a confidence which had no support but a mistake, they felt a deeper, stronger confidence which rested on no mistake at all. They were often like their spokesman, Peter, when "he wist not what he said," though he wist well enough why he said it. The light was in their heart, and they felt vastly more than they saw; indeed as to the objects of Christ's coming, and His methods of securing them, they saw scarcely anything. But "they beheld His glory, the glory as of the only begotten of the Father;" and they felt the attractions of His character, and the sweet and powerful influences of His spirit. There was a secret force that drew them, a hidden bond that bound them

to Jesus; the strength of which was shown in resistance to so much that startled and stunned them, and was felt when the thought of leaving Him was suggested to their minds. "Lord, to whom shall we go, but unto Thee?—Thou hast the words of eternal life."

We too feel more than we understand. It were a poor thing if our confidence in Christ and Christianity were based on learning and logic, or even distinct opinions. Much that we think we understand is either a blank or a blunder, and our theological phrases conceal our ignorance often rather than express our knowledge—a fact soon proved, if all those theological phrases could be obliterated from our memories, and we had to find some other words ourselves. It is by no process of argument that most men get to believe in a God, and a Christ, and a world to come, and sin and redemption; and many would be sadly plagued if they had to frame an argument to prove them. Facts that had no existence, reasonings that begged the question, or were irrelevant, or contradicted each other or themselves; texts of Scripture, whose meaning was mistaken, or whose reference was unrecognized—these would often be furnished as the reasons of faith. And for its matter you would as often be supplied not with what was really believed—that is, what had taken distinct and intelligible shape in the mind—but what it had been taught was proper to be believed, or more likely with accredited forms of words which, not being understood, actually contradicted the real belief. The mass of Christians believe to-day in the same way that the first disciples believed. Their faith has little to do with reasoning, and still less with right-reasoning;

little to do with clear conceptions of any kind, and still less with correct conceptions. Beneath the surface current of their creed and their confession, there is another current going quite the other way. The moral fitness of religious truths, their felt excellency and glory, their comforting and purifying power, engage their belief. It is really true—though Paul's words might not express the exact idea—" with the heart man believeth unto righteousness," and that faith may exist without very precise or very accurate notions of Christianity. In other words, a man may believe in *Christ*, the person, " the image of the invisible God," " the man Christ Jesus," may believe in His spiritual perfectness, His pure and blessed life, His infinitely worthy death, and the Father's boundless love to Him, and to us for His sake, and cleave to Him and follow Him, and yet be miserably at a loss if asked for a scientific or a satisfactory exposition of his faith; and as to many a word of the Great Teacher, have to confess with the disciples, " We cannot tell what He saith."

II.

They believed, but they did not know *how*.

" Do ye now believe? Behold the hour cometh, yea, is now come, that ye shall be scattered, every man to his own, and shall leave me alone." Christ did not mean, as we have seen, to question the *reality* of their faith, but its *intensity*. They did believe, always had believed, and, under the influence of this affecting scene, and thinking that they understood His meaning, believed more than ever, and imagined that they believed more than they did now. But they little knew how frail and feeble was their faith, in comparison with the burden it would have to bear. They felt strong, like a convalescent invalid, but, like him, as soon as strain and pressure were on them, their strength was that of a little child. It might do for the present quiet hour, but would not do for the hours soon to come; for the peaceful place in which they were, but not for the dark and troublous scenes before them; for the company of Jesus and His friends, but not for rough friction with an evil and angry world. It might do for the Paschal Chamber, and evening meal, and frank and affectionate fellowship, but not for Gethsemane, the Hall of Judgment, and Calvary; not for the seizure, trial, and shameful death.

Apply this thought to the faith of *contemplation* and the faith of *action*; in other words, to man looking on truth as an object, and obeying it as a claim.

While the disciples had Christ before them, and had only to listen to and behold Him, they believed; but when they had to follow Him, to show their practical regard, "they all forsook Him and fled." Whether or not they understood Him, they could not but be awed and melted by His presence. Such words as His did not need to be understood, to have effect. The best teachers are more than what they speak; more than their language or their lessons. And while they were quiet observers and hearers, it was easy to believe that He came forth from the Father. Oh! it was pleasant to listen to the tones of that sweet voice, and note that eye so full of tenderness and truth, and catch here and there a sentiment of deepest sympathy and love, and drink in the impression, like that of distant music in the evening air, or of the beauty of a soft summer landscape. But it was another thing to meet the actual demand of Christ's Messiahship, to *will* as well as feel, to do as well as see, to be faithful in the active service of coming hours, to fulfil the duties of life as followers of the Christ.

And still there is a difference between the quiet thought of truth, and its embodiment in act; between perceiving and receiving the truth, and doing it; between admiring and approving it as revealed, and performing its high behest. "Faith worketh by love." No other faith can save a man. How "can faith save," if it *does nothing?* How can it save from sins, if it does not destroy sin? Truth is given us, not to be a pleasant object, but a living power. The Word of God is "a lamp to the *feet*," not only to the eye.

Do not deceive yourselves. It is very possible to have faith in Christ when looking *at Him*, beholding the graces of His character, the credentials of His mission, and the glory of His work, and to be sadly wanting in loving and daily obedience to His will; possible to have faith in propositions, with practical unbelief in duties; to combine a form of sound words with a substance of unsound conduct; and yet the faith which is "more precious than gold," must bear the test of gold. I ask not if you believe in the sense of recognizing and admitting the truth of God, but do you believe with a faith that goes into the world with you, "keeps" you as in a garrison while prosecuting your daily business, raises you above the pleasures and supports you under the tribulations of ordinary men, and directs your intercourse in domestic and social life; by means of which your common way is a "walk with God," your common deeds are "wrought in God," and your "life is hid with Christ in God."

Apply the thought to the faith which receives Christ in *peace and prosperity*, and that which receives Him when His claims conflict with our *fond beliefs and wishes*.

Christ made no demand upon the disciples in the upper room, at least they thought not. They did not see Him as the friend going away, and not returning in the same form, as the friend dying a victim to the malice of His enemies. And, of course, they only believed in a part of the Messiah—a part which excluded the shame and pain in His image and history. And how easy it is for us to do likewise! Peter realized our thought on the Mount, and the nine Apostles on the plain: he had a faith which, seeing the transfigured Christ, exclaimed, "Let us make here three tabernacles;" they had a faith which asked with "whispering humbleness," "Why could we not cast him out?"

Truth of all kinds, and especially spiritual truth, comes to us in many ways and guises, and few men reject it in all, and few perhaps in all accept it. We admire revealed principles when they fit in with our preconceived opinions, but when they conflict, how voracious is our demand for evidence. We can think so calmly and speak so eloquently of the goodness and equity of Providence when "the lines are fallen to us in pleasant places," but how mysterious it becomes when He "destroyeth the hope of man." What was a pleasant study becomes a perplexing, perhaps insoluble problem. We can recommend so persuasively the cheerful drinking of the cup of sorrow when in the hand of others, but what wry faces we make when put into our own! We can expatiate on the blessedness of obedience, the nobility of self-control and self-denial, the luxury of doing good, but how different they appear when these lessons have to be wrought out in hard toils and hard endurance. It is as it was in that upper room: Jesus in peace and safety, speaking like an only son, of a dear Father, and of His joyful home, speaking like a kind teacher of His love to His disciples, and great comforts in store for them, is one Christ; but Jesus in circumstances of trial, and danger—the dark, cold night, the flickering glimmer of lamps, the rude tramp and strange voices of men—Jesus betrayed by a disciple, and seized by soldiers, is quite another Christ. And we may welcome Christ as He comes in quiet, pleasant modes and moods, and be only astonished and offended when, as truth, or duty, or outward circumstance, or inward impulse, He makes a claim hard or distasteful on practice or patience. Faith acts the scholar, when the soldier and martyr are far to seek.

Apply the thought to faith in *enjoyment of strong and stimulating privileges* and faith *deprived of them.*

There was every thing in that upper room to excite and gratify every religious and Christian feeling. As men, the disciples were with brethren; as Jews, they had observed one of the most solemn and delightful festivals of their nation; as friends of Jesus, they had seen Him open His heart as He had never done before, had been admitted in the holiest of all within the veil that had hitherto been drawn, and had partaken of another feast, whose significance they could not but feel to be very great, though now in part concealed. Everything about that scene gave it an untold impressivenesss—the time, the place, the acts, the words; its occurrences, its reminiscences, its anticipations; while the shadows of a great mystery infused into it a tone of awe and pathos in affecting harmony with its nature. But when this scene had passed as a dissolving view, and wintry barrenness had taken the place of summer loveliness—when the spell had been broken, and nature was left to its ordinary action—faith failed.

Brethren, you know what times of unwonted spiritual impression and excitement are, when the spiritual world seems opened to your view, and your spiritual sensibilities have a strange susceptibility; when the unseen is more vivid than the visible, and the future nearer than the present; when the glory of God passes by; when "alone" with Jesus, "he expounds all things to His disciples;" when "the secret of the Lord is with them that fear Him, and He shows them His covenant;" and when they "know the love of Christ which passeth knowledge," even their knowledge at other times. It may be so in the lonely, silent chamber; it may be so in seasons of great and peculiar exercises of the soul or flesh; it may be in communion with choice specimens of the elect of God; it may be in public service, when speaker and hearers are under a special ministration of the Spirit, or when they who are one body partake in token, and confession, and realization of the fact, of the "one bread." But these times do not last. They cannot. I do not mean they cannot from any miscalled "sovereignty" of divine appointments on the one hand, or from the defectiveness of human religion on the other, but from the laws of our being and the demands of practical life. And how soon the fair vision vanishes. A return to the worldly lot and the society of man dissipates it all; aye, a walk in the cool air and the common street is quite enough; and we ask ourselves if it was a dream! And we find that the faith to which just now the world was but a trifling toy, and heavy troubles "light afflictions," and stern "commandments not grievous," can scarce resist the fascinating temptation, or bear the painful yoke, or fulfil the onerous duty; and it requires all our effort and care not to "leave," in heart, the Jesus we had felt to be our "life," and "peace," and "hope."

The subject teaches us how to try ourselves and others. Not by clearness of views or sensibility of feelings, but *life*. We cannot be in the upper chamber, or on "the holy mount," always or often. And if we could, it would not be right. We are in a world that we may deal with worldly things. We are amongst men that we may walk and work with them. A solitary, separated, contemplative religion, in us, cannot have the right type, nor accomplish the right purposes. Let us aim to walk before man, before "our houses," before the social, public providence of God, with "a perfect heart." And let us devote our more private hours, and our more solemn and stimulating experiences, to the purpose of fitting us to fulfil our course, to serve our age, to "fight the good fight of faith, and lay hold on eternal life."

CHRIST ALONE WITH HIS DISCIPLES;

OR,

THE PARABLE EXPOUNDED.

MARK IV. 34.—"*And when they were alone, He expounded all things to His disciples.*"

THESE words are chosen as a text, not merely as a motto, but in honourable reference to their meaning and design. I love to look upon the Gospels not as records only, however faithful, of things which have been, but as pictures most precious of things which are to-day; things which were in Judæa long centuries since, because they were to be, and to the end of time, in another and a better way. The Gospels would, like all other records, lose half their interest, if they were merely ancient histories. But they are ancient histories because they are everlasting types—types, that is, in the only sense in which anything is typical. They are not forms of future realities, understood and complete, but the realization in forms imperfect and adapted to the times, of things which should afterwards appear in higher forms: a sort of metempsychoses of ideas and powers. The oldest things are the newest: what never began to be never becomes old: it is the recent that becomes old and passes away.

The "good news" of Christ's history is an "everlasting Gospel," and the interest of it is derived in part from its being a revelation of the permanent providence of Christ and of the character of man. Christ is "the same yesterday, to-day and for ever," in His views, objects, feelings, and general modes of action; and men are the same, and Christians are the same, in the leading facts and features of their condition and character. And as He who "ascended is the same also that descended," and the men of this time are but the children of Christ's time "of a larger growth," we may expect that Christ's modes of dealing with His disciples are essentially one with His modes of dealing with us; that His truth and cause in our day will have the same fortunes as in His; that ungodly men will resist and pervert, and be borne with or exposed, as they were then; and that He will teach and comfort and rebuke His friends on the same general principles, and in like manner as of old. He will still be gentle to weakness and stern to wickedness, still often be harsh in manner when most kind in meaning, still reserve much which is beyond present power of understanding, and utter much which can be only understood in part. He will still supply our wants in methods combining prodigality and economy, put the utmost honour upon human agency when fixing thought upon His purpose, and seeking information to "prove" His disciples, and not from any necessity of His own. He will still visit us on stormy seas, and in dark nights and strange forms. He will still make a distinction between some and other of His followers; and between all His followers and "them that are without;" permitting these to mistake or abuse His teachings, and giving those to "know the mysteries of the kingdom of heaven;" "sending the multitude away," and "expounding all things to His disciples."

We cannot read these words without wishing that there could be, or were, something of the kind in the Church of God in these "last days;" some systematic provision for practically recognizing in the ministrations of the Church the varied capacities of men, and especially the great and vital distinction between the carnal and the spiritual. Surely that distinction still exists. It would be a poor compliment to the Church, to be supposed to have no powers or cravings of instruction beyond the world, and a poor compliment to the "pastors and teachers" of the Church, to adjudge them incompetent to meet the greater need. There are truths and experiences, privileges and duties, speaking of which to the unregenerate is like speaking of an unknown science, or in an unknown tongue. I do not mean "doctrines," which are often the shallowest of things, or metaphysical and scholastic theology, but "the deep things of God," which "the natural man receiveth not," "the height and depth, and length and breadth" of the temple of truth, the "heavenly things," compared with which Jesus declared the being "born again" but "earthly,"—views of God in His revelation and dispensations, and "the exceeding greatness of His power to usward," and "the riches of the glory of His inheritance in the saints," which "the spirit of truth whom the world cannot receive, because it seeth Him not, neither knoweth Him," vouchsafes, or is able and willing to vouchsafe, to such as have "the knowledge of the holy" which is "understanding."

But what may we learn from the fact that Jesus gave a private exposition to His disciples of His public teaching? In what respects and in what manner may we conceive of Him as pursuing the same method as "Minister of the true sanctuary," as Teacher of the Church? And may that gracious and only effectual Teacher speak to our hearts, and bring us, by all that is plain and all that is perplexing in His instructions, to Himself!

I.

The Parables a Puzzle.

It is very striking that the very means of instruction should have hid the truth, and even from His followers. The parables of Christ were sometimes obscure and confounding to His foes; *that* is not strange. Where there is no taste or desire for instruction, the clearest and simplest lessons may be vain. How much sooner we detect what we are familiar with, than what is strange; how much sooner understand what we love, than what we hate; how much sooner recognize what we expect, than what we have no thought of meeting! "Therefore speak I to them in parables; because seeing they see not, and hearing they hear not, neither do they understand." It was a judgment, but not an arbitrary and cruel one. It was a punishment which the blinded deserved, and it was one which they inflicted upon themselves. Parables were among the easiest and most interesting methods of instruction. They addressed a variety of powers; and thus were suited to a variety of minds, and a variety of faculties in the same mind. They suited all ages, and stages of mental development, were windows through which any kind of eyes might see the truth. But if the eye was at fault, and could not see, or could not see aright, then the windows had no use; and the means of light conveyed no image, or a false one. There is often, and especially in moral matters, more in the learner than the lessons; and, as an ancient heathen said, "Wise men learn more from fools than fools learn from wise men." The carnal listeners to Christ suggested more truth to Him than they received from Him. Even the symbolic illustration of the truth, which should have revealed it, concealed it. It is so still. To the gross and earthly the sign hides the reality it should make known; the instrument obscures the agent it should discover; the form weakens the power it should assist; the symbol covers up the truth it should display; and however much men may, like the Jews, admire the *miracle*, they, like the Jews, care nothing for "the sign." Parables would have been no judgment, if there had been no obtuseness and perverseness in the hearers. Only the weak of sight are chastised by light; only wrongdoers have "coals of fire" heaped on their heads by love.

It is harder to understand how "*the disciples*," who had some insight and sympathy, should have been perplexed. And still more surprising that such parables as that of the Sower, and of the Tares, should have required an explanation. For these parables did not invoke any new or strange doctrine, anything beyond their present attainments and powers. We can easily see how some of Christ's parables should have severely taxed and utterly defied their best endeavours at interpretation, because they expressed ideas unfamiliar, and indeed quite foreign to their minds, but they were no strangers to either the matter or the form of *these* parables. All men not wholly thoughtless know that teaching, and truth, and the minds of men have fitting types in the scenes and processes and the results of agriculture. The fault was in themselves. They were sluggish and gross of thought. But why did Christ employ a method which had the effect of concealing what, if stated without a parable, they must have seen and appreciated at once? Why did He use figure to convey what might have been more easily and clearly conveyed without it? Why did He say what they would probably have caught at once, in a way to occasion any difficulty? Why did He clothe thoughts, simple and beautifully true, in a dress that, instead of setting them off, only hid them from the eye? Was this to teach, and teach most wisely?

We are here, my brethren, right upon a great and blessed truth. The parable taught minds *by taxing them*. It made truth plain to the *thoughtful;* but required sometimes more, sometimes less thought for its comprehension. It was a way of teaching, but by calling out the desire and effort to learn. If a man only *heard* it, the truth was hidden; if he were bent on getting at its sense, the truth became more plain and powerful by its means. To look *at* it was to see nothing; to look *through* it was to behold most beautiful and glorious things. When it fell upon a passive nature, it left no impression; when it fell on one quick and active, and in quest of truth, it realized a blessed end. As soon as the disciples, failing to apprehend Christ's sense, came to the prayer, " Declare unto us the parable," they had reached the highest end of teaching: they not only were in the way to know, they were exercising the powers of knowledge; and it is a greater thing, in some respects, to set the faculties at work about truth than to impart it, to make a man a learner than learned; and, when both are combined, and that method of instruction is employed which both puts a gentle strain upon the mind and makes the lesson clear, which goads the faculty of the scholar and shows the meaning of the teacher, which agitates thought, and by means thereof conveys light: teaching becomes both the best proof and the best instrument of wisdom.

There are many parables in God's grand system of human education, and, no doubt, of angelic also. What we have in the case before us, we have in connection with everything of chiefest value. The method which Christ adopted in teaching, and its reasons, are to be found in all departments of His ministration. All things He does as well as says, in this sense, are parables: they are intended to teach, but they teach in the way of training; they have in them an element of difficulty mercifully fitted to make easy, an element of obscurity mercifully fitted to make clear. He wishes to excite, to awaken the dormant and stimulate the sluggish; to call out our powers; not only to bless us, but to bless us by quickening us; not only to impart knowledge, but make us knowing; not only to enrich us with goodness and happiness, but to enlarge our capacity for both. We often think that He might have said things more clearly, given things more easily, done things requiring of us less endurance, and exacted things requiring of us less exertion; and we exclaim, like Israel complaining of the prophet, "Doth He not speak parables?" Verily, he does. Christianity is a parable. Providence is a parable. Nature is a parable. Life is a parable. Duty and privilege in all their kinds are parables. "Without a parable speaketh He not unto" us. But, then, parables are *to teach*, and the difficulty of them is only as a thin veil upon a lovely face, forbidding the rude gaze of the vulgar, but which for friends is drawn aside. They are "an open secret," "a revealed mystery." If they seem to distance objects, it is to draw them nearer; if to forbid recognition, it is but to make it more full and sweet. If they wear a mask, it is not for concealment, but that without one they could not make their way to you so well. The lesson might have been easier, but the truth would not have been so glorious. The action might have been more facile, but the principle would not have been so precious. And a heaven on lighter terms would be a heaven of smaller joy. Parables arrest, excite inquiry, bring men to God for explanation, help to produce the conditions as well as give the materials of what is good. "Every place that the sole of your foot shall tread upon, that have I given to you," is the title, as of Israel, of the sons of grace; and in the fullest sense, and the worthiest things, we possess nothing we have not mastered.

II.

The different ways in which the parables were treated.

On some occasions Christ's worst enemies caught His meaning, and were angry. When He described their conduct, conscience helped the interpretation. But, most probably, in a majority of instances they listened without knowing, or caring to know His sense. They were like men with their eyes open but not looking, or looking but not seeing. But the disciples listened more attentively, and, failing to understand Christ's words, but dissatisfied with their ignorance, took measures to have it removed. They felt uneasy from their inability to apprehend, and sought rest in knowledge.

Now here we have a type of the manners in which all the parables of truth and providence are treated by the children of men. His object, we have said, is not merely to "instruct," but to "educate;" not merely to put in, but to draw out; not only to give us what we have not, but to exercise what we have; that as to the blessing of chief account, He cannot make them ours in fullest measure, and sometimes not at all, unless we are moved to seek them, unless we care for them, and put forth effort, and not of a trifling nature, to secure them; that it is not an arbitrary ordinance, but a natural necessity, that we must "dig for wisdom as for hid treasure;" that we must reap "joy" as a harvest of "light," and "work out our salvation with fear and trembling." And in respect of these things,

and others, men are just as men were in respect of
Christ's parables. The blessing is put before some,
and, not being forced on them, nor made available
without some toil or suffering, they reject it, or, with
equal fatality, neglect it: it is put before others, and a
painful sense of defect and want moves them to make
it theirs. Some gaze upon the mystery scornfully or
listlessly, others seek with deep anxiety to have it
solved. Difficulty offends or disheartens these, but
stirs up those to activity and zeal.

Truth is often difficult. What is needful to salvation is within the reach of all, for an inaccessible
boon cannot be an indispensable blessing. But truth
of most sorts, as well as religious, is not unavoidable,
and frequently it is hard to get. It requires search,
calm and impartial judgment, moral affinities, and a
resolve to " buy " it at any price and " sell " it at none;
and while many are wishing that it were before them
in a form they could but see, and with evidence they
could but accept, the law and blessing runs thus wise:
" Blessed are they that have not seen, and yet believe."
And this is quite enough to deter them from the pursuit. But others find in it the strongest argument for
it. Because it is not necessary, because it is not self-
demonstrative, because it takes strange forms, because
some truths seem to conflict with others and some
parts of a truth with others, they cannot rest. What
if there should be hid treasure? Or, having got a
truth, they feel there is more—more within and more
around. Newton gazes on a falling apple; here is a
common law. Franklin gazes on a flying kite; here is
a common law. And so moral facts are but instances

of moral powers, and moral truths are parts of a vast economy of truth. And so they go from the outer to the inner, from the lower to the higher, not contented with ignorance, or partial or superficial views, until the "parable" is wholly open, and all its secret wealth and beauty are exposed to view.

And if we pass from what is to be *known* to what is to be *done*, from the difficulty of *apprehension* to the difficulty of the *performance*, the same kind of remark applies, "Is there not a warfare to man upon the earth?" Is any promise of good in other than the apocalyptic form, "To him that overcometh will I give"? "The kingdom of heaven is taken by force." "The strait gate" is entered by "agony." "Eternal life" has to be seized. The fact is that most good has to be acquired, or to be kept and increased by dint of labour, watchfulness, the ruling of our own spirits, and the resisting of the spirits of others. Even moral qualities and conditions are frequently the fruit of self-control and self-culture; and the most precious of slowest growth. All this is parable to many, and they care not to solve it. They will not take the trouble to unlock the mystery and make it theirs; and some are lost for ever, and others are lost even here as well. Some hear the hard conditions, and go away from Jesus, though "sorrowfully," giving up the thought of "inheriting eternal life;" and some fail to possess "the life which now is," letting the man sink into the brute, and the brute become more brutish than the beasts of the field. But there are others who are only goaded and roused by obstacles. They know the blessing is great, is vital, and the harder to be won, the more worth winning; and, the difficulty being in themselves, the more needful to be mastered. A thing of little worth might be abandoned; but this must be sought for with greater zeal.

III.

The private solution of the Parables.

When the multitude were sent away, Matthew says that the disciples came to Jesus, requesting an explanation of His teaching. This is not the only occasion mentioned (Matthew xv. 15), and we may be sure there were many. They had the right, and availed themselves of it. And there are now those who have access, so to speak, to the solitude of the Saviour. Many only know Him in the world, and the face of day; in His written word, in His general providence; as the teacher of crowds, as the worker of wonders. They might know Him otherwise. Had this multitude cared for His intimacy, they might have had it. Had they possessed His spirit, they would have possessed both the power and the privilege of freer intercourse and fuller truth. There was not one of them forbidden but by his own carnality and dulness. They were in the outer circle of mere hearers, simply because they had not the spiritual affinity characteristic of the inner circle of friends. But those who had that affinity, in whom the love of Christ was quickened with an attendant disposition to know and do His will, could draw near to Him, and hold communion with Him, stating their doubts, proposing their questions, reporting the marvel excited by His public works, and expressing the perplexity occasioned by His public words.

We, like the disciples, may be "alone," and alone with Jesus. It is not necessary, in order to this, that we should be absent from men. There is a solitude of the flesh, and a solitude of the spirit. The spirit may be lonely in the midst of "the great congregation;" and far away from the busy world, beyond the reach of voice or eye, it may be surrounded by a company which no man can number. Loneliness is not a question of place and outward presence. The soul is lonely in all "great searchings of heart," in the day of conversion, and day of judgment. It may be made more deep and awful by others being near: the sense of separation may be quickened by the fact that though others are at hand, there is no communion; and, as "if the light within is darkness, how great is that darkness," so if in company we are solitary, how great is our solitude! But there is one with whom we may be, when all besides go their way: one with whom we may converse when all besides know not the heart's bitterness, and are strangers to its joy. Christ is still to be found in secret. We are not ignorant of His private life—not banished from His presence. He may still be found in secret. He has other communications than those he makes in public—not different, but deeper and yet clearer; expositions which only love will seek, and only love receive; and if moved by sayings that all listened to, and acts that all perceive, we seek the solitude of His spirit, and ask the interpretations of His grace, we shall prove that "the secret of the Lord is with them that fear Him, and

He will show unto them His covenant." It is no disproof of it that the mass of men do not find it so; it is no disproof of it that the mass of Christians know but little of it. There are but few who know any but a public Christ. The carnal and worldly-minded, the money-getting, fashion-following of all classes, and, in so far as they are so, the strangers to solemn, quiet thought and patient study, and wrestling supplications, cannot visit Christ in "the house;" they cannot draw near when the people are gone away; they care not to receive His profounder instructions, and choicest tokens of affection. But to those that can, there is a light to which all other is as shadow: it may be a light to remove difficulty, and reveal parables; but, if not, a light disclosing *Him*, so making manifest His glory to the heart, so "full of grace and truth," so witnessing to the inmost spirit His goodness, purity, and faithfulness, that difficulty unremoved loses its painful pressure, and parables not expounded cease to trouble and to vex, and the soul can break forth in gladness, gratitude, and triumph: "I know but little, but I know the Lord; truths are mysteries, but the teacher is no problem; facts are startling, staggering, but the worker is no marvel. *He* is 'the way, the truth, and the life,' and, though surrounded by perplexity and stumbling evermore, in his path I shall have light and strength, to reach the true peace and 'joy unspeakable' of God."

Are we asking, "What is truth?" Do we feel that this is the first of questions, and one sometimes difficult of answer? Are we "hardly bestead and hungry" in the search for it? Are we distressed by the fact that no man can work out the sum for himself of Christianity by means of independent study—the sum of credentials, and canon, and translation, and interpretation—that questions disputed by the equally learned, and equally intelligent, and equally good, are not to be answered by such means as most possess, such efforts as most can put forth? Are we sore vexed and confused by the hard sayings that have strained, and vainly strained, the finest intellects since the birth of thought? Do we feel that there is no solution of the mystery of the will, and the mystery of evil? And even with the word of God in our own hands, and translated into our own tongue, are we conscious of immense, if not insuperable difficulty in fitting fact to fact, and word to word, and all to the moral judgment of our own minds? Brethren, there is an exposition for us—it is from Christ; it is in Christ. It is not vainly written that "he that is spiritual judges all things;" that "he that wishes to do God's will shall know of the doctrine" needful thereto, that there is "an anointing which teacheth all things." God has direct and immediate access to the spirit of man; and Jesus is "the Word." Let lexicons and grammars, criticism and comment have their place, and do their utmost work; they may leave the soul without the truth, and may leave the truth without the power of God. Christ is the best *revelation* of spiritual truth, its strongest *evidence*, and its only quickening *force;* and we may say of Him and Christianity, what Cowper says of God and Providence—

"He is His own interpreter, and He will make it plain."

Perhaps your parable is evil, the evil in the world, in yourselves. The difficulty that pressed on Job and on David, and on all that have thought, especially if they have suffered, presses upon you. You wonder why *you* should be afflicted; why any man should be afflicted. There is no one can expound it but Christ; and no one can make the exposition satisfactory and soothing. There is *something worse* than pain and sorrow, and something better than ease and quiet, or even peace and joy; and if this better thing may be secured by means of the pain and sorrow, is not there, in part, a solution? Is there not the dawn, at least, upon the mountains? Christ has this explanation: He is it. He is the *example*, the *medium*, the *agent* of this blessed mystery. It is *He* that puts "the soul of good in things evil;" and more than "soul"—*spirit*. Paul gives this solution. Hear him, with the "thorn" still piercing his "flesh," and his prayer unanswered, "I will glory in my infirmities, that the power of Christ may rest upon me." *She* found it (Alexandrina d'Alopius) who, looking back on many days of bitter bereavement, could say, "Those were cruel and dreadful days; but now, by God's grace, I mourn for my Albert *gaily*."

And the same remark applies to *duties*. There is a striking passage in Luke bearing upon this. Christ had warned His disciples against offences, and had preached the doctrine of prompt and full forgiveness, even unto seven times a day. And the Apostles said unto the Lord, "Increase our faith." That is, their faith in *Him*. He had given no doctrine, but *a duty;* and the *hardness* of this made them crave an increase of confidence in Himself, that they might not be offended by it, but might obey it. And when the parable of duty is before us, and we tremble as we contemplate particular obligations, or the whole responsibility of life, we must seek Jesus, and ask His exposition. More faith in Him will lighten the burden and ease the yoke, however hard and heavy. "I can do all things through Christ which strengtheneth me." He is *model, motive, might* of all obedience; and the life we live is His life, and we follow Him, and all we do is from His love constraining us.

There is a lesson for all. Some are painfully exercised with doubts and difficulties. Their "misery is great upon" them. They "walk in darkness," "a darkness that may be felt." Let me entreat such to "come to Jesus in the house;" to seek the secret Saviour. Whether perplexed by ignorance or pressed by sin, or agitated by fear, or burdened with woe and care. Seek Him for light, the peace of pardon, the rest of love. Seek Him alone, in the solitude of the closet, in the solitude of the soul; in the stillness of the night, in the stillness of quiet thought and prayer. And, as surely as His ear was open to the request of these disciples, shall you say, "I have found it!" "I have found *Him!*"

But if, like the carnal Jews, His teachings awaken no desire to understand, and their real or apparent difficulty deter you from faith and following, you must depart with the multitude, and never see the light; and be yourselves an unsolved parable of sin and folly for ever!

After Jesus had expounded the parable of the

Tares, Matthew records that "Jesus saith unto them Have ye understood all these things? They say unto Him, Yea, Lord." My brethren, Jesus will make requisition of us too. He knows our opportunities, and requires that we should use them. And many times, in the searching thoughts of our own hearts, and the testing discipline of His providence, He will surely ask us our knowledge of His ministry; and blessed are they who can answer "Yea, Lord."

THE TRANSFIGURATION OF CHRIST;

OR,

THE REDEEMING MAJESTY OF THE SON OF GOD.

LUKE IX. 28—36.

"*And it came to pass about an eight days after these sayings, he took Peter and John and James, and went up into a mountain to pray.*

"*And as he prayed, the fashion of his countenance was altered, and his raiment was white and glistening.*

"*And, behold, there talked with him two men, which were Moses and Elias:*

"*Who appeared in glory, and spake of his decease which he should accomplish at Jerusalem.*

"*But Peter and they that were with him were heavy with sleep: and when they were awake, they saw his glory, and the two men that stood with him.*

"*And it came to pass, as they departed from him, Peter said unto Jesus, Master, it is good for us to be here: and let us make three tabernacles; one for thee, and one for Moses, and one for Elias: not knowing what he said.*

"*While he thus spake, there came a cloud, and overshadowed them: and they feared as they entered into the cloud.*

"*And there came a voice out of the cloud, saying, This is my beloved Son: hear him.*

"*And when the voice was past, Jesus was found alone. And they kept it close, and told no man in those days any of those things which they had seen.*"

WE accept this as strictly true. There is a school which puts all such records into the class of myths, or mistakes. It is not my design to deal with this school now, but to make a remark suggested by the narrative itself. Besides the reference, distinct and clear, of 2 Pet. i. 16-18—which must be quite sufficient for for those who believe in the authenticity of that Epistle —the record of the transfiguration, one is inclined to imagine, is enough to prove that it describes a historical event. At any rate, it suggests anything rather than the presence of a myth, or a mistake. The whole account forbids the notion that here we have only the exaggerated description of a common matter, or the formal representation as fact of the vague ideas of unenlightened disciples. When we find the scene introduced with a particular reference to its date, and followed by a circumstantial account of an act and a conversation which took place the day after; when we find that in this scene glory and death are connected together—a most unlikely union on the mythic hypothesis—and are told that immediately after it had passed away Christ discoursed with His disciples concerning it, and gave them a prohibition as to divulging it, we can scarcely, even without going away from the narrative itself for proof, help concluding that the Lord Jesus Christ was glorified in circumstances of surpassing grandeur, heaven and earth contributing most richly to the magnificence and solemnity of the scene.

This is the *most glorious* passage in our Saviour's history. His career was not attended with worldly honour. "He was a man of sorrows and acquainted with grief." *Spiritual* sublimity often marked His course, and when He was least in carnal eyes, He was not seldom "greatest in the sight of the Lord:" His mighty works were evidences of an omnipotent *physical* energy, which not seldom arrested and impressed the most sceptical and most debased; once, indeed, He rode in symbolic triumph amid the plaudits of the people. But never did He rise to so high an elevation of outward distinction as on "the holy mount," when matter and spirit, God and man, the living and the dead, united to honour Him who "bore our griefs, and carried our sorrows."

I.

I shall, first, ask you to look at the circumstances which the Evangelists record.

The transfiguration took place upon a "mountain." It is generally supposed that Mount Tabor is meant. The history does not mention it; and there are several things that make it very improbable that Tabor is intended. A tradition not earlier than the fourth century, and the fact that Tabor was the highest mountain in Galilee, seem to be the only grounds of the common opinion. But to these are opposed the facts that the history rather points to the North of Galilee (Mark viii. 27), whereas Tabor is in the South; and that the expression used by Matthew and Mark, "a high mountain *apart*," and Peter's words, "let us make three tabernacles," imply that the event occurred in a solitary place, whereas there was a fortified town on the top of Tabor. It is, however, a matter of but little importance on what particular mountain Christ was transfigured. Yet is it interesting to notice that a mountain was the scene of His glory. You cannot be ignorant that mountains appear as the sites of important transactions in the Bible, and in the history of

Christ they are described as the chosen spots of its greatest passages. Mountains are connected with His chief teaching, His sufferings, His glory, His prayers, His death, His ascension. It is not fanciful to say that mountains seem to have a power of attracting to themselves the great things of men. Natural advantages may account for it in part, symbolism may account for it still more. Physical qualities present a strong claim, spiritual significance a stronger. However some may disesteem the more ethical relations of the material to the mental, we believe that men have been wise in seeking for types as well as space in the outward world, and that their religions, whether of human origin or of divine origin, as among the Jews, have embodied a deep truth in connecting their sacred scenes and sacred services with "the ancient mountains," and everlasting "hills." When the Son of God appeared in glory, the earth assisted in his temporary enthronement, and the local accident harmonized with the spiritual import of that august event.

The *second* thing to be noticed is the *company* that Christ selected for the purpose of witnessing His transfiguration. It consisted of Peter, James, and John—Peter who, without conceding his apostolical supremacy, cannot but be held to have been highly distinguished, the keys of the kingdom having been given to him; James, who was destined to be the first martyr among the apostles; and John, who was emphatically "the disciple whom Jesus loved."

These witnesses were enough to attest the reality of the occurrence. But why select them? Why not permit all the apostles to be thus privileged? The answer to this may not be within our knowledge. It is, however, probable that they were more intimately related to the Saviour than the rest. On other occasions we meet with them in His company alone. At the raising of Jairus' daughter they were present. They witnessed His sufferings in the garden. We therefore conclude that, for some reason or other, they were the inner circle of Christ's followers. To say that they witnessed the glory because they were to witness the sufferings of Christ is no explanation. The question occurs, why were they to witness His sufferings? And the only answer within our reach is, that they were objects of special regard, and required and could profit by special training. There was a great difference among the apostles, in their characters, attainments, and destinies. They had not all equal sympathy with their Lord; they were not all equally advanced in His truth; they were not all appointed to the same career. As, therefore, Christ's general disciples were nearer to Him than the world; and the apostles nearer to Him than the disciples; so, we may believe, Peter, James, and John were nearer to Him than the other apostles. They had a closer fellowship; they could follow Him further; they required a higher preparation. They perhaps loved more, could bear more, and needed more. And thus, as He showed Himself to all of them more than to the world, so He showed Himself to some of them more than to the rest, admitted them to the deeper things of His spirit, and the stranger facts of His history, now permitting them to behold His "sorrowfulness unto death," and now permitting them to be "eyewitnesses of His majesty."

The *time* of the transfiguration is worthy of attention. Matthew says it was "after six days;" Luke, "about an eight days after these sayings." The expressions are consistent, though various—different modes of computation being adopted; according to one, the days from and to which the time was reckoned being included, according to the other those days being omitted. The reference is to the conversation which Christ had with His apostles at Cæsarea Philippi, when Peter declared his belief in His Messiahship, and Christ predicted His sufferings.

The immediate season was night; for what took place on their descent from the mount, Luke says, was "on the next day." Hence the disciples fell asleep. Christ went, as He did on other occasions, to spend the night in prayer to His Father. The darkness of the night would add to the solemnity of the scene. And may we not say that the seasons of our greatest glory are commonly connected with gloom, and that the evil of sorrow and shame help the display of the moral lustre of the soul? But the circumstance to which I would especially call attention is that Christ *was "praying"* when He was transfigured. And is there not important instruction to us in the fact, not only that Christ was a Man of prayer, and frequently withdrew to solitude for prolonged supplication, but that the more significant and momentous scenes of His life were connected with earnest intercession. His forty days in the desert were days of "fasting," and doubtless of prayer; the night before the appointment of His apostles was spent "in prayer to God;" in the garden He prayed; on the mount of glory He prayed. The obvious lesson from this is, that not only should we always indulge the spirit of prayer, but that we should enter into the greatest events and experiences with peculiar devotion; that special temptations, special duties, special sufferings, and special good, all call for special wrestling with God; that instruction and strength, fortitude and honour, are to be sought from heaven; that only in prayer can we meet our enemy, only in prayer can we fulfil our vocation, only in prayer can we drink the cup of love, and only in prayer can we gain "the spirit of glory and of God."

The transfiguration itself is described in language which does not satisfy our curiosity. The account given of our Saviour's person is not scientific, but according to appearance. The strongest language is, however, employed to represent the splendour with which He was invested. He was, as the word is, " metamorphosed." Luke says "the fashion of His countenance was altered." Matthew says "His face did shine as the sun." According to Luke, "His raiment was white and glistering;" according to Matthew, it "was white as the light;" according to Mark, it "became shining, exceeding white as snow; so as no fuller on earth can white them." It is not said how this took place, whether from without or from within. Moses and Elijah are said to have "appeared in glory," and thus the whole scene seems to have been filled with a supernatural brightness. Probably Christ's person became luminous for the occasion; and science teaches us that objects which are opaque may by a slight change become transparent. It is, however, the meaning and not the mode of this transformation that is important. That there was miracle here none can doubt, and it is equally evident that the display was in harmony with all our natural ideas. Light is the highest emblem of the highest excellence. The language of men never associates evil and sin with this object. Darkness is the image of all that should be hated and feared, brightness of all that should be loved and cherished. It is the symbol of Deity. "God is light." "O Lord my God, Thou art very great; Thou art clothed with honour and majesty. Who coverest Thyself with light as with a garment."

The scene was signalized by *the appearance of Moses and Elijah*, the Greek termination of the name of the latter being substituted for the Hebrew. These "appeared in glory; and spake of the decease which He should accomplish at Jerusalem." These came as visitants from the spiritual world. But they were visible to the eye; they had a bodily form. It is interesting to remember that there was something remarkable about the corporeal destiny of both these men. Of Elijah, it is written (2 Kings, ii. 11), "Elijah went up by a whirlwind into heaven." Of Moses, we are told (Deut. xxxiv. 6), "And He" (the Lord) " buried him in a valley in the land of Moab, over against Beth-peor: but no man knoweth of his sepulchre unto this day." The language is strange, suggestive of something unusual, although not necessarily importing more than that God interposed, as we might suppose, to prevent any idolatrous regard being paid to the body of the great lawgiver on the part of His besotted people. But, in Jude 9, we read "Yet Michael, the archangel, when contending with the devil he disputed about the body of Moses, durst not bring against him a railing accusation, but said, The Lord rebuke thee?" This throws no light upon the subject, but, like the passage in Deuteronomy, implies a peculiar destination of the corpse of the lawgiver of Israel. But if we cannot answer the questions that are thus provoked, we need be at no loss to guess why Moses and Elijah were selected to appear with Christ. The one represented the law, the other the prophets. They were two of the most worthy and wonderful men of the former dispensation, both for what they were and for what they did, their personal qualities and their public work. The first established the preparatory system; the second revived it: the first brought it into existence, the second laboured to breathe into it new life. No men could have been chosen more fitted to commune with the transfigured Jesus; and as they appeared in His glory, and spake of His departure which He was about to accomplish at Jerusalem, was it not shown that a greater than the greatest of ancient worthies was here, and that His humiliation and death were not inconsistent with His Messiahship, but in fullest keeping with the highest honour that could be put on all the law and all the prophets?

The *impression* of the scene on the minds of the apostles was such as might have been expected. They had slept, as was natural, and had not seen the commencement of the Transfiguration. But "when they were awake, they saw His glory, and the two men that stood with Him. And it came to pass, as they departed," or, rather, were departing, "from Him, Peter said unto Jesus, Master, it is good for us to be here:

and let us make three tabernacles; one for Thee, and one for Moses, and one for Elias: not knowing what he said." If he did not know what he said, it is obviously unnecessary for us to know it. It is not always when people know best what they say, that they have the greatest thoughts or the best feelings. The highest condition of the human soul is often that in which the tongue and the understanding are both inadequate to put its sentiments into precise form, when no expression can be given to what is passing in the heart, and like him with the unknown tongue but without an interpreter (1 Cor. xiv. 28), a man must be content with "speaking to himself and to God." But if Peter did not know what he said, he knew why he said it. It was a foolish request, but a natural and necessary desire. He wanted to prolong the glory. He did not like the thought of losing the heavenly company and the Divine radiance, and descending again to the beggarly scenes of common earth, and the inferior fellowship of common men. "Oh, that this might last!" would doubtless have been the wish of any of us in such a case. It accorded, too, better with the imperfect conceptions of Christ's disciples that he should thus be honoured than that he should be humbled and afflicted. But it was not meant to be continued. This elevation of sense and soul was intended not to take from toil and travail, but to fit for them. The garden must follow, with its anguish and bitter cries. Such brilliance and blessedness can only be transient in a world of stern duty and manifold trials. And so, likewise, when we are elated above measure, and far removed in thought from the ways and works of daily life, an unusual light falls upon our souls, and we hold unwonted converse with the invisible world, and the wish is cherished that this experience might not pass away, did we listen we should hear a voice, as did Peter, "while he thus spake," "This is my beloved Son: *hear Him*." This vision is not for joy, but for obedience; go from this place of glory, and let your active, holy service show that your unusual privileges have but prepared you for the less brilliant, but not less honourable scenes of earth and life." It is useless to object to the language said to have been used by Peter, "How could he know that the two men were Moses and Elijah?" Explanation is easy. It may be supposed that they were discovered by their conversation. It has also been finely said, that "to any one living in the spirit of Scripture, such characters as Moses and Elijah must be conceived of as bearing a peculiar impress that could not be mistaken." There is no need, therefore, to have recourse to the hypothesis of some, that they did not know till afterwards, and that the names were not mentioned at the time by Peter, but were only inserted in the record of his words.

We now come to the close of this extraordinary transaction. Matthew says, "A bright cloud overshadowed them," and a voice came out of the cloud, commanding attention to the glorified Jesus. There can be no doubt as to what this cloud indicated. It was the emblem of the Divine presence. We meet with it of old. There are implications of some visible token of Jehovah, in the earliest tokens of the Old Testament, and specific references to the cloud in the history of the chosen people. It attended them in their journeys in the wilderness, it rested on the tabernacle, and abode in the Temple. The voice which came from this cloud at the Transfiguration, proceeded from the presence of the Lord. It proclaimed Jesus to be the great Prophet promised to the fathers. Moses himself had said (Deut. xviii. 18, 19), "I will raise them up a Prophet from among their brethren, like unto thee, and will put my words in His mouth; and He shall speak unto them all that I shall command Him, and it shall come to pass, that whosoever will not hearken unto my words which He shall speak in my name, I will require it of him." Now was this promise made to Moses fulfilled, and fulfilled in his presence. The greater Messenger had come, and the disciples were turned from him, whose continued presence they had fondly desired, to their glorious Master, with whom they companied, and to whom they listened. Christ is installed as the Lord and Lawgiver of the New Dispensation, and his claims to reverential homage and implicit obedience are enforced by the presence and the voice of the Father of all.

The vision is ended, and Jesus is left alone with His disciples. When they heard the voice, they were exceedingly afraid, and fell on their faces. But Jesus restored them by His touch and gentle words, "Arise, and be not afraid." Matthew and Mark add, that Christ forbade the telling the vision until after His resurrection; which prohibition, according to Luke, the disciples heeded. It is easy to understand why this prohibition was given. There would have been the greatest danger of the perversion of the fact to improper purposes on the part of the people generally, while the rest of the Apostles were not sufficiently advanced to be safely entrusted with its knowledge. In the sense of fully comprehending its meaning, none of them were far advanced, for we find that Christ's mention of His resurrection gave rise to reasonings among the three, "what the rising from the dead should mean." His death was still a mystery to them, and as it was presupposed by His resurrection, they could not conceive of the latter. Two of the Evangelists give another particular. The prevalent opinion was, and Christ declares it to have been correct, that Elijah must precede the Messiah, and restore all things. The appearance of Elijah on the mountain suggested their inquiry as to the truth of this belief; his disappearance perplexed them on the supposition of its truth. Christ confirmed the notion, but explained it in a new sense, applying the prophecy, on which it was founded, to John the Baptist, thus adding another sign of Messiah's coming, to those which had already pointed him out as the servant of the Lord.

II.

I shall, secondly, call your attention to the meaning and design of this glorious scene.

1. *It had immediate reference to the circumstances of Christ and His disciples.*

It must be remembered, that Jesus was now entering upon the last and most sorrowful portion of His career. He was probably within a fortnight of His death. But a week before He had begun to inform His disciples of

His mournful end. After Peter had confessed His Messiahship, we are told (Matt. xvi. 21), "From that time forth began Jesus to show unto His disciples, how that He must go unto Jerusalem, to suffer many things of the elders and chief priests and scribes, and be killed, and be raised again the third day." Now, it cannot but be known to careful readers of the New Testament, that " the man Christ Jesus " was subject to all the sensibilities possible to a sinless nature in His circumstances. He suffered, "feared," trembled. His mysterious association with Deity did not make Him proof against the natural suggestions of an evil condition, or an evil prospect. It did not prevent the free exercise and development of His human virtue. The God did not overbear the man. He was not rendered superior to the need of strengthening and fortifying influences. We are expressly told, that in the garden of agony an angel came and "strengthened him." And we may be sure that while His own history was a teaching to others, it was also constructed and arranged with a view to the education and maturity of His own being. It was meant to minister to the instruction and nourishment, the preservation and invigoration of His humanity. Taking this view of Christ, and of His treatment, it is not difficult to see wherefore He was transfigured. The hours of darkness and of anguish were at hand. It was not the dying, but the attendant circumstances that made the future so distressing to the mind of Jesus. In another sense than that of the disciples, " He feared as He entered the cloud." He was chastened and oppressed by the anticipation of His peculiar woe. And, doubtless,

"He received from God the Father honour and glory," on the occasion before us to strengthen Him for the coming conflict. It was, in part, a foretaste of "the joy that was set before Him," for which "He endured the Cross, and despised the shame." The supernatural brightness that invested Him, anticipated the "glorious body" of His heavenly state. The presence of messengers from the unseen world, symbolized the dominion He should receive over heaven as well as earth. The discourse of these visitants about His death brought vividly before His mind the magnificent relations and results of His approaching sufferings, and afforded Him the sympathy of the noblest spirits. And the presence and the proclamation of His Father gave a seal and a satisfaction, which could only be felt and appreciated by one doomed to rejection and affliction like His own.

But if the Transfiguration was meant for Christ, it was also meant for the disciples. It was intended to reward and establish the conviction of His Messiahship, which they had lately expressed. It was intended to extend and exalt their conceptions of His character and work. Had they remembered the Old Testament history, they might have been struck with a somewhat similar passage in the life of Moses. When he entered the clouds, to receive the law upon the mount (Exod. xxiv. 15-18; xxxiv. 29-35), his face so shone on his return to the people, that he had to put a veil upon it. He was transfigured. The lawgiver of Israel was glorified. So here, the "Son," as well as servant of Jehovah, was formally honoured in the presence of His friends and followers, as the Head and Founder of the new kingdom. There was everything in the vision to impress the minds of sensuous, but sincere disciples; men who were convinced of His peculiar character and mission, but were yet unable to appreciate their spiritual qualities. They could not but have a deeper sense of His greatness and dignity, as the Son of God, from what they saw and heard on this occasion. Albeit, they might not gain any accession of accurate ideas, they must have received a profounder impression of the majesty of His person, and the importance of His career. And as they were to witness His mysterious sufferings in Gethsemane, they would be in part prepared for that vision of distress by the honour now put upon Him, and the pleasure now proclaimed in Him. It is quite true that when Christ reached the close of His course, was apprehended and crucified, they, with their brethren, appear not to have profited much by this event. But the fact was, that they were stunned and stupified by those occurrences. They were as men that dream. A conflict of thought raged in their minds. Light and darkness contested it within them. They knew *Him*, but not His work. His death was an event for which their conceptions had no place. It was an element in His case with which they knew not what to do. Yea, it confounded and contradicted their notions. Still, we cannot doubt, that they were in some measure sustained by the things that had gone before. The full effect of His sufferings and crucifixion was resisted by the remembrance of His glory, and if His end was not explained, they would be enabled, perhaps, to treat it as a problem inexplicable now, but to be solved anon, and to bear that which they could not understand. The force of the blow was broken by their knowledge of the past, and though they might not tell their brethren what they had seen, they might comfort and strengthen them by the assurance that they had seen something of unearthly grandeur and significance. But it was after Christ's resurrection that the full impression of the fact was to be felt, and information of it was to be diffused. Then it would be understood. So it was with much of Christ's history. It was not understood till it was past. His sayings fell upon the ear, but conveyed no clear ideas to the mind; His works were seen, but their meaning was not discerned. The key to both was wanted. When He rose, having suffered and died, His disciples reviewed former occurrences in a new light. They lived over again their brief fellowship with their Lord, listened again to His discourses, beheld again His miracles, and a truth, not seen before, appeared in many a word, and many a work, and just as a man who has travelled in the dark looks back, at break of day, from some lofty eminence, on the way that he has gone, and admires the beauty and magnificence of objects that he passed, aware of their presence, but not their claims, or deeming them objects of fear and not of delight, so the disciples, when the full light had come, recalled the scenes of their Master's life, and the sayings of His mouth, and rejoiced in many things that, at the time, perplexed and grieved them. The Transfiguration was not, altogether, one of them. Still, though they had "rejoiced in its light," they had not entirely comprehended its meaning. But when they had been made to receive the idea of a suffering and risen Messiah, and when, moreover, they had beheld Him ascend into heaven, and the Holy Spirit had revealed to them "the mysteries of the kingdom," they would understand the full import of that event, the discourse of Moses and Elijah about His death would be no longer a puzzle, the whole scene would be extended and sublimated; it would become a symbol of the Saviour's heavenly rule, a material representation of His spiritual glory, as the possessor of "all power in heaven and earth," the bearer of "the keys of death and the unseen world," the end of the law, the beloved of the Father, the central object in the Providence of God.

2. *This leads me to remark that the transfiguration has a meaning to ourselves, as a type of the redeeming majesty of the Lord Jesus Christ.*

Christ is glorified. He is personally transfigured in heaven. He is "changed," and His body is a "glorious" one, the beauteous type of the restored bodies of all who "die in" Him. This body exists in light. Ineffable brightness invests it. Far different is it from what it was below—the seat of infirmities, and pains, and death. Far different is its state from its state below— one of want, exposure, injury, and shame. True, this personal glory of Christ is but a comparatively poor element in His mediatorial majesty. We must not think of *it* as constituting "the joy set before Him," and "the honour" with which He is "crowned." Still it is something to a man; and Christ is human, though the Son of God. And most seemly is it that the physical personality of Him who is the Head of all things should be dignified and blessed in the highest possible degree. Nor can we, surely, feel aught but the deepest joy as we contrast the humbled and afflicted lot of our incarnate Saviour on earth, and His ennobled condition as He dwells in light which no eye can see. When He ascended the mount of honour, it was to receive and reflect a brief brilliance, and that preparatory to deep anguish and an awful death; now He has reached an abiding glory as the well-won recompense of all His toil and tears.

The glory of Christ is the glory of *One who is appointed the Lord and Lawgiver of man.* He is to be "heard." God has ever delighted to appear and speak to men by men. He has made His communications by their mouth. He has moved them to declare His will, and thus we possess His revelations and His laws in words which they have uttered, in works which they have written. But the greatest of all His communications are by Christ. "God, in these last days, has spoken unto us by His Son." He has always been the reason and ground of divine communication. He is now its immediate organ. He is the Prophet of the Most High. He is the Teacher and Ruler of the new world. From His lips fell the words of grace and holiness which contained the germ, the seminal principles of the kingdom of heaven, and by His spirit they were expanded and developed into the complete Christianity of the perfected revelation. He is speaker and truth. His doctrine is embodied in Himself. All the realities that give life and glory to His system are found in His person, His work, His spirit, His history. The last utterance of God to man is by one who is Himself the greatest theme for the fellowship of glorified men. We are to "hear Him" who instructs us in *truths* of which He is the best form and evidence; we are to "hear Him" who gives us *laws* best interpreted and commended by His lips; we are to "hear Him" who establishes *institutes* whose meaning and spirit are derived from His work and blessing.

It is the glory of One *who passed to honour through suffering and death.* Most notable is it that the theme of conversation with the glorified messengers was His "decease," and that this transcendant majesty shortly preceded and fitted for inconceivable woe. Christ had not thus been honoured, but in expectation of His humiliation in the garden, His "obedience unto death, even the death of the cross." And do we need to learn that all the might and renown of the Mediator is indissolubly connected with His sorrow and shame? He was "made perfect through sufferings." This is the law of providence. Its richest gifts descend on those who have endured affliction—its "crown of glory" is "received" by those who withstand temptation—its highest offices are given to those who are made meet by misery for power. Christ's glory is a reward for sorrow, and in Him we have the grandest specimen of wrong and recompense, the mystery of undeserved distress, and requited faithfulness. But far more than this, Christ's glory is spiritual, and His power to bless is the result of His self-sacrifice. Our spiritual usefulness is the rich result of self-sacrifice, of love that ignores self, and makes a cheerful offering of all that is most prized and cherished. And Christ has gained His throne whence He dispenses gifts, His force to reach and open the hearts of men, His merit to restore to the guilty the favour of God, by "bearing our sorrows and carrying our griefs," by "dying the just for the the unjust," by becoming "a curse," by presenting "His soul as an offering for sin."

It is the glory of One *whom both worlds obey and honour*. It was not enough that the disciples should witness His transfiguration: the state of the dead must furnish its representatives on the occasion. The earth is the theatre of events, according to the Gospel, which attract the attention and awake the interest of other worlds. Christ was "seen of angels." We are not to estimate the importance of Christ's work by its immediate circumstances. Christianity is a revelation to more than man. Principalities and powers learn "by the Church the manifold wisdom of God." And as Christ is the object on which all gaze, so He is the power to which all submit. Earth and heaven, matter and spirit, men and angels, are placed under Him, and do His bidding. "The Lamb is in the midst of the throne," and with "seven eyes" and "seven horns," perfect wisdom and perfect power, rules unerringly and irresistibly all things visible and invisible.

It is the glory of One *in whom all history finds its meaning and its honour*. When Moses and Elijah appeared, it was not only as representatives of the invisible world, but as representatives of the preceding history of this world. Had mere messengers from Hades been wanted, there need not have been chosen the great legislator and great prophet. It was thus declared that Christ was the end of the former system, now waxing old; and, as these two conversed with and comforted Jesus respecting His approaching end, it was indicated that to prepare for His death was the purpose of the institutions and predictions of the Jewish law. Nor of that law only. History, prior to the settled system of the Israelitish Church, had pointed to the Messiah. The promise of Him had ruled its events and moulded its character. Its every form and feature had relation to the " heir of all things." All the influences that composed it had, like Moses and Elijah, met together on our earth to do honour to the Christ, and when, like them, they " appeared in glory," it was ever in the glory derived from Him.

And as with the past, so with the future. As the former looked forward to His death, so the latter looks backward to His death. "He is to come," was the proclaimed or hidden meaning of things and persons prior to His advent ; " He has come," is the known or unknown sense of all that has happened since His advent. This is "the day of Christ's power." He has given life to a new history. The Lamb has prevailed to "open the book" of the future. All things are influenced by His Cross. It has put new spiritual forces into operation. The leaven is leavening the whole lump. The Kingdom of Heaven is ruling and moulding society. Grace and truth are assimilating to themselves large massès of humanity ; and evil, unsubdued and unconquered, appears and operates in other forms because of them. It may be excited, provoked, and aggravated for a time by the action of opposing principles, but only to prepare for and signalize the final triumph of the Lord of Glory. It is written that "all things shall be subdued unto Him," that " every knee shall bow, and every tongue confess to Him," that "the kingdoms of this world shall become the kingdoms of our God and of His Christ." And so it shall be. And *when it is*, when the end is accomplished, when God's counsel is finished, when the mystery of Godliness is fully revealed, and all the then designs of mediation are attained, to the holy mind, the entire history of the world shall appear as one prolonged transfiguration of the Son of God; its material and moral incidents, its powers and its personages, shall be seen as if communing about the great things of His redemption, and shall be bright with the light that is shed from His presence. The unity of providence shall be revealed, and the Cross appear as its central truth. "And every creature which is in heaven, and on the earth, and under the earth, and such as are in the sea, and all that are in them, heard I saying, Blessing, and honour, and glory, and power, be unto Him that sitteth upon the Throne, and unto the Lamb for ever and ever."

THE FAMILY AT BETHANY;

OR,

NATURAL VARIETIES IN RELIGION.

JOHN xi 5.—"*Now Jesus loved Martha, and her sister, and Lazarus.*"

LUKE x. 38—42.—"*Now it came to pass, as they went, that He entered into a certain village: and a certain woman named Martha received Him into her house. And she had a sister called Mary, which also sat at Jesus' feet, and heard His word. But Martha was cumbered about much serving, and came to Him, and said, Lord, dost Thou not care that my sister hath left me to serve alone? bid her therefore that she help me. And Jesus answered and said unto her, Martha, Martha, thou art careful and troubled about many things: but one thing is needful, and Mary hath chosen that good part, which shall not be taken away from her.*"

THE absence from the Bible of any recommendation or injunction of friendship has been urged as an objection against it. But if there were no other answer to it than the facts connected with the text, they would be amply sufficient. The Incarnate One, the master and model of men, who came in the likeness of men, and to whose "image" men are to be "conformed," was a friend. Filling all the generic relations of humanity, He filled this among the rest. Possessing all the capacities and yearnings of our nature, He had those which friendship fills and satisfies. Needing, and more than others, all the succours and solaces of our nature, He sought and found those which friendship yields. Hence among His *Apostles* there was an inner circle of three, chosen and favoured above the rest, and of these, there was one blessedly marked as "the disciple whom Jesus loved;" and, among His *general followers*, there was the family of Bethany, the scene of His most familiar fellowship, and of His grandest miracle—where "the Man of sorrows soothed His wearied spirit," and "the Lord of Life triumphed gloriously."

It is delightful to think of Jesus there. It often happens that great men have *some home* where they may unbend, retire from the bustle and battle of the world, throw off the professional, and find in the freedom of love, and confidence of affection, repose and solace. Great authors, statesmen, preachers have had alliances of unusual intimacy with particular families where they need not be other than *men*, saying what they thought and felt with no fear of perversion, and with more likelihood than otherwhere of being understood, and with the certainty of being loved and sympathized with. Jesus had such a second home—and yet not a "second," for He had no other; and it was more precious because the only one—where He found not only rest and refreshment for His wearied flesh, but "the comforts of love" and hearts disposed to learn; and there, as "the hour and power of darkness" came on, and He yearned for human sympathy, as in the garden when asking, "Could ye not watch with me one hour?" He betook Himself after the labours of the day, and there He felt *at home*.

Who would not like to have seen Him there? Home

is the best school and sanctuary of the heart, where its purest affections are both drawn out and rested—find exercise and repose. It is an evil sign when it ceases to attract, loses its interest, and when strong and more stimulating influences than it supplies are needed. Methinks I could have missed many scenes in Christ's life rather than this; that to others fonder of the awful and exciting, I could leave the temple where He harangued the people, the lake where He stilled the storm, the mountain where He held battle with the prince of the demons, to have a view of Christ at Bethany, in Martha's house; to see Him as the member of a family, interested in their private and personal affairs, asking and answering questions, dispensing familar instructions, smiling benignly on their happiness, shedding peace and love on hearts that honoured Him without fear, and served Him with exceeding joy.

There were three dwellers in that house—two sisters and a brother. I do not know that He would, or that He *could*, have found, apart from female society, what He wanted and craved. The greatest men have always a feminine element in their natures, and have always pleasure in female fellowship. It has been so with those of the roughest, hardest lives—men of war as well as work. Was not this imaged in woman's production? She was made *for* him, and *of* him; for him, that he might not "be alone;" of him, because he too was womanly. And as it is with the first-born of our race, with Him who was born of God, so with all His grandest sons—*like her* and *loving her*, even their manhood finding its counterpart and supplement in her more strictly feminine qualities. Had the house of Lazarus been without them, I doubt if Jesus would have graced and gladdened it so often. And there were other women among His followers, who "ministered unto Him" in life and death. Oh! let not woman think that there is anything but loss and shame in approaching to the likeness of men. We have men enough; too many, if they are not to be under her benign influence. Her glory is to be woman—herself, and—

> "Set herself to man,
> As perfect music unto noble words."

What I have to say about this family, on the present occasion, will find a fitting place if I select one subject of discourse—*Religious Varieties.* The household which Jesus loved

I.

Presents them *in actual existence.*

There are three occasions on which we meet them in the Gospel narratives. The first is recorded in Luke x. 38-42, where Martha is busy and troubled about much serving, and complains of Mary, who sits at the feet of Jesus and hears His word. The second is in John xi. 1-32, where Lazarus is sick, and his sisters send word to the Master of his condition, "He whom Thou lovest is sick," and on His coming to the house, Martha meets Him, while Mary sits still in the house, and both express their conviction that had He been present, Lazarus would not have died; Martha adding her confidence in His Messiahship and His power to raise him even now from the dead. The third occasion is in John xii. 1-13, where we find Jesus with the family at supper in the house of Simon, probably a relative or intimate friend: Martha serving, Lazarus sitting at meat, and Mary, in "the extravagance of love," anointing Jesus with very costly ointment.

These passages bring before us three types of character. Two of them are very distinct—Martha and Mary answering to Peter and John among the Apostles. On each occasion Martha is in action, "serving" either in her own or another's house, "careful about many things," going out to meet Jesus; while Mary is hearkening to Christ's words; sitting still in the house, pouring out her affection in an unselfish and, as it might be deemed, and by some was deemed, a useless homage. Of Lazarus's words or acts, we have nothing at all. The only thing said of him is that he was "one of those that sat at meat"—a thing not very significant of character, and that might be said of many people who have no character at all. But as "Jesus loved Lazarus" as well as his sisters, and as they could speak of him to Jesus, as "he whom Thou lovest," we cannot imagine there was nothing in him, or that what was in him was not good; and therefore conclude that it was of a kind which does not seek publicity nor oblige self-expression. I think it fair, allowing for the brevity and incidental character of the Gospel records, to say that we have here specimens of the three great departments of our nature—*thought, feeling*, and *action;* Lazarus representing the more quiet, and passive, and reflective class, Mary the tender, affectionate, and confiding, and Martha the natures that find their chief delight in external activity. We do not mean, of course, that these were their exclusive features, for they never are of any one; nor is it necessary for our purpose to prove that they were their prevailing and predominant features; it is quite enough that they were their features at all: but, as the occasions on which the Bethany household are brought before us are those which most naturally and powerfully reveal the inner nature—those of fellowship, and sorrow, and joy —we may innocently and correctly assume that the contemplative and emotional and practical are typified in this loving and beloved group. For all their diversities were consecrated by spiritual discipleship, by faith in the Son of God, who came to reveal and to create a higher and holier relationship, who has declared Himself the brother and the son of all who do the blessed will of God, who came to sanctify all the properties and endowments of humanity, and, like "the fir tree, the pine tree, and the box tree together," are to "beautify the place of God's sanctuary, and make the place of His feet glorious," to adorn and enrich the spiritual temple by all the glorious varieties of human intellect, and heart, and active will. They all loved Jesus, and after a natural manner, and Jesus loved them all, and His love has given to them an immortal fame, and conferred an immortal honour on the several characteristics by which they were marked.

Men are naturally different, not less different in soul than in flesh. As no two men are exactly the same in form and feature, however marvellous may be occasional resemblances, so no two men are perfect copies of each other in mental and moral constitution and temperament. Had man not sinned, we have no reason to suppose it would have been otherwise. There is endless variety in nature. There is difference in heaven above and earth beneath; in stars, and trees, and animals. There is difference in the Church— even in its miraculous endowments—diverse " operations " of the " same God," diverse " ministrations " of the " same Lord," diverse "gifts " of the " same Spirit." And in its common attributes still more. As man is not made alike in all individuals, so he is not remade alike. Regeneration is not a new beginning of a man, but a beginning of the best good in a man. It confers no fresh faculties or sensibilities, but awakens, restores, and controls those already in existence. The only thing bad in man is sin. That is the root of all other evil, of darkness, weakness, and corruption. And the grace of God is to put that away. It is as with a painting, covered through long years with dust and smoke, looking as if one dark surface; the divine grace cleanses that surface, and restores the portrait, not by making fresh features, but bringing out the old ones. It is as with natural life: a man has little vital power, the action of the heart is feeble almost to death, and it shows itself in different effects according to the several functions of the body, causing torpor, pain, or disfigurement, as the case may be, or all together; and the divine grace quickens new life, and without adding or altering organs, secures the regular and energetic action of each. And all this is true, not alone of the main divisions of our nature already mentioned, but of minor parts, and separate powers; not only of thoughts, but kinds and tones of thinking; not only of emotions, but of orders and qualities of feeling; not only of actions, but of the natures and conditions of action. There is thought of the sure foot, and thought of the strong wing; there is feeling of the distant harp, and feeling of the near trumpet; there is action of the gentle light, and action of the scathing lightning. There is the intellect which analyses, and the intellect which generalizes, which cunningly dissects, and which gorgeously clothes; there is the heart which is quick to resent, or quick to love; sanguine to believe what it hopes, or timid to believe what it fears; and there is the active energy which seeks its ends by quiet, steady labour, or by vigorous single efforts, which works best alone or best in company. And, however a man is marked in respect to all these things before he knows Christ, he may be marked by them after he knows Him, remaining the man when he becomes the Christian, and not losing his individuality when he joins the general assembly and Church of the first-born. And just as the varieties above and below make the sky more glorious and the earth more beautiful, and the diversities of Christian gifts and powers contribute to the greater strength and usefulness of the Church, so all these individual distinctions, when inspired and ruled by the Son of Man, become both a grace and power.

These varieties exist and show themselves under the action of other things than religion, and why not of it? Take the cases before us. We have this blessed family in their quiet common life, and the presence of Jesus brings out their characteristic qualities. We see them under the shadow of a great woe, and their peculiar qualities are still revealed. And lastly, they are presented to us at a social feast, perhaps intended to celebrate the resurrection of one of them, and they are still the same. And if death and life, if joy and grief, if privacy and publicity, do not conceal, but only develope and manifest their characteristic differences, and if the same holds still of all such things, it is only natural that the most powerful of all influences will reveal while it sanctifies the individual varieties of men; and that the Father of all, in doing His greatest work on His greatest creatures, while He frowns on that which is not His own, will honour that which is. The souls of men are so constituted as variously to absorb the different colours of the light of heaven.

II.

Consider these natural varieties *as manifested in connection with Christ.*

For not only are we told that they who exhibited them were His followers, but they were exhibited in the very way of following. If, as we are assured, "Jesus loved Martha and her sister, and Lazarus," so as to take up His abode with them, we may be quite sure that they loved Him, but their love is displayed according to their several temperaments. If, as we know, they believed Him to be the Son of God, gifted with wondrous power, their faith worked in harmony with their prevailing dispositions. Let us remember that they had faith and love : there is, says Jesus, "One thing needful," one thing of vital importance, and all that can exist without that is of very secondary account; and if that one thing does exist, there will be something, more or less, of all the qualities we have supposed in the family at Bethany, although one or other may subsist in a stronger or purer form than the others.

The practical, in Martha, honours Jesus. It has been a great question, whether the world is more indebted to men of action or of thought. The question is rather useless. "Both are best," and both are necessary. To take the lowest view: strong coupling chains are as necessary as good engines, and "the eye cannot say to the hand, I have no need of thee." Martha was the hand. Christ needed refreshment, and she prepared it; and this was only part of her general activity, for she was "careful about many things," not only serving in her own house but her neighbour's, the leper's, when Christ was there, and, perhaps, sometimes when He was not, and coming out to meet Him, and carrying His message to her sister, and reproving her for her apparent neglect. I fancy her the bustling housewife, of robust health and good animal spirits; clear, but not remarkably deep in mind; generous and warm-hearted, but not very deep in feeling; ready to do anything to help another, but judging help almost chiefly by the coarser tests; really anxious to honour Jesus, but not entirely forgetful of self, or her own existence; honestly wishful to have Mary do something for Him, but not displeased to have it known how much she was doing alone; a woman of the glib tongue and ready hand, who had no idea of letting "grass grow under her feet," and could express a bit of her mind; who, as the strength of some is to sit still, was on the other hand, never so still as when thoroughly busy.

Now, there are people of this sort in the Church— men of practical genius and active habits; very clever at devising expedients and using means. I have known some never cool but when in hot water, and who never slept but as a top, on the spin; who have no insight into deep thought, and no sympathy with delicate feelings—who think the one a sign of weakness, and the other of disease; but who yet perform functions of indispensable importance. They do the lower, rougher work of Christianity. Like Martha, they feed the body. They are at home with all that appertains to the external things of religion. They "serve." They say what needs to be said, but others would not like to say; and do what needs to be done, but others would not like to do. They come out when others sit at home. They provide material appliances. They can "find grace to be faithful" to those who do not. Christianity, as an object of contemplation, and as a spring of emotion, might have justice done to it without them, but as embodied in men, as the power and rule and aim of a human society, the spirit incarnated, as Jesus is the word made flesh, it "hath need of them." It requires buildings and agents and books; and they provide them. It requires plain, bold statements, and sharp rebukes, and rough appeals; and they can make them. There was a Vulcan among the gods, an Andrew among the Apostles of Christ, and a Martha among His friends.

Let them have their place and praise. They are the sappers and miners of the army, the Levites of the congregation. Let none usurp their office, and let not themselves neglect it. But Martha warns them against two dangers: first, the danger of *putting their external activity in the place of the heart and essence of religion*; and, secondly, the danger of *depreciating and interfering with the fitting, and it may be the better, sphere of others*. They may put work for life, and machinery for motive-power. They may mistake being busy for doing good; keep agencies in action after their use has wholly passed away, as a drowsy nurse repeats her lullaby when the child is fast asleep. "One thing is needful," which, in the fuss and flurry of such spirits, is liable to be forgotten, and which alone can make their labour of any value in the kingdom of heaven. And they are sometimes apt, and partly for this very reason, to rebuke and spoil the different moods and temper of their fellow-Christians. It is their infirmity not to be able to appreciate the more devout and sentimental and retiring of the Church, their own special tastes and gifts unfitting them for doing so; and their besetting temptation is to judge of value by outward and visible signs. Their very strength arises from sources which forbid them to either understand or sympathize with the philosophers and mystics of the Church.

Christ did not disdain Martha's activity, but accepted it. He received her hospitality, frequented "her house," and partook of her provision; nor would He have probably even gently rebuked her, had not her love for the outward and material endangered in her case the better things of the heart, and her coarser and more boisterous zeal intruded on the "quiet resting places" of Mary's soul. The turmoil of her secular activities might hush "the still small voice," and their extravagant appreciation interfere with others' calmer, but nobler ways.

Mary represents *the quiet, tender, sentimental disciples*. Gentle, retiring, with a deep power of emotion, she preferred listening to labouring, privacy to publicity, and worship to work, while yet her heart could well up on occasions in acts of unwonted and almost reckless love and homage. If she slept, she slept like a volcano. The mildest natures are often capable of the most violent outbursts of passion. John, the Apostle of love and holy insight, was no unmeet companion for James, and could wish with him "fire from heaven," on the offending Samaritans; the rough and awful Apocalypse came from the same mind as the fourth Gospel so calm and gentle; and Mary, the quiet, modest Mary—was it in gratitude for a brother's life, or in sorrow for the Master's speedy death?—Mary performed a service of self-denying affection and devotion that would never have entered Martha's busy brains.

There are Marys still, and they are not always feminine; as the Marthas are also often masculine: persons in whom the heart is the head, if I may so say, whose intellect is rather the instrument than the quickener of their affections, and who would rather dwell with complacent delight on worthy objects than study them with curious criticism. They take pleasure in divine things, and truths, and persons, as Adam and Eve took pleasure in the Garden of Eden, when neither botany nor cookery were known. They are not good at general action, and when attempting, are more remarkable for the fervour than the efficiency of their labours. As a rule, their conception of ends is too high, and their conception of means is too low; what is impossible in the first, they deem within an easy reach—what is indispensable in the last, they deem of no account. If they work at all, it is by impulse, and now and then, and on special occasions, and for a short time; and then they do more than others, or nothing. They are too uncertain and ethereal for common fellowships, are apt to be disgusted with ordinary procedures and practicable projects, but realize the loftiest ideal of friendship. They are the enthusiasts of the Church. They have their function, and though some, like Martha, may somewhat disesteem them, Jesus holds them in high honour: "it shall not be taken away from her;" "let her alone."

Is it nothing that they contribute to the gracefulness of religion, which requires "whatsoever things are lovely, as well as of good report?" They tend to the elevation and refinement and adornment of the Church—they infuse a finer sense and feeling into its necessary but lowlier life. They add taste to its talents, and luxury to its toils. Marthas supply the business-like prose, Marys the poetry of religion, which—though some may ask, as did Sir Isaac Newton, when "Paradise Lost" was read to him, "Very good; but what does it prove?" and others, "What does it *do?*"—soars into a region too high for evidences, and performs service too refined and subtle for ordinary tests. Marthas rear the needful things of life in the garden of the Lord, Marys cultivate its flowers. Marthas "serve" the meals of "the household of faith," Marys bring the costly spikenard. In the divine ceremonial, Marthas give the sacrifices, Marys the sweet incense; and as "the house was filled with the odour of her ointment," so the spiritual temple of God is fragrant with their perfumes. Robertson, speaking of the refining influence of poetry, says, that "under it passion became love; selfishness, honour; and war, chivalry." And if the refinement and sensibility of some did nothing else than breathe a softness into and spread a bloom over service and work otherwise hard and coarse, they would still be precious.

But this temperament of Mary which delights in communion with Jesus, this reliant, sympathizing, loving spirit, is pre-eminently the spirit of *devotion*. Worship is the duty and privilege of all, but it is not *equally* easy and pleasant to all. To pray well may be to preach well, but some may be better at prayer and some at preaching. The mood and temper in which we address God most effectively, and in which we address men most effectively, are not necessarily the same: or, at least, their aspects and exercises are not the same. And thus with one man prayer is more an act, and with another a mood of mind; with one a service, with another an exhalation of the soul. A confiding, expectant, cleaving spirit pervades some, and they "pray without ceasing." And this is vital to the Church. For the Church is a body, and it is animated by one spirit; and it is not what one man or another does, but what one *with* another, that makes up the whole work of the Church; and so, likewise, not what one suffers in conflict with evil, nor what one man prays. There is of course every importance to be attached to individual prayer, and patience, and labour, for each one will bear his own burden, and the whole mass is composed of units; but there is a great human embodiment of spiritual truth, and right, and love in the Church, and to this there is a work assigned, and that work entails warfare and suffering, and the success of that work is dependent upon prayer. And as some are called to greater toil, and others to greater endurance, so others to greater supplication. Not individuals only, but members of a body. The prayers that are offered by some, speed the toil of others, returning like the rain: and, like the rain, blessing other scenes than those from which they rose. The Marthas little think when in the full swing of their absorbing engagements, and inclined to boast how they are safe in contact with powerful evil, and powerful against it, how much of their security and success are owing to the quiet hours and unspoken prayers of the Marys of the Church; and as the disciples, while toiling with rowing in the midnight storm had One upon the mount who saw and supplicated for them, so they enjoy a strength which others partly win.

We have suggested Lazarus as a type of the more *reflective, recipient, passive class.* Had he been a man of much speech or action, addicted to many words or strong deeds, it is likely, considering the prominent position he occupies in the evangelical narrative, that something of his, as well as something about him, would have been preserved. A man loved by Christ, and raised by Christ—a man the object of the most precious affection, and the subject of the greatest miracle of Messiah—could not have been a cypher; and therefore we infer that he had excellences, but such as do not force themselves into notice. He had a heart open to Christ's influence, he pondered His discourse and deeds, and, as he "sat at meat" with Him, lost no syllable of "the gracious words that proceeded out of his lips," and enjoyed a feast of wisdom and love while many only partook of what was needful for the body. There are still such men; they know more than they say, and feel more than they know. They are too sensitive for the rude friction of common life, and their silent and retiring ways prevent their being appreciated, or perhaps understood. As most people expose all their mental goods, and some goods not their own, these are apt even to be thought poor; but they do not believe in spiritual socialism, nor consider a community of thought better or wiser than a community of property. Very often they have no such conceit of their inner processes as would dispose to their exhibition; for, as a rule, modesty is the mate of greatness. And so they are better recipients than dispensers, and better subjects than agents.

And as a subject Lazarus is presented to us: and as a subject he honoured Christ. We read of him as sick, as buried, as quickened again, and as becoming the object of the senseless hate of the Jews, and in that way, the occasion of bringing on the "hour" of the Messiah. That sickness and death revealed the Christ, and told upon His course as did no individual experience or outward event. They displayed His knowledge, tenderness, sympathy, and power. They manifested His glory as Lord of life and death. They hastened the consummation of the cross. They aroused the vengeance of Christ's enemies to a murderous fury. The raising of Lazarus was the death of Jesus, and, indirectly, His resurrection and exaltation. And thus as Martha by service, and Mary by sacrifice, so Lazarus by suffering honoured Christ. And there are those now who can do and say but little in His name, who can yet show forth His praise by bearing the impression of His likeness and His power. Like Paul, "the power of Christ rests upon them." They are kept from evil; they are sustained in good. They glorify God in the fires. They endure affliction, preserve their souls in patience, and rejoice in hope. And in a world of trial and disappointment, of sickness and pain, of woe and worry, and sinful associations and satanic assaults, it is a great thing *not* to "defile one's garments," and not to lose one's self-control—and they *on* whom Christ works may honour Him as well as those *by* whom He works.

III.

Let us more specifically notice *how Christ treated these varieties.*

He *recognized* and *honoured* them. He allowed them to be displayed in connection with Himself. He sat at Martha's table. He proclaimed His pleasure in Mary's offering. And on Lazarus, in his utter helplessness and prostration, He wrought His most wondrous work. Special qualities, even when in excess, He did not reject. Martha's extravagant activity, and Mary's extravagant generosity, did not offend Him. He looked at the *motive*, and knowing that was right, He did not disdain the deed. He saw in the one a desire to honour Him in life, and in the other a desire to honour Him in death—and the desire consecrated the meal, and made of the anointing an embalming. And whatever may be your native characteristics, love to Jesus will render them all acceptable to Him. And without that love, they will all be to Him an offence. Though some or all faculties and sensibilities be developed in you to the utmost possible extent, though you had all knowledge, and could remove mountains, and gave your body to be burned, without love you would be nothing.

He *guards* these varieties. When Martha would intrude on Mary's sphere, He forbade her. And when the apostles censured Mary's offering, He reproved them. And still He looks with no kindly eye on those who are impatient of their brethren's different excellences. We are all apt to disesteem and disparage those who possess qualities that we are destitute of, and the disposition to do so is in proportion to the destitution. There is a bigotry of character as well as creed; a disposition to "forbid" those who "follow not with us" in respect of modes of manifesting, and means of applying the "good things" which may be "in us towards the Lord God;" and Jesus says, as of old, "forbid them not." And, on the other hand, there is in some a tendency to despond when conscious of the want of features and powers which others, unquestionably excellent and holy, exhibit. In such cases remember that you are called to be yourselves, to cultivate and control the gifts which God has bestowed upon you. If you were to try to imitate the objects of your admiration, you would probably spoil yourselves, and caricature them. It was the lazy man's charge that his master reaped where he did not sow, and this reproach became his condemnation. Take care that you do not suffer from acting as if you believed that your responsibility was greater than your powers.

He *controls* them. He gently chastened Martha's anxious and troubled mind, though He approved of Mary's apparently wasteful offering: as much as to say—the very opposite of what men are accustomed to say—" If there be excess and extravagance, let it be in honouring Me, and My work." If enthusiastic, let it be for good; "if beside yourselves, let the love of Christ constrain you." But there is danger in letting marked peculiarities run to seed. Very many men are not content with maintaining their peculiar attributes, but they allow them to become morbid extravagances. It is so with authors, orators, artists; the Carlyles of literature, the Turners of art; and it is so in private life: and thus what was a grace becomes a disfigurement, and what was a power becomes an infirmity and an offence. Now, although we are not called to denude ourselves of mental specialities any more than bodily ones, we are called to see that they answer the purpose for which they are given—to let them have their perfect work and that only—to make full proof of their ministry, and not encroach on the service of others. And especially those which most naturally run into evil should we watch with unusual care. Martha's activity was in danger of becoming worldliness, and therefore required expostulation; but Mary might go a great length in the expression of her strong affection without equal peril of losing her soul. The world reserves its praise for the enthusiasts and devotees of business and mammon—and the world is *wrong*.

THE APPARENT NEGLECT

OF

SELF-DENYING LOVE.

JOHN xi. 5, 6.—"*Now Jesus loved Martha, and her sister, and Lazarus. When He had heard therefore that he was sick, He abode two days still in the same place where He was.*"

THERE are a thousand things in the Gospels which are nothing in themselves, but much in combination; not having force as independent evidences, but fitting into and connecting together the beautiful mass of truth and proof, and possessing great interest in all connections—little incidents and traits of character, which are delightfully at one with the reality of the record, which are a great deal more if the record be received as true than otherwise, and which make the record more also. We have one of them here. John is the only Evangelist who speaks of the friendship between Christ and Martha, and Mary, and Lazarus—and, excepting one reference by Luke, the only one that mentions the family at Bethany at all. Is it not strange? I do not refer to the resurrection of Lazarus; different hypotheses have been adopted to explain the fact that he only mentions that: but I mean that he only gives us the picture of Christ in social life, Christ unbending, Christ in the intimacy, the freedom of tender, personal affection, Christ *as a friend*, just as he only gives the *social 'miracle* of Christ at the marriage in Cana. *He only*—the apostle of love, "the disciple whom Jesus loved," the expounder of the truth of love, who teaches that love is the seminal principle of all things good, the essence of the divine character, the light of all truth, and the life of all law—he, and he only, gives us this aspect of Christ's nature and history. Is it not natural? Is it not beautiful?

I choose just one expression in the narrative in which this view of Christ is most powerfully and touchingly presented; this feature of His moral visage, which was "fairer than the children of men." The text is a significant, and, at first sight, a strange sentence. To most thoughtful persons, noticing it for the first time, it might seem as if there was a mistake, or an omission. It certainly does not run as if in perfect and natural harmony with things. The stress is on the "therefore." The reference is to the fifth verse. "Now Jesus loved Martha, and her sister, and Lazarus. When He had heard, therefore, that he was sick (should we not expect, "He went to Bethany," or, "sent to say that He would come"?) he abode two days still in the place where He was;" in Peræa, whither He had escaped from His foes (John x. 39-40). That is, *because He loved them,* He did not go to them; because not only they loved Him, but He loved them—loved them more than others, not with general benevolence only, or spiritual sympathy, but that peculiar affection which needs more than nature, or relationship, or even moral complacency for its base and bond—because of *that,* He remained away!

I.

The Mystery of Suffering.

"He, Lazarus, was sick." We are here face to face with the great mystery which casts its dark shadow on the path of all our love, and confidence, and hope—a very "shadow of death;" the mystery of evil, evil in connection with love, and love in one who *could* remove it; which has sorely tried the thoughts and hearts of men, and led them to seek relief in abridging the powers of God, or vent their vexation in denying His perfection—made them now set up another God, and now deny Him altogether. Whatever else may be said to lessen or to lighten this mystery, we only say now *the facts are so*. "He whom Thou lovest *is sick*." There was no doubt about the malady of the man, and none about the mercifulness of the Master. And so we say still. Whatever your theory, the existence of evil is not to be questioned, and yet whoever made the world and men would have made them very differently if He had wished to make them miserable. He need not have given pleasure at all, much less so much of it, and have mixed it up with our pains. There *is* love and there *is* sorrow. Christianity is not responsible for the difficulty, nor for *any* difficulty; for, as Sir W. Hamilton observes, "no difficulty emerges in theology which had not previously emerged in philosophy." Christianity did not create moral difficulties, but it has done something to mitigate them. David was not the only one who "understood" what had previously puzzled him, by going into "the sanctuary."

"He whom Thou lovest is sick." It is true to-day. Christ did not prevent it, though He could—as did not His servant Paul, who yet could work miracles, heal his dear friend who "was sick nigh unto death." God does not prevent His *chosen ones* suffering; those who are more to Him than others, and dearer—those He calls His friends and children. They belong to a system of physical forces and social influences—they are bound up with matter and men in such a way that it would require a perpetual miracle, that is, another world, for them to escape. He causes, could not help causing, "His sun to shine, and His rain to descend, on the evil and the good," and sickness comes alike to saint and sinner from the scorching heat and the damp air. And so it is with all besides.

It is difficult for us to realize the consistency of sickness and love—love in the Almighty, All-knowing Master, and sickness in His servants and friends. The fact is, that, looked at *alone*, they are *not* consistent. They are absolutely and necessarily opposed. A God of love and a world of woe, regarded as bare facts, are a moral contradiction. And no wonder if, through the veil of tears, we cannot always see His goodness; no wonder if "the clouds and darkness round about Him" sometimes make us forget that the sun is shining still. Pain is evil, only evil in itself, and that continually. It suggests evil; the hidden consciousness of sin interprets it as the token of the Father's frown. And the Bible teaches that suffering came by sin. It is hard to separate calamity from crime, to think that those on whom towers fall, or who are slaughtered with their sacrifices, are not "sinners above all men;" and sufferers are seldom without kind friends, like Job's, to remind them faithfully that great trouble is indicative of great transgression. But the Bible says, "not so." "Whom the Lord *loveth* He chasteneth." The Old Testament, in which, according to Lord Bacon, prosperity was the blessing, as adversity is the blessing of the New Testament—the Old Testament, which knew but little of a future world, and knew nothing of it as an argument for peace or patience, for love or labour, even that spoke of sorrow being discipline, and discipline a proof of parental regard. And the New, as you well know, makes suffering the *necessary* evidence of love, and the *choicest* instrument of profit. Look at it. "He whom Thou lovest is sick." Take the thought with you through all the haunts of human wretchedness. Turn the lamp of God's love towards every object of distress—let its light fall full upon it. It is a dark world else. If *evil means evil*, how great must be the evil! If the light be darkness, how great is that darkness! If God hates all He afflicts, if pains of body, and soul, and spirit, come from His wrath, are only products and prophecies of His displeasure, don't talk of a creature-devil, we have no need of His services to curse and crush us. No. Whatever thy trouble and terror, thou mayest be one whom He loveth. No—look at that poor, shivering skeleton wretch—a caricature, not specimen of man—almost afraid to eat, it is so long since he had a meal; "he whom God loveth" is famishing. Look on that worn frame and livid face, and gasping mouth; "he whom God loveth" is dying. Look on that lone, stricken man, he has buried "the desire of his eyes," and now is "weeping for his only son;" he whom God loveth" is bereaved.

II.

The Resource of Sorrow. "When He had heard." How?

The sisters sent to Jesus, saying, "Lord, he whom Thou lovest is sick." As the words of the message are given, it is perhaps lawful to suppose that they literally comprise the communication—though, had it been simply said that they sent to tell of the fact, we might have imagined more.

They sent to tell Him. It was natural, even if they thought only of telling Him. Deep fellowship of heart suggests and requires other fellowships as well. Community of goods—often a foolish fancy, and a frightful failure—was but a truth awkwardly and insufficiently expressed, the inarticulate blessings of infant lips, the tottering steps of infant feet. But it is a fact that oneness of heart cannot be alone; and if in goods it cannot be—for property is perhaps the last thing that will be reclaimed—it will in other things. True love will always seek joint-participation. It will *tell* what befalls it, tell it from natural dictate, tell it because it likes to tell it, and because reciprocal affection has a right to know it. When so great a trouble came to this loved household as a brother's dangerous, and perhaps sudden sickness, it was a thing not to be thought, but to be done, to let the Master know—the spontaneous suggestion of *their* regard, the proper meed of *His*. They knew that He would value their confidence, and that they should have His sympathy. When John the Baptizer was killed, " the disciples went and told Jesus." And so should we, whenever our hearts are full. If nothing came of it, we should speak to Him of what is in us. He knows little of souls and of speech who does not know that we must sometimes pass through others to ourselves, that our words are modes of *receiving* as well as communicating. The voice gives an objective existence to our thoughts —reflects our personality. We are more impressed in solitude by our uttered than our silent thoughts. Soliloquy, often deemed a sign of absence or weakness of mind, may be rather of its presence and strength. Christ was God's " Word," before spoken in flesh, before there was any but Himself to hear it. And I believe that God hears best our prayers when *we* can hear them too— in other words, we pray best for ourselves *aloud.*

I said, they *merely informed* Jesus of the sickness, as the record seems to say. But we can hardly suppose they did not mean and expect something more. Can we not read their wish in sending to Jesus, from their words when they saw Him ? Both these sisters, each for herself, exclaimed, " Lord, if Thou hadst been here, my brother had not died." Was it not to *prevent his dying* that they told Jesus of his sickness ? They doubtless had faith in His *power*, mingled though it was with insufficient thought of His other prerogatives. They *did not know He knew !* Had they, they might still have sent. *We* know He knows, and yet we tell Him—tell Him too *because* He knows. Our prayers are not to inform God : He knoweth the things we need without our praying, but He wants, as Whately puts it, to know *our prayers*, and He cannot know *them* unless we pray. It would be a sorry thing for us if we had to tell God our needs in order to inform Him; for He has to *inform us*. " We know not what we should pray for as we ought; but the Spirit itself maketh intercession for us." He judges of our prayers from us, not of us from our prayers—He wants the expression of our feelings, not the instructions of our wisdom. " Who, being his counsellor, hath taught him ?" We pray because God knows; it would be useless else: because He knows what is in man and needeth not that any should tell Him; because He remembereth our frame, and understandeth our thought, and can tell how to separate the wisdom from the folly of our prayers—can tell what we mean when we do not say it, and cannot say it, and when we say the opposite; and can answer us as He answered Moses and Paul, by denying our request, and yet doing " more abundantly than we ask or think."

They evidently expected and intended that He would come and heal Lazarus, but *they did not ask it*. They did not ask anything. Was it modesty or faith ? Did they shrink from asking so great a boon, or were they satisfied that He would grant it without asking ? We cannot tell. But this is certain, that the more we approach to this mode of prayer the better, at least as to things of an earthly and a temporal kind. The more we leave them to God, the more we remember that we are to " ask according to His will" if He is to " hear us," and that only *spiritual* blessings are blessings always and for ever the better. Many a parent has prayed the life of a child whom afterwards he has wished had found an infant's tomb. Many a merchant has craved the success of a venture, whose success has been the beginning of a course of worldly and soul-destructive prosperity. We know God's will in the greatest gifts: "He will have all men to be saved;" "this is the will of God, even your sanctification;" "He is willing that all should come to repentance:" there is no danger of error or excess while we make *these* boons—*salvation, holiness, righteousness of mind*—the objects of our request; we may "pour out our hearts before Him," however full, and "open our mouths wide," without fear of disappointment, while we pray for these; but, as to other things, we do best when we say least; if they are good we may expect them, if not we should not wish them. God sees and foresees all things; and the more we are at one with Him in purpose and sympathy, the less we shall miss them if withheld, and the more enjoy and profit by them if bestowed. "Delight thyself in the Lord, and He shall give thee the desire of thy heart;" thy lower desire, if best; thy higher in any case.

There is something striking in *the way in which these sisters said what they did say*. Taking the words as a *real wish*, though in form a mere statement, it is instructive that they do not mention themselves, but Lazarus, and not Lazarus' love to Jesus, but Jesus' love to Lazarus. They might have put it as the afflicted mother did, "Have mercy upon *me*, for my daughter is grievously vexed with a devil." They might have said, "Him we love is sick," or, "He who loveth Thee is sick." But they say, "He whom Thou lovest is sick."

They thought the best argument was Christ's own love to him,—and, verily, if He loved him so much that he *needed not to be named*, if they could be sure that Jesus would and could make no mistake as to who was meant, it was the best argument. Brethren, we always prevail with God when we make *Him our plea*, when we ply His own nature, His own character, His own feelings, "for Thy name's sake," "as Thou usest to do unto those that fear Thy name." Christ comforted the disciples thus—"I say not unto you that I will pray the Father, for *the Father himself loveth you.*" The more we plead God's love, and the less we obtrude ourselves in any way, either in wants or wishes, the more we "lay hold on His strength."

III.

The Triumph of Love.

"Therefore He abode two days still in the same place where He was." He tarried where He was, did not go to them, *because* He loved them all. Surely, one might say, and doubtless many *have* said, why did He not hasten to Bethany? Even if He did not choose to prevent Lazarus dying, He might have soothed him and his sisters by "the grace that was poured into His lips." He might have cheered the silent thoughts of Mary, and nerved the strength of Martha, and comforted the poor sufferer by speaking of the "Father," and the "Father's house." Here we come upon the most wonderful of Christ's words—words I never read without being awed afresh by their mystery and unutterable tenderness, without "fearing" as I "enter the cloud"

—bright, but still a cloud. He did not go to Bethany because He wished Lazarus to die; and He intimates (we should not have dared to think it else) that if He were at Bethany, *He could not let Lazarus die.* " Then said Jesus unto them plainly, Lazarus is dead; and *I am glad for your sakes that I was not there, to the intent ye may believe.*" I am almost afraid to breathe a word on this wondrous sentence, " I am glad for your sakes that I was not there." Why could He not have been there, and yet let Lazarus die, and then raise him ? It seems not. It seems as if the sight of His sinking " friend," and the sight of the sorrowing sisters would have been too much for Him, and moved Him by compassion to a premature interposition. We say no more; but remember that He was the image and the Son of Him who of old was " afflicted in all the affliction" of His people, that He himself was "made perfect through sufferings," and that He is now, in all His glory, " touched with the feeling of our infirmities." Let us believe that He is *our* Saviour and succourer, our almighty friend, who could not trust Himself at the bedside of dying Lazarus; and think, that having " suffered being tempted, He is able to succour them that are tempted."

And all this was because He meant *to raise that friend.* As Paul said of Onesimus, Lazarus departed only that he might be received back—" departed for a season that he might be received for ever," and " as a brother beloved," " both in the flesh and in the Lord," the more for having gone away. The sisters' joy would be heightened by his four days' absence from their home; their love be made more sacred by his tenancy of the tomb and of the unseen world. He would be a connecting link between the two states, and the thought of him who "died and was alive again" would make earth more solemn and heaven more sweet; while the glorious display of Jesus' power in His master-miracle, the most signal proof of His authority yet given, as bearer of the keys of death and Hades, would mightily excite and strengthen the faith of all—Lazarus, sisters, apostles, and many more —in the Resurrection and the Life. "This sickness is for the glory of God, that the Son of God might be glorified thereby," "to the intent ye may believe;" this is Christ's description of the end and object of His seeming neglect and His real delay. Lazarus received a higher life than coursed through his corpse when Jesus said, "Come forth;" the sisters loved both Christ and Lazarus more, and were objects of a deeper love in return, and the transient loss was an immortal gain; the apostles received a grander impression of the powers and claims of their Lord and friend; and many of the Jews who "came to Mary, and had seen the things which Jesus did, believed on Him." Thus "the shadow of death was turned into the morning;" "the sorrow was turned to joy;" the love of Christ was glorified by the very thing that seemed to throw upon it doubt—was glorified by aiming at a higher good than had been wished, and by being able to sacrifice a lower good and bear suspicion and distrust in order to it.

Herein is a picture of Providence. God does these things many times with men. There was *transformation* here—*of evil into good*. And this is the light which Jesus and His Word throw on evil. It is *not* evil only, or for ever. There is a "soul of good in things evil." He may tarry at a distance, but it is only to get nearer soon—nearer to the heart than if He had gone at once. He may "answer not a word," as in the case of the Syrophenician mother, but it is only that He may have to say, "O woman, great is thy faith!" These are the sayings of the "Word of life" "tribulation worketh patience, and patience experience, and experience hope;" "He chastens us for our profit, that we might be partakers of His holiness;" "the light affliction which is but for a moment, worketh out for us a far more exceeding and eternal weight of glory."

There was *elevation* here. The *material* made instrument of the *spiritual*. The body and grave were made sacramental by the power of Christ. And thus, as in the world of matter, we get transparent glass from hard flints, and nearly all the properties of gold and platinum, the most precious metals, in a metal (aluminium) obtained from common·clay; and the brightest lights reside in lumps of coal and blocks of wood; and the diamond is only charcoal; so in the world of minds and morals, purest lustre and richest worth are, by "the faith which worketh by love," extracted from things which, in their natural state, are both offensive and pernicious. There was *fellowship* here. One *sickening* and *dying* for the *health*, and *joy*, and *higher life* of many. "For us they suffer and for us they die."

We have talked of love and sorrow—Christ's love and man's sorrow. Let me conclude by reminding you that *here only* can the two be found together. There are two states before us—one, in which there will be *sorrow without love;* and another, in which there will be *love without sorrow.* Yes!—suffering without Christ— suffering with no tender sympathy, no eye to pity, and no hand to help—this is *hell.* Love with no pain, or trouble, or death—love having no scope for patience and no need for self-restraint, able to exercise itself without let, and rejoice without limit—the love of Christ ever present, and ever felt, filling the heart with joy unspeakable—this is heaven. Brethren, seek heaven; set your affection on things above; follow Christ, and now, so let Him dwell in you, and sanctify your griefs and wants of every kind, that you may soon be with Him where He is, and behold His glory!

CHRIST AT A GRAVE.

JOHN xi. 38—"*Jesus therefore again groaning in Himself cometh to the grave. It was a cave, and a stone lay upon it.*"

IF the external evidence of the authenticity and genuineness of the Gospels were not, as it is, as full and varied as, considering the circumstances, could be reasonably expected, the internal evidence would be quite sufficient to a fair and practical mind. There is, as has often been remarked, a striking difference between the Gospels we possess and those rejected by the Church of old, and between each of these and the rest. Passing from the evangelists' to the spurious lives of Christ, is like going from a school to a nursery, or from the fresh air to a close room. The whole mode of thought and language is different. The few *undisputed* interpolations—not half-a-dozen of any importance—found in Greek manuscripts of the Gospels, betray themselves by their internal character. I cannot think that any man of average intellect and healthy heart could imagine the fourth Gospel an imposture, in any sense. Take the chapter before us. It *cannot* be a fiction. I go further, it *must* be inspired. What it says, and what it does not say, and its manner of saying things, and the whole tone and air of the narrative, prove it. Considering the character of the circumstances, its simplicity, brevity, naturalness are not human *only*. If not inspired, it could not have been better if inspired. If not inspired, it might have been.

This is the flower and crown of miracles. Of course there are no degrees of power in miracles. Of miracles it may be said as of creation, the first and grandest miracle,

"In creating the only hard thing's to *begin*."

To raise a body is no more than to feed it; to raise it after four days is no more than after one; to raise a man is no more than to raise a child : and we cannot but feel that the resurrection of Lazarus was the greatest of Christ's wonders. Events reveal God and man, and derive their importance from so doing. It was not the physical magnitude, if I may so call it, of Christ's miracles, so much as the *moral manifestations* which they contained, that made them so valuable—not their greatness as exhibitions of power, so much as their character as expressions of a spiritual nature, attestations of a divine claim, and means of a spiritual purpose. Surprising and impressive as a flash of lightning, they revealed things unseen before. And while they were divine revelations, they were human also. They brought out the qualities of men. *This* miracle was a grand unveiling of hearts—the heart of Jesus, the hearts of the sisters, and the hearts of the Jews. We shall consider the *groans*, the *words*, and the *work* of Christ at the grave of Lazarus; and may He bless our thoughts to the quickening and raising of our souls.

I.

The groans of Jesus..

We are familiar with Christ's sorrows. He was "a Man of sorrows." It was said of Him long ago, that He often wept, but never laughed; for though laughter is for man, it was scarcely for one who as the representative of divine rights and human woes came into the world to bear sin, and destroy the devil. He was tried as we are in all respects, says Paul, but He had sources of sorrow peculiar to Himself. What to others were indifferent scenes, to Him were charged with profoundest meaning; and things joyous to them, opened up to Him fountains of grief. He rode in triumph, such as it was, into Jerusalem, but as "He beheld the city, He wept over it." He approached a grave as the conqueror of death, but did it "groaning in Himself." Many had gone "to the grave to weep there," but he went thither as a prince of life, to release its occupant—to restore him to a loving sisterhood and sympathizing crowd—and yet "Jesus wept," and "groaned in the spirit, and was troubled."

Why ? "A lost friend," is the ordinary reply, but an insufficient one. He had the sensibilities of friendship in all their purity and strength, and His friend was dead; but He was not to remain so. Christ had come to "awake him out of sleep," and would soon say, "This my friend was dead, and is alive again." It was not, then, the friend *as lost* that He mourned for; but there were other griefs—indeed there were griefs of all kinds in His bosom then—griefs over the *physical*, and *mental*, and *spiritual* miseries of men.

1.—He mourned over *mortal man*. "Where have ye laid him? They said unto Him, Lord, come and see. Jesus wept." Those tears were from the thought of Lazarus' tomb—not that his friend was *lost*, for that he was not—but that he was *dead*. There is a striking instance in Mark vii. 34. A man deaf, and unable to speak freely, is brought to Jesus. He takes him apart, puts His fingers into his ears, touches his tongue, and, "looking up to heaven, *He sighs*, and saith unto him, Ephphatha, that is, be opened." Why did He sigh? Not from doubt or fear; not for show or instruction, for He was alone with the man, and the man was deaf. There could be no other reason than that His sensitive nature was affected by His close contact with human suffering; so affected that, though about to remove it, He could not restrain emotions of grief and sympathy. He generalized this instance. The woes and ills of our common nature came up before Him. He felt, as with an electric shock, that he was in a world of pain and infirmity—that He had become the brother and head of maimed and miserable humanity, and, looking up to heaven, was moved by the contrast of its calm brightness, and even His "Ephphatha" was preceded by a "sigh."

His tears now were from the same cause. He was come into immediate contact with death, and tears flowed freely in this scene of desolation. But not only for the death before Him. That was but a specimen of a common fate—an instance of a common law. The good, the kind—the man in the prime of life—the brother, the friend, the esteemed neighbour, the honourable citizen—and in spite of all, was dead. A dying world came before Him. The long history of the reign of death and sin flashed with lightning speed through His mind. The earth, with so much in it of the "goodness" and "beauty" of God, became one vast mausoleum. And "Jesus wept."

And death *is* an affecting thing. It is not so much an evil, as the epitome of all evils. As such it was threatened as a curse "in the beginning;" as such, says Paul, it "hath passed upon men." Dreadful in itself, it comprehends and stands for dreadful things. And it is shameful too. It is a di grace for a man to die. It means decay, and weakness, and humiliation, and corruption. It means all that can make the dearest friend glad to lose the object of his love; and to make a man glad to part with himself—the organ and instrument, the dwelling-place of his soul. It means the end of time, and beginning of eternity—the end of probation, and beginning of judgment. Regarded alone, as the seeming end of possibilities reaching far beyond itself, and often the cessation of powers which have just reached their prime or their promise, it may well extort the Psalmist's cry, "Wherefore hast Thou made all men in vain?" But it is more. *Evil is always a kind of death*—death within or death without; death in the object or the power to enjoy and use it. This "king of terrors" has for its subjects, and ministers, all pains, weariness, disappointments, and sorrows. It is part, and token, and effect of the great separation from the Father and Fountain of life. The tomb thus becomes a text of universal misery. And no wonder, when His sensitive heart was approaching one under the circumstances before us, "Jesus wept."

2. Jesus now mourned over *sorrowing man*. "When Jesus therefore saw her (Mary) weeping, and the Jews also weeping which came with her, He groaned in the spirit, and was troubled." He knew He was about to turn those tears of grief to joy, by restoring him whom death would have invested with an awful charm; but the sight of the weeping crowd and weeping sisters moved Him. It mattered not that they would soon be glad according to the days wherein they had been afflicted—that they "would forget their misery, and remember it as waters that pass away." But they were weeping *now*; and seeing them He thought of others, thought of all, thought of hearts sobbing and breaking everywhere, thought how the ties of nature and society become, through sin and death, conductors of grief, and how our very love, by their agency, is like the ancient punishment—a binding of the living to the dead; and His "eye affected His heart" as He beheld in image "the whole creation groaning and travailing in pain together."

Surely we do well to remember Jesus, in this touching exhibition of His nature, in His *sympathy* with sorrow, as sorrow, sorrow which He was about to comfort with an exceeding great delight; weeping with tears that He was on the very point of wiping away. We have nothing, I think, that gives so true and so tender a view of the sensibility of Christ as this. It would have been something if He had felt for woes that *could* not have been healed, to weep with mourners who must needs weep on without cessation or mitigation of grief; it would have been something if He had wept *because* He could not assuage the sorrow of His friends, could not rifle the tomb: but for Him to be so moved, not because their tears had sufficient cause, but while, had all been known, they would not have been shed, while He had the present power and purpose of filling the sorrowing hearts with gladness and with song, to be so moved by the *mere contagiousness* of grief, this is at once most wonderful, most blessed!

Let not anything obscure or weaken this fact. Let us not be afraid lest the full recognition of it should at all interfere with other, equally true, views of His nature, lest the "Son of God" should suffer from such honour done the "Son of man." It shows what sin and theology have done between them, that it should ever have entered the mind of man to imagine that the thoroughly Divine could ever be discrepant and contradictory; that pure human affections should be other than expressions of Divine; or that Christ was was not *more human*, if I may so put it, than other man, because He was *more than* human. And let us not think that this sympathy was only during His *earthly* sojourn, and that He does not feel so now. Heaven is not a place where hearts grow cold. "Jesus Christ is the same" in the "yesterday" of His abode below, and the "to-day" of His heavenly and glorified existence, and "for ever." "We *have not*," now, "a high priest who cannot be touched with the feeling of our infirmities."

3. He mourned over *unbelieving* man. "And some of them said, Could not this man, which opened the

eyes of the blind, have caused that even this man should not have died? Jesus, therefore, again groaning in Himself, cometh to the grave." Here is an intimation that the scepticism of the spectators, whether expressed in mockery or wonder, saddened His soul. Nor were the sisters without participation in this grief. They both complained, "Lord, if thou hadst been here, my brother had not died;" as if implying that they deemed Him able to have *prevented*, but powerless to cancel his death. And though Martha went further in her profession of confidence, even to God's granting Him whatsoever He would ask, yet, on the removal of the stone, she observed, "Lord, by this time he stinketh: for he hath been dead four days." We cannot doubt that this was a principal element in Christ's distress. It was that no one there thought that He would or could interpose effectually. Even in this connection we see how high was His honour for faith. "It was all to the intent ye may believe." "Said I not unto thee, that if thou wouldest believe, thou shouldest see the glory of God?" "I am the resurrection, and the life: he that believeth on me, though he were dead, yet shall he live: and whosoever liveth and believeth in me, shall never die." "That they may believe that Thou hast sent me."

You need not be reminded that with Christ faith was the great thing, spiritual faith above all other, and faith in Himself as the best of spiritual faith. It was the want of this, the refusal to be gathered by Him, as a brood under the parent wing, that made Him weep over the doomed city: and when, on one occasion, the Pharisees sought of Him "a sign from heaven, tempting Him," "He sighed deeply in His spirit, and said, Why doth this generation seek after a sign?" So here, the grave of Lazarus, and the tears of the sisters and bystanders were not the most troublous elements of this scene. There was a worse death and a sorer bereavement there—a death, aye, many deaths for which there were no graves; rather, deaths for which bodies themselves were graves; bereavements, not of brothers and neighbours, but of the Lord of glory. Faith in Christ is life, for "He that hath the Son of God hath life;" and here there were souls who had not Christ, and, therefore, not life: and dead souls were more offensive to the Saviour than dead bodies could ever be; and while the Jews were saying, "Behold, how He loved him," they themselves were the objects of a love which made Him groan.

There might be more than one feeling here. Perhaps there was (1) *an oppressive sense of loneliness*. This He always had. Of Him, more than any, were the words true, "The heart knoweth its own bitterness, and a stranger doth not intermeddle with its joy." The foremost of His followers would have prevented the fulfilment of His mission. Hence, when pouring out the deepest contents of His spirit in prayer, He had to be alone. None could join in or comprehend His prayers. (2) *A deep conviction of the guilt of unbelief.* He saw in it, not a misreading of prophecy, or a mistaking of miracles merely, but a symptom of spiritual blindness and deadness, a proof of alienation from God; for if they had known the Father, they would have known Him. (3) *A distressing feeling of the miseries of unbelief.* For it was a dreadful thing then, as it is now, to be without faith at *a tomb;* not to know " the *Resurrection* and the *Life,* in the presence of death, and in prospect of immortality ; to look upon the graves of others, and expect our own, in ignorance of Him who giveth us the victory, because He hath destroyed him " who had the power of death."

II.

The Words of Jesus.

1.—He spoke to *God.* " Jesus lifted up His eyes to heaven, and said, Father, I thank Thee that Thou hast heard me. And I knew that Thou hearest me always : but because of the people which stood by I said it, that they may believe that Thou hast sent me." These words, the first spoken aloud for all, and the last, perhaps, in a lower voice for His disciples, are wonderful. It was not a prayer, but *a thanksgiving for an answer to prayer.* No prayer is recorded, perhaps no *vocal* prayer had been offered. For prayers— meant for the Omniscient—are *seen* as well as heard, and seen in their earliest germs, as well as in their perfect flower and fruit. " Hannah spake in her heart ; only her lips moved, but her voice was not heard ;" yet the Lord " granted the petition she asked of Him." But the striking thing here is, that Christ thanked the Father for *hearing a prayer not answered*—not answered *yet.* There was that oneness, that perfect sympathy, that interflow of all holy feelings between Christ and the Father, that He heeded not the *fact* of fulfilment to assure Him of its *certainty*. " He felt in Himself that God had heard Him. And so may *we*. I do not say we do, or that many do. We may be so one with God in purpose and principle; we may live in such communion with His Spirit; we may have such intuitive insight into His thoughts and feelings, as of friend with friend, or of child with parent, as to know that we " ask according to His will," and thus know we shall be answered. Indeed, faith in prayer, so far as it goes, is faith in the answer; for if " we know that He hear us, we know that we have the petitions that we desired of Him ;" and even we, therefore, need not postpone our thanks till in receipt of blessing, but may rejoice in being heard before we are answered; and thus, " by prayer and supplication *with thanksgiving*"—thanksgiving for that, too, which we are now supplicating—" may make our requests known unto God." And this was said " because of the people that stood by, that they might believe that God had heard Him;" not for His own only, or God's, but theirs, that they might connect His work with His relation to the invisible Father, and regard it as His attestation of His claims, and believe in Him, as they believed also in God. And He thus teacheth us, that even in our intercourse with God we may sometimes have respect to men, that we may not only seek their good directly, but indirectly, and speak to God for them to hear.

2. He spoke to *men*. " Jesus said, Take ye away the stone." " Jesus saith unto them, Loose him, and let him go." It may seem strange at first, and would be somewhat absurd, but for the principal and moral

meaning of the directions, that Christ should engage the services of men on such an occasion. The idea of helping at a miracle is, of course, a contradiction; but here, as elsewhere, men were employed, not for Christ's sake, but their own; they were honoured by being used; and their acts became Christ's ordinances.

Surely, it is very striking that Christ should thus direct men in connection with such a work. Of course, one word would have been sufficient if Christ had put *all* into that word. The removing of the stone, and the unloosing of the bands, might have been included in the miracle. He who did the greater could have done the less. He who could perform the work of God, in making alive, could have performed the work of men, in giving liberty as well. But there you have His reason for not doing it—it was *the work of man*, the work within man's power and wont. Christ had great respect for human agency, and employed it when He could. Men must cast in the net, though the draught of fishes is miraculous; men must carry the baskets, though the bread is divinely provided; men must fill the water-pots with water, though Jesus turns it into wine; and men must open the grave, and unbind the body, though He only "quickeneth whom He will." And it is so still, and in all things. The use of man's agency is an ordinance of God. It is not that God needs it, for God provides it; it is that men need it. And, therefore, as a merciful appointment, in every department of life we have to do what our "hand findeth to do," the thing to which it is fitted, and for which it is competent, and in connection with that we may expect His rich and varied blessing.

And things *beyond our power*, and in which the agency of God is *specially revealed*, are still associated with our acts. There are parts of the divinest works which may be done by men, and circumstances of the divinest scenes which they can bring about; and as a master artist or mechanic assigns the simpler, coarser portions of his work to some " 'prentice hand," or inferior agent, reserving the more important or more prominent to his superior and more practised skill and taste: so God, even when performing His "strange work," exhibiting Himself in unwonted ways, yet loves to leave what is subordinate and subsidiary to our dimmer wisdom and feebler powers.

The life of souls, the life of the Church, is a grand, yea, the grandest of all God's works. It is not miraculous only because God's grace has made it common, has connected it with the use of means, and regulates it according to fixed rules. But it is extraordinary, if not miraculous. We are not born again of blood, or of the will of man, but of God. And His agency sometimes appears in surprising forms and in alliance with strange incidents. The birth of the Church of Christ was "life from the dead." It was connected with miracles of surpassing majesty. Jesus was a miracle. The Holy Spirit was a miracle. The human agents were miraculously endowed with speech and deed. And the life of each man who walks in the spirit is a new birth, a resurrection from the dead. He "is quickened together with Christ." "He saves us by the renewing of the Holy Ghost." But yet there is a place for man, both *before* and *after*, in preparation for and in developing the life: stones to be removed, and bands to be unloosed.

Take the soul. Regeneration is always a divine act. It is the beginning of "the life of God" in the soul of man. And sometimes it seems as if it had little or no dependence upon means. Yet, as a rule, men can "frame their doings to turn unto the Lord," and there are "works meet for repentance," not only in the sense of being *fit fruits*, but *fit seeds*. The parable speaks of the merchantman who "seeks goodly pearls," finding "the pearl of great price." But always *afterwards* Christians are consigned to the care of ordinary instrumentalities and appointed rules: however apparently unusual the process of conversion, and though God has seemed to be "found of them that sought Him not." Henceforth the divine power is to be expected and enjoyed in association with the diligent exercise of human faculties, and the regular employment of fitting means. `For the soul may be quickened, yet not wholly free—may have life, but not perfect liberty. There is light in the reason, but clouds of ignorance and error have to be dispersed; there is purity of affection, but the cravings of the flesh, and the memories and associations of sin make its preservation and increase a work and a warfare; there is vigour in the will, but only training and exercise can give strength and steadiness to its volitions. The spirit is alive, but has not perfect use of its powers; and its own watchful care and sedulous efforts, and the appliances of social godliness, are demanded to secure the full inheritance of life; and the law of liberty runs on this wise, "Work out your own salvation with fear and trembling, for it is God that worketh in you both to will and to do of His good pleasure."

3. He spoke to *the dead.* "*Lazarus, come forth.*" Of course, the word was nothing but a sign to connect the resurrection of Lazarus with the volition of Jesus. But He might have done it otherwise. Jesus spoke thus, addressing the subjects of His power when inanimate. "Peace, be still," was an order to the elements. And it is delightful to think of "things without life" being thus addressed, being all His servants, and obeying His bidding. But, of course, this mode of address has a peculiar propriety in the case of persons: as when Christ commanded men to be whole, and commanded the demons to depart from men, and they obeyed him. But here was *a dead man* spoken to—one in his grave—one dead four days! Yes, but still he could receive the orders of the Lord; and who shall say he knows so much of spiritual being that he knows that he did not? Perhaps the resurrection of Lazarus was an act of voluntary obedience on his part; and in coming back to earth, he served the Lord!

But one remark I would make on all these words of Christ: they were all for men's good. He did not require their help; He did not need to make known His prayer; He might have raised the dead without calling on him to come forth. All was for their sakes. And no wonder, when the miracle itself was, and Lazarus' sickness and death, and Christ's own death and resurrection were so.

III.

The Work of Christ.

1. For it was His act by which Lazarus rose. "His word was with power." It was a King, "the Lord of all," and "where the word of a king is, there is power." "Death heard the mighty voice, and starting at the sound, shrunk from the contest with superior power, and, though reluctant, gave back his prey."

We will not endeavour to glorify the scene or the record. Let them be in their simple majesty. It is vain to perfume the rose, or paint the marble. But we may make one remark. This miracle, and such as it, are separated by a wide gulf from all the miracles of impostors. It was of a kind not to be counterfeited, for there is no collusion with death. It was in circumstances in which deception was impossible; public, and in the face of enemies. There is no one point in which it was akin to the favourite feats of ecclesiastical legerdemain. No dubious case, no select audience, no uncertain result. "Truly this was the Son of God!"

There is "a better resurrection," a resurrection of the spirit; and it is still by the word of Christ, as the sign of His almighty power, that it is effected. We are "born again by the word of God." And of this probably speaks Jesus, "The hour is coming, and now is, when the dead shall hear the voice of the Son of God, and they that hear shall live."

2. "Then many of the Jews which came to Mary, and had seen the things which Jesus did, believed on Him." We cannot gather from these words anything

beyond the fact that they were impressed in favour of His claims; the faith of some would go further and last longer than that of others. There would be the difference between an admission of His prophetical, and an admission of His Messianic office; between a transient impression and a permanent conviction. But so far as it went, it was in the line of Christ's purpose, and their own highest good. So far as it went, it was a resurrection. It was a quickening of thought in the direction of God and eternity. It was thus *a raising of their souls*, a calling forth of sensibilities and powers that had been dormant. It was a raising of their *former faith*. They could not get any true impression from that scene without receiving new life and vigour into the ideas they had held before. The faintest spiritual contact with Jesus would affect and better their religious thoughts, which, however feeble and corrupt, could not touch even the hem of his garment without receiving some virtue from Him. And, my brethren, all good in man is of the nature of resurrection, for all good is in the measure of the quickening and liberating of his powers; and spiritual good of all of them. "I am come that they might have life."

3. But some of them went and told the Pharisees, and they gathered a council to consider what they should do, admitting that Jesus did "many miracles." But you think it scarcely credible that men should behold such a miracle, and not believe; still less so that they should admit it, and yet regard the worker of it with feelings of animosity; and, least of all, that they should take measures for His destruction. But Jesus had said, "If they hear not Moses and the

prophets, neither would they be persuaded though one rose from the dead." The conviction of the truth is but a small part of the way to salvation; a mere setting out on it; rather, a mere seeing it. "The truth may be imprisoned in unrighteousness," "the light that is in us may be darkness." The Pharisees had interests opposed to Christ. They were too shrewd not to see that He was opposed to them, that His teaching and His character all expressed another spirit and purpose from theirs; that if He prospered, they would perish; and, therefore, the more they were convinced of His claims, the more needful it was to put Him away; and everything that should have been an argument for homage and submission, became an argument for rejection and hostility. "They will reverence my Son," was the dictate of reason: "This is the heir, come, let us kill him," the conclusion of selfishness. How differently things appear from different points of view, as beheld from truth or falsehood, from righteousness or wrong!

My brethren, take care that you have no interests against Christ. They may lead you to disbelieve Him; but if knowledge, custom, tradition, and conscience are too strong for that, they will lead you to reject Him practically. Many boast that they are not infidels, as if that were anything—anything but an insult! As if a man should rob you with a profession of honesty, or strike you with a polite bow! Christ came not into the world to be a creed, but a Saviour; not to receive your permission to exist, but to give you life; not to have your respectful homage, but to save you from your sins; "not to be ministered unto, but to minister."

You may admit His claims, and make them, and make the very admission of them a means of dishonouring Him, and of injuring and destroying yourselves; and you will do so, if, like the Pharisees, while knowing right you do wrong. Beware, I say again, of having interests against Christ, whether of repute, or profit, or pleasure; of pride, vanity, or love of the world. Sacrifice them at once and wholly, or they will turn the truth of God into a lie, and He who might be the Saviour into the worst destroyer of your souls!

CHRIST AT JACOB'S WELL

OR,

THE TWO FOUNTAINS.

JOHN iv. 10.—"*Jesus answered and said unto her, If thou knewest the gift of God, and who it is that saith unto thee, Give me to drink, thou wouldest have asked of him, and he would have given thee living water.*"

IT was a matter of prudent precaution for Jesus to depart into Galilee when the Pharisees had heard of the large increase of His disciples. For He did not unnecessarily expose himself to danger. He would not "tempt God." Prepared to meet His "hour" when it came, He would not hasten it. Unlike fanatics, He looked on pain and death as things to be suffered, but not sought; to be received calmly, and even welcomed, in the way of duty, but not to be wished for their own sakes.

He therefore went into Galilee, and "He must needs go through Samaria," because it was the common and directest road, though avoided by some Jews, from a superstitious feeling; not the only instance by many in which superstition has taken needless trouble and the longest route. Theological bias and geographical ignorance have found another reason for Christ's conduct, and have found the "needs must" in a purposed interview with the woman of Samaria. It would have been well if doctrinal prepossessions had done nothing worse than discover a high spiritual purpose in a matter of custom and convenience.

In passing through Samaria, Christ came to the city of Sychar, where was Jacob's well, on which, being wearied with His journey, He sat down, while His disciples went into the city to buy bread. A woman of Samaria came to draw water; and this gave rise to a most beautiful and instructive interview. The materials were not promising. A sinful, and an ignorant woman; a pitcher; and a well. But they were abundant for Him: He needed but little as the text, occasion, and vehicle of the divinest truth. He was full of wisdom, goodness, and love; and the merest contact of objects and events was sufficient to draw them forth. If, so to speak, they did "but touch the hem of His garment," virtue went out of Him.

We must confine our present thoughts to the beginning of this conversation. Jesus said unto her, Give me to drink. The woman was astonished at the request, perceiving Him to be a Jew, and thus one of a rival race and Church, who, being near to the Samaritans as neighbours and religionists, hated each other with a bitterness worthy of Christians. Christ responded in the words of the text, assuring the poor woman that it was only ignorance that prevented her craving of Him a far greater boon than He had asked of her.

I.

Here is a contrast between Christ's present bodily need and His permanent spiritual satisfaction and abundance.

"Give me to drink." "He would have given thee living water;" the reference being to water clear and flowing, which the Jews called "living" in distinction from still, stagnant waters of a pool. So that He who had enough and to spare of the higher good, was yet dependent on the casual kindness of a stranger for the lower good.

The contrasts in the life of Jesus are very striking. The union of weakness and power, even in physical things, is so. He sleeps, to refresh his weary flesh; but at the call of His terrified disciples, He awakes to hush the storm. He is hungry, like another man; and yet He dooms to perpetual barrenness the tree whose leaves made a vain profession of fruitfulness. He is too poor to pay tribute-money; but He can obtain it from a tenant of the deep. He is being taken as a prisoner to endure an unrighteous judgment and a cruel death; and in that very hour miraculously heals a wound received in His apprehension.

But the most glorious contrasts are those between Christ's outward condition and His spiritual authority and wealth; as when sinking into the arms of death, "crucified through weakness," he promised life and blessedness to the wretched supplicant at His side; or when thirsty and weary, and asking a draught of water at the well of Jacob, He had the power and the will to slake a far sorer thirst, and renew and refresh a far greater life.

The "living water" which He had, and had to give, was not mere happiness. Though including that, it was a nobler and more necessary thing. "In the last day, that great day of the feast, Jesus stood and cried, saying, If any man thirst, let him come unto me, and drink. He that believeth on me, as the Scripture hath said, out of his belly shall flow rivers of living water. But this spake He of the Spirit, which they that believe on Him should receive." It was, then, the Holy Spirit, "the Lord and Giver of life," whose gracious influences both exalt and satisfy the powers and cravings of the soul, that Jesus spake of. There is in man a thirst for righteousness, a thirst for rest, a thirst for God though unknown, which the divine Spirit only can quench. I say, "a thirst," not necessarily a conscious desire, but a want, a craving, a feeling more or less distinct of defect and discomfort; for the soul's thirst, unlike the body's, can be, and often is, separate from any longing for specific objects. Or, more properly speaking, there is the thirst of need, and there is the thirst of desire. And Christ can meet them both. What a contrast! Behold Him in the hot noon and after a toilsome way, looking with wistful eyes upon that woman's pitcher, and asking of her the luxury of a cooling draught; and, at the same time, able to fill her nature with renovating and exhilarating grace. We all know, but we often forget, that the highest spiritual power is independent of physical and worldly things. Like "rivers of water in a dry place," it may spring up in the dreariest deserts of life. The body and outward lot may be but a sorry lantern holding a bright light. The glory of God may shine in the tabernacle with its "rough planks and black hair-cloth." The forces and fulness of a divine life and righteousness and love may be allied with poverty and fleshly feebleness and worldly meanness. "As poor, yet making many rich; as having nothing, and yet possessing all things."

And this does not exhaust the truth. Jesus would not have had living water to bestow upon that sinful woman, if He had not been in a condition to require the refreshment which He asked of her. It was because He took our nature in our state; assumed a humanity which could suffer, and did suffer; felt all the instincts and trials that flesh is heir to; "was tempted in all points like as we are;" knew hunger and thirst, and weariness and pain; it was because of this that He could give the water of life freely unto men. The heat and fatigue which made rest and refreshment precious to Him belonged to the process by which He became our benefactor. His need of a stranger's help was part of the condition of His power to bless. The purest, strongest influence, the greatest and best power to do good, cannot be separated from the actual experience of evil. Pain is both the softener and the strengthener of the soul. It gives the deepest, clearest views of all things spiritual. "We learn in suffering what we teach in song." And, after all, in dealing with the wills and affections of men, in seeking to win them to virtue and godliness, there is more in the speaker than the speech, the doer than the deed. Words and actions have their chief worth in expressing and conveying the spirit of goodness, sympathy, and love.

II.

There is a contrast here between the narrowness of religious prejudice and the generosity of Christian grace.

"How is it that thou, being a Jew, askest drink of me, which am a woman of Samaria? for the Jews have no dealings with the Samaritans." Christ therefore chose a Samaritan in His parable to teach the doctrine of neighbourhood and humanity. Religious faith and feeling, if divorced from the natural instincts and sentiments of benevolence and justice, become merciless tyrants and oppressors. Satan could not accomplish his masterpieces of wickedness without the aid of religion. The greatest traitor was an Apostle. The worst despotism has been a Church. To tell a thirsty man that he belongs to another religion!

But see Jesus, the representative, not of sectarian littleness and bitterness, but of the divine generosity and philanthropy. "Thou wouldest have asked of Him, and He would have given thee living water." The gift of man is hindered by what should have assisted and inspired it; "the gift of God" knows no obstacle but our unfitness to receive it.

The desire to bless was strong and constant in Jesus. He saw in this woman one to be taught, to be stirred to the desire for high and holy blessings. Though worn and wearied, he was "ready to this good word and work." He cared more to impart His boon than to receive hers, for it was His word that "it is more blessed to give than to receive," and "it is not the will of the Father that any should perish." Nor was there anything forced, or even abrupt, in His introduction of religious things. His good was not like unripe fruit which must be plucked from the branch, but like fruit, mellow and juicy, and falling at the slightest shake or touch. He had not to fetch His wisdom from afar: it lay before Him. Nor had He to present it in strange, unwonted forms; He could use those that were at hand. And as He made the sycamore tree the tree of life to Zaccheus, so He made Jacob's well the water of life to the woman of Samaria. "The wise man," says Bacon, "makes more opportunities than he finds." But the wisest man can find them without making them; find them in things that seem to others unmeet for use. You never feel, in reading Christ's life, that He was making opportunities of usefulness. It was itself the flow of living water, running through all the channels of ordinary events and casual intercourses, and diffusing gladness and fruitfulness on either hand. The corn white for harvest, the great vine on the Temple gates, the unseemly strife for the best seats, and here the woman's errand to the well, and other such like things, enable Him to begin or illustrate the holiest and most gracious teaching with all the facility of nature, and its grace and impressiveness also.

As we possess Christ's spirit and mind, we shall do likewise. Do we want occasions of doing good? It is occasions rather that want those who can employ them. A mind filled with the divine truth, and a heart filled with the divine love, will use occasions as they present themselves, just as water flows through the channels made for it, or molten metal seeks the curious devices of the prepared mould. None will be too mean or low to engage our interest; and every scene, however common and bare, will be suggestive and symbolic. An ignorant, sensual woman made Christ forget the claims of thirst, and a pitcher and well of water gave Him a subject for the sublimest discourse.

In proportion to our likeness to Him will be our disinterested generosity. Spiritual goodness and power have this property of diffusiveness. To recur to the figure before us: living water is, of necessity, flowing. Love is the essence of the highest good. Love is of God. God is love. And love must be in us "a well of water springing up into everlasting life," as to its ultimate destiny, and also flowing abroad among all our worldly ways as to present and social influence. I wish to impress this fact. "The gift of God is eternal life," and that cannot be restrained. The grace of Christ is a fountain. Mere belief, transient feelings, custom may be still and stagnant ponds, but the power of the Divine Spirit in man is fresh, sparkling, running water. The one may become corrupt and fetid, and if not kept pure by change and addition, must; the other is sweet, healthy, and life-giving. *Its movement keeps it fresh.* The pool becomes offensive and noisome because it is quiescent, the stream is pleasant and wholesome by constant motion. Love must act to live. Without action it degenerates into a morbid sentiment, or dies out utterly. Grace gains by giving. Other bestowments impoverish, he who dispenses most of this is richest. "There is that scattereth and yet increaseth." And this is truest, and is always true of the divine principles that lead to the scattering. For herein, though the work be lost, the worker succeeds; and he who gives, hoping for nothing again, finds in his very disinterestedness the best and worthiest recompense. "He would have given thee,—poor, guilty, carnal, erroneous creature though thou art—living water."

III.

Here is a contrast between this woman's relation to Christ, and her own conception of it.

She regarded Him as one to whom she could minister, whose bodily wants she could satisfy; for whom she could obtain the cooling, assuaging draught. But, if she had known God's Son, and God's salvation, she would have seen and sought an infinitely greater service. He was to her view a mere worn, parched traveller; He was, in fact, a messenger and message of mercy. She thought that she could refuse or grant His request for a transient blessing: He was even now in the act of conferring on her life everlasting.

She did not know Him, or the boon He bore. Expecting, with others, the Messiah, she little thought that He was now talking to her. Ignorance keeps us from unnumbered blessings. It prevents the possibility of their enjoyment. It is the darkness of the mind, in which he who walketh stumbleth. A man may know and not do; but he cannot do unless he know. And knowledge, in many kinds, inspires the will as well as affords the instruments for action. Knowledge of the laws of nature would be a manifold blessing to thousands, lessening and prospering the work of their hands, and guarding them against a multitude of grievous ills. Knowledge of the laws of the mind would often secure health and power where now there are disease and weakness; would dissipate many a distressing personal mystery, and account for many a disheartening, moral failure. And knowledge of the truths and principles of religion would secure its possession, and keep the heart free from evils and abuses on every hand.

Here, Christ speaks of knowledge of Himself and the gift of God, the nature and medium of God's great and greatest blessing, His "unspeakable gift." And surely if men knew *that*, had any right thought, and proper sense of that, they could not fail to seek it. It is easy to understand the words by which it is expressed, and yet not to know it; just as you may understand the words by which a gorgeous sunset, or a magnificent waterfall are described, and yet have no true idea of the scenes themselves. And men may know all about Christ and the benefits of His Gospel, so far as intellectual conceptions are concerned, and yet be, to all intents and purposes, as ignorant as if they had never heard of them. And ignorance of Christ, and the grace which is through Christ, places an insuperable barrier in the way of spiritual blessing. *He* gives it, and God gives it through Him, and, apart from Him, we have nothing to draw the water of life with, and the well is deep.

But the point I wish now to notice particularly is this: this woman's ignorance of Christ made her look on Him as one to be ministered to, not as one to minister to her. Had she known Him truly, she would have been the supplicant, feeling that He could help her to what infinitely transcended any favour within her reach. And our ignorance of Him, and of our relation to Him, is continually blocking up the path of blessing, and misrepresenting the nature and object of His requirements.

He asks of us many things. He meets us often in the ways of life, and seeks our service, and we think not that we have greater need of His aid than He of ours; that, in fact, He has no need at all of ours, but such as He wills to have. He requests our obedience, lays upon us laws: and we consider whether or not we shall do His will, as if in doing it we were to oblige and benefit Him. We think we are contributors, but did we know Him, should feel far more that we were recipients. It is because we have a superficial and partial view of duty that we can think so. A deep, full knowledge would make us realize our infinite indebtedness to Him, make us see in His mighty help the only possibility of doing His will, and in His requirement of it a means of moving us to crave it. Instead of supposing that there is any merit in our best obedience, we should confess that we are unprofitable servants, after all was done; and placed under great obligations by being aided to do anything. The spirit of true obedience is the spirit of dependence, desire, and prayer, and we shall never "work out our salvation," or the salvation of others with any effect, but as we pray to that "God who worketh in us to will and to do of His good pleasure." While Jesus, then, is asking of us the obedience of heart and hand, true knowledge of ourselves and Him will lead us to supplicate that holy energy, which can give purity to our affections and vigour to our wills, and fill the forms of service with the life of God.

The thought applies to the efficiency of works of faith and love. In the ministry of grace Christ employs the agency of redeemed men. They work, but it is He that causes them to triumph. We misconceive the whole matter when we labour in the temper of independence, as if we were used by Him on account of any intrinsic value and efficacy in our deeds. He employs us, but then He renders our work effectual. Self-confidence and self-conceit will miss the end, or rather will prevent our having any end, that Christ can bless. If we have His end in view—if in the light of His work we do our own—if we know anything of the evils we endeavour to remove from men's souls and lot, and anything of the strength in Christ which enables Him to remove them, and must enable us to remove them in His name: instead of having pride or complacency in the service we render to Him and to his Gospel, we shall never be so humble as when we are most earnest, and while feebly heeding His request for our poor and feeble help, shall still more fervently ask of Him the blessing which alone can make our work or ourselves rich.

Once more. The thought is applicable to *rewards*. The idea of reward is inseparable from honest toil. And Scripture sanctions it in its highest relations. There are rewards, and great rewards, in heaven as well as earth. But such is the grossness of our thought, and the besetting power of our pride, that we are always prone to force the figure and strain the fact. The truth is that, properly and strictly speaking, there is no such thing possible as a divine reward of creature worthiness; and if there were, merit in the sinful, even if they had been sinful in the slightest measure and for the briefest period, would be out of the question; and in those whose only goodness is a gift, and a gift perpetually renewed, would be an absurdity. And if there were a reward, in accurate language, it could not be heaven. No; knowledge of Christ and his gift will make the eternal glory a thing to be sought but not deserved, to be striven for with humble earnestness, but not demanded with confidence as a right. In this sense, as well as every other, we must receive out of His fulness, and grace for grace, the grace of reward for the grace of obedience. Looking forward to the infinite and eternal good promised to holy servants and faithful workers, good without defect and without end, good so perfect as to exclude all we know of evil and to exceed all we know of good below, and thinking of the greatness of our guilt, and the insignificance and imperfection of our worthiest services, we shall feel that nothing in us has any value or relevancy as a desert of that; we shall feel that if we are glorified, it must be the crowning act of mercy, and in the weakest possible sense the recompense of aught we are and do; and, while meeting His demand for such tasks as are within our power, shall expect and supplicate from Him " the abundance of grace, and of the gift of righteousness," " looking for the mercy of our Lord Jesus Christ unto eternal life." If it be ours to render any little service to Him in his Gospel and his Church, even no more than the giving a cup of cold water to some fevered follower in His name, we shall do it with the chastened trust and lowly joy of those who are hoping for the time when "the Lamb in the midst of the throne shall lead them unto living fountains of waters," and "make them drink of the rivers of his pleasures;" and the greatness of that hope will awe as well as stimulate, and fire with an ambition of meekness equal to its strength.

IV.

A contrast between the eagerness for the lower good, and the indifference about the higher.

This woman had come out, as doubtless had been her constant wont, to draw water, and yet plainly showed that she knew nothing of the refreshing and satisfying influences of the divine grace. And when she mistook the Saviour's words to mean mere fresh, running water, she replied, "Sir, give me this water that I thirst not, neither come hither to draw;" and yet we are not told that when she learnt the sense of Jesus, she asked to be supplied with His spiritual gift. You may remember, also, that when, on another occasion, He spoke of giving the true bread from heaven, the Jews, thinking the reference was to some immortal material nourishment, exclaimed, "Lord, evermore give us this bread;" but when they discovered their mistake they were offended, and forsook him.

There is nothing in one view more strange, or in any view more sad, than the fact thus presented, the possibility of man's utter ignorance and insensibility of his greatest want and danger. The natural ordinance is that the need of food and drink shall be accompanied with a desire for them, and that the intensity of the desire shall equal the severity of the need. But in the case of the spiritual necessity there is no such craving; for this necessity is not natural, but sinful, and its curse is that in proportion to its extent it prevents the consciousness of its own existence, until at last the soul, entirely lost to spiritual grace and goodness, is entirely lost to spiritual sensibility also. A man dying of starvation would give a fortune for a meal, but a man sinking fast into the second death cares not for the life immortal; and, while all his instincts and appetites for bodily provision are quick and strong, and goad him to incessant exertion for its possession, his nobler powers and aspirations die out, and leave him but the mockery of a man. There can be no more striking instances of the contrast between the sensual eagerness and the spiritual unconcern than those to which I have referred; for they are brought together, are shown at the same time, and in connection with the same objects. "Give me this water," "Give us this bread," showed how men could value what they supposed to be material, while the very same occasions proved their carelessness when they found it to be spiritual.

My brethren, be not deceived. You may be needy unto ruin, in the things of the Spirit, and yet think you have need of nothing. You may be perishing for lack of the necessaries of spiritual life, and yet feel no hunger and no thirst. The worst of sin is, that it not only damns the soul, but destroys all desire to be saved, and makes it unconscious that it is being damned at all!

CHRIST SEEKING AND SAVING THE LOST.

LUKE xix. 10.—"*For the Son of Man is come to seek and to save that which was lost.*"

THE very perfection of consistency is for a man's words respecting himself to express the loftiest conception of human character, and for his life to be a visible embodiment of that conception. Some men do not pretend to be anything in particular, nor even commonly good; and many more fail to realize their own low estimate and declaration. They mean to be but little, and they manage to be less than they mean. Their pretensions are low, and their reality is lower still. There are others who, in describing themselves, would only give vocal utterance to the thoughts of all observers—their language would be but the weak echo of the impressive sayings of their whole course and conduct. In speaking of their aim and principle, they exhibit the noblest ideal, but one entirely realized in their actual being. Their words are but the brief descriptive guide to their life—the worthiest sight. *They are in harmony with truth*—and their account is in harmony with themselves. Thus was Christ. He calmly, boldly said of His own motives, aim, and rule, things that cannot be surpassed for excellence; and yet you never feel in reading them that there is aught of pride or self-conceit. The most delicate conception of humility is never outraged or offended by His strongest protestations of sincerity, holiness, and love. And why? Because you feel most intimately that all He said, *He was*. Did He say, "I know Him, and keep His saying"? He was revealing His Father's name, and maintaining His Father's cause, among those "who sought to kill Him," and "took up stones to cast at Him." Did he say, "My meat is to do the will of Him that sent me, and to finish His work?" He was sitting on the well where He had both created and slaked the thirst, in a poor, guilty soul. Did He say, "The Son of Man is come to seek and to save that which was lost"?—he said it in *the house of Zacchæus*, to whom He had " brought salvation," "teaching" him, with renewing power, "the weighter matters of the law, justice and mercy."

Let us dwell, for a short time, upon this glorious saying; and may He, who thus describes His mission and work, cause us to prove the truth and to possess the likeness of this blessed character. May we be sought and saved—may we, under God, seek and save our brethren!

I.

Let me bring before you the interesting statement of our text.

You are aware, that though it was intended to describe the conduct of Christ *on earth*, it may be taken as the just description of all His ways and works. The whole mediatorial proceedings of Christ are thus fairly represented. They contemplate the condition of the "lost." They involve a search and pursuit for them. They design their salvation. We shall not, therefore, be very careful to confine our remarks to the fleshly life and doings of Christ, but endeavour to illustrate the spirit of the words, by reference to the character which, as Mediator, He always bears, to the design He always proposes, and the disposition he always displays.

1. *The " lost," then, are the objects of His care and love.*

There are two ideas comprehended in the expression. When Christ would illustrate the condition of those who were lost, on one occasion, he selected three objects: *a sheep—money—*and a *prodigal* (Luke xv). One of these could only be lost in the sense of its owner being deprived of its use. Having no consciousness, the evil of its being mislaid fell upon the "woman." But the other two being lost, suffered or were exposed to evil of their own, as well as occasioned evil to those to whom they belonged, or were related. The loss of the "sheep," included danger and trouble to itself, as well as anxiety and deprivation to its possessor; the loss of the "prodigal," entailed distrust and shame upon himself, as well as affliction on his "father's house." And these are the most fitting and forcible symbols of the sinner's case. He is lost to God—he is lost to himself. This great and blessed Being that made him misses him, so to speak—is defrauded of his services—deprived of his affections and his work—receives not from him the honour and homage to which He is entitled, nor from his life the illustration of His truth and honour, the promotion of His cause and will. But this is not separated from his own loss, nor can it be. He who is not with God nor for Him, is not in safe and healthful possession of his own faculties and powers. As all things are "God's servants," and do His bidding, and glorify His name, they who are without and against God are fatally at war with their own destiny and their own souls.

Let me entreat you to consider this, that an evil man is a lost man. *He* is lost. It is not that he loses, but *is* lost. It is not what he *has*, but *is*, that is lost. True, the loss of other things is involved—he who is himself lost, must lose all things. All things are evil to the evil—it may not be or appear to be so now—but, ere long, it will so be and so appear, for who can speak peace, if God speak truth; who can escape wrath, if He order destruction; who can dispense a blessing, if He pronounce a curse? But this is grievous only as he feels it. If perdition were not felt, it would not be. It is the suffering that makes it loss. And he who suffers, thus and wholly loses his powers of happiness and peace. So far as his consciousness is made the means of pain and grief, in an important sense, his consciousness is lost. But the powers of being and of doing are far nobler than the powers of suffering. There is all the difference of the passive and the active, the receiving and dispensing, and "it is more blessed to give than to receive"—more noble to work than to suffer. Sin involves the loss of the highest powers of man, his power of spiritual perception and service; and if you could entirely prevent all other evil—if you could avert the wrath of God, and pain, and mental anguish, it would be a sad thing that he who was fit, and was designed for obedience, for intelligent submission to the claims of God, for noble and blessed fellowship with things and beings holy and divine, for the sight and sense and service of the glorious Gospel, should be found without taste and temper for them; should be without " the knowledge of the holy"—the " images" of the Creator—"righteousness and true holiness." Zacchæus was rich, in office, and a Jew; he had many of the objects that were, and are still, prized; but he was yet a " lost" man, till Jesus found him.

And is not this the state—the woeful state—of our nature still? Look around upon it, and how small a portion is not, speaking spiritually, destitute and astray? Who can contemplate it, under whatever religious name, civil rule, social influence; whatever its moral or physical condition, and not perceive that the description still holds good? Of what is it possessed compared with that of which it is capable? Bring the image of a really holy Christian man—who is living in the action and the hope of Gospel truth—loving God and his neighbour, finding his blessedness in blessing, bring this image into comparison with men in general, and see how wide the distance at which they are, from what they were intended for! How vast the mass of rich material lying waste—how large the force of spiritual vitality bearing weeds and thorns. Leave out the future altogether—take no account of eternal death

—the awful and unending portion of the lost—and what a wretched picture is presented now! How few say, really, practically, "there is a God." How few say, really, practically, " I have a soul." Choose your spot —go not to China but to Christendom—take not the people under the darkness and bondage of the great religious lie and tyranny, but under the light and liberty of full and free Gospel teaching and Gospel rule, and is not your nature desolate and low? Is it not broken, spoilt? Does it not deny its dignity? fail of its function? caricature its essence, origin, and end? By the standard of *this Book*—not of sensuous, scientific, or merely moral conventionalisms, but by the principles which God has taught, which Christ has lived and died to honour and impress, and which the Spirit of holiness and grace quickens in the hearts of all that truly believe—does it not show, as a lamp without its light, a temple forsaken of its glory? Are not men "lost"?

But we may go lower still, and find a similar result. Is it not sad and solemn fact that the mass of men are not even moral? What class is without its notorious vices? What circle has not its characteristic sins? How few are there who never lie, never break their faith, never overreach, never transgress the rules of strict sobriety, never offend the laws of purity, never give way to impulses of wrath and anger and revenge? What besetting selfishness binds and oppresses men's hearts? What tyranny of custom and of creed, inflicts injustice on the honourable and the free? How many a Zacchæus takes advantage of office to defraud the weak? What a general subjection of the highest passions to unworthy ends? I saw but yesterday, a cow enticed along the road by the side of its calf carried in a cart, and I thought within myself, "This is man—but a picture of a great procedure—thus are the purest, tenderest affections made to work for low and earthly purposes: thus love is harnessed for selfish ends; and seeming service rendered that personal ease may be secured." Is it not so; is not the money-market the place to learn the value of all ethereal sentiments and spiritual powers: are they not worth what they will fetch? Are not the holiest gifts and faculties regarded, but too often, as the Nethinims, "the hewers of wood and drawers of water" for the sanctuary of worldly ease and gain?—Are not men "lost"?

This suggests another idea. Going lower still, what is the general character of human toil and care? Is it not for the mere instrumentality and outward show of life? Go where you will, and what do you find to be the chief anxiety, desire, and labour? Does it not respect the *material* of existence? Is not the main burden of discourse the condition and prospect of food, commerce, dress, and outward law? Are not the early and late thought, the midday toil and midnight dream concerning property, business, and secular plans? Is not the one oppressing care of the great mass, "How shall we live?" Say not this must be—there is no help. Was it God's design that man should be always trying to live, and never living; that they should be for ever labouring to keep mind and body together, without opportunity or power of cultivating their mental powers, their moral sentiments?—that the great mass should have no nobler office in view than barely providing themselves with necessaries, and no nobler prospect in decay than entering the workhouse, or depending upon alms? But leaving this—is our nature healthy, when the whole soul is engrossed in pursuing earthly things, when the "heart is united" only to amass wealth, when a competency or a fortune is sought as if it were the chief end of man? his whole energies employed in covering himself " with thick clay;" when "what shall we eat, what shall we drink?" are the most interesting of all questions, the most momentous of all problems; when the richest endowments of our nature are regarded chiefly in their subserving to animal advancement, gratification, and adornment; intelligence enabling to seek them skilfully, imagination infusing into the pursuit a little ethereality of sentiment, and conscience imparting something of a moral element? Is not man "lost"?

2. Man, thus lost, thus spiritually lost—lost to God, and to himself, is the object of Christ's care. He loves us in our weakness, and worldliness, in "our crimes and our carnality." He proposes our *salvation*: to bring us back to God, to bestow His knowledge, love, and image; to impart a spirit of holiness and grace; to bind up our broken, and unite our separated powers; to regain the dominion of affection over flesh, and conscience over all; to infuse his "saving health," by means of His mediatorial "stripes" and purifying spirit; to deliver from the bondage of social custom and individual depravity; and, by the influence of His Gospel, taking hold on the world, to correct the sinful and selfish principles and

passions that have so great a place in the production of wretchedness, want, and death. Let it be remembered, however, that Christ's chief aim is to secure inward and *individual* salvation. Whatever may be done *for a man* is very little while *he* is lost, in reference to the highest things; you cannot *save him*, unless you *convert* him. The best plans and institutions are but trifles, while men are personally subject to the rule of injustice, unkindness, and ungodliness. Christ knows this: and, therefore, instead of propounding a scheme and system of human welfare—" He went about doing good"—doing good to single souls—talking at a feast—calling from the receipt of custom—meeting a woman at a well—beckoning a man from a tree, and, at last, in the fulness of His risen power, sending forth His representatives, not to establish a mighty apparatus of machinery, but to preach the glad tidings of the kingdom, to say, "*He* that believeth shall be saved;" "Examine yourselves whether ye be in the faith;" "Every man shall bear his own burden."

And let it be further observed that Christ, in pursuing the good of the lost, omitted not, but rather selected, those *most lost*. This was His reproach in His day, as it is often in our own. "And when they saw it, they all murmured, saying, That he was gone to be a guest with a man that is a sinner"—(Verse 7). They meant *a great sinner*, and it is in reference to this complaint that the text was uttered, "The Son of Man is come to seek and to save that which was lost"—which meant, "Is it true that the publicans are worse than others? Then are they the proper objects of my care, for I came to save the guilty; and the most guilty though they would have least claim upon a judge, have most upon a Saviour; for who, and what, are the immediate objects of interest to men—is it the sheep enclosed in the fold?—is it the money safe in the chest?—is it the child happy at home?—and not rather the wandering animal, the mislaid coin, the prodigal son." The more we love ourselves, the more we shall avoid the reprobate and wretched; the more we love our brethren, the more we shall seek them out. The consideration of personal ease and convenience in the Priest and Levite led them to avoid the sight of the poor waylaid traveller—disinterested charity in the Samaritan prompted him to approach, and comfort and provide for him.

3. *Christ* "SEEKS" *to* "*save.*" He goes in quest of men. He had His eye on Zacchæus when he visited the sycamore tree—His "delights were" at the work ere His charity had utterance there. He knew where the objects of His pity were to be found, and directed His course and shaped His plans that He might meet with them. He did not sit in solemn pomp—did not dwell in quiet glory—awaiting the approach of the miserable and guilty. His love was not of the easy nature that merely listens to the cry of woe and want —that stretches out the hand when power is supplicated—but of the nobler kind, that goes after the lost and ruined. He was the missionary of salvation, not alone its magnificent dispenser. And rightly, the worst cases are not those that present themselves— the greatest ignorance is that which knows not of its own existence; the grossest depravity is that which feels not its own shame; the deepest woe is that

which covers up itself, and turns its face to the wall that it may die.

And now the Saviour contents not himself with "receiving sinners," but searches for them. And is it fanciful to say that in the case before us we have a beautiful suggestion of the various means by which He compasses their paths, attracts their attention, and brings them into contact with Himself? See how agencies and events, see how good and evil, see how mind and matter are all His "servants" in His work of men's salvation. Had His fame spread—the report of His mighty works gone before Him? Behold how knowledge, especially the knowledge of history, and still more especially of Christian history, is employed to stir and stimulate the mind. Was His coming talked about at Jericho? Behold how the human voice is at His command. Did Zacchæus look forward to His passing thither? Behold how expectation of the future, and especially the future in its relation to the Son of God, seems to quicken thought. Was curiosity excited in his breast? Behold the influence of craving and inquiry subservient to salvation. Was he little of stature? Behold how personal disadvantages may have to do with the greatest good of souls. Did the crowd obstruct his view? Behold social position and pressure preparing for conversion. Did he climb the sycamore tree? Behold nature contributing to the triumphs of grace. Did Christ command him thence? Behold the force of personal influence bringing into the presence of the Lord. Did His "words take hold" of him even unto renewal? Behold the effectual working of redeeming truth and love!

4. Once more. Christ not only proposes the good of the " lost," even their " salvation," and " seeks " them for this purpose, but " He is come " to do it. In looking at His interference for our race, we may not dwell alone upon His actual course on earth, or His present work in heaven. It would be to exclude the most important facts and features of His history and those which give to all the rest their chief importance, charm, and power. What He did on earth—His life and labours and sufferings and death ; what He does in heaven, by the agency of men, the ministry of Providence, the operations of the Holy Spirit, are all to be considered in relation to His coming hither— the fact, the manner, and the meaning of His advent. Had He not existed prior to His appearance as a man —had our knowledge of Him been confined to His manifestation in the flesh—His course would have been single and alone ; but when we call to mind that He " came " that He might " seek and save "—that His coming was voluntary and from another and a higher state—that He chose to come and to come " in the flesh"—that He who was found in "the form of man" was previously adored in " the form of God "—that He who was a man of sorrows was, " before the world began," glorious with the Father—that He assumed the nature of them He loved and laboured for, first putting Himself, in a manner, on their own level, taking their own place, uniting Himself with their own sympathies, and subjecting Himself to their wants and woes and dread mortality—that He made a descent which men could never make to pass through an ex- perience that they could never feel, and die a death

which they could never die, is anything wanting to the perfection of His history ?—and do not the few plain words before us present a scene which fact can never equal, and imagination may only miserably explain—" The *Son of Man* is come to seek and to save that which was lost." " This is a faithful saying, and worthy of all acceptation, that Jesus Christ *came into the world* to save sinners."

II.

Let me ask you to consider some important bearings of the statement now illustrated.

1. *You have in our subject an evidence of our religion—the religion of " the Son of Man."*

Take His character and course as here described, and all the notices we have of Him in the Scripture and elsewhere are to the same effect—if He was, which none will doubt, He was what we have represented Him to be; if He wrought, He wrought as we have sought to exhibit His work—and you have a strong proof of the true divinity of His mission and life. Think of His object, principle, and method, and say whether, in the circumstances of the case, they do not necessarily indicate one come from God ? He set before Him a high object—spiritual salvation; and He laboured for it with an entire, self-sacrificing zeal. This appears, if you leave out the peculiar nature of His death, an atonement; if you reject the peculiar nature of His birth, an incarnation. Look at Him simply as He was on earth, and among men—mark His career as it was apart from strictly Scriptural intimations of his original dignity and mediatorial office—regard Him as "seeking and saving the lost," proposing the real, highest, personal, and perpetual good of man; pursuing it with the devotion of His life and heart; going among the wicked and worthless, Himself the holy and unstained; falling like light upon the sinful and cleaning them, Himself most free from all pollution;—e sacrifice at last to His love and pity, but all along a living offering too, combining the noblest object with the noblest methods, and say, "Truly, this was the Son of God!"

For remember, to do justice to this history, when He appeared and among whom. Men are according to their age—he is the greatest man who *seeks* the best objects; he is the best being in opposition to the strongest influences of his time and people. Strength is according not only to exploit, but to resistance. Stormy wind as well as lofty flight indicates the power of wing. The "life" must be considered together with the "times." While Christ was all alone in any case, all that He was He was in opposition to the people among whom He "dwelt," and the marks and tendencies of the period in which He lived. His was at constant warfare with prevailing sentiments and tastes and tempers. In aiming at the moral, evangelic welfare of souls He had to reject the most besetting notions of the world and Church to which He came; in following it with utter self-abandonment, He had to disregard and suffer from the policies and principles of all that were around him. It was a reproach that He cared for the "lost;" it was an offence that He endeavoured to effect their "salvation" after the Spirit, not the letter; it was a novelty that He went in quest of it, giving up all things to this end. There were no materials in that "half-barbarous nation in wholly barbarous times" out of which could have been formed the *living* "Son of Man," and no materials out of which *His image* could have been formed. He must have been, or none could have conceived of Him; and if He were, He must have been from heaven.

2. *You have in our subject a beautiful model of Christian life and labour.*

What Christ was, we should be. "He that saith he abideth in Him ought himself also to walk even as He walked." We derive from Him not only spiritual life, but spiritual life like that which was in Him. He creates us after His own likeness, fills us with His own spirit. He is the "corn of wheat" which, falling into the ground, bringeth forth fruit "after his kind." He is "the vine" from which, as "branches," we derive vitality and fruitful force. The same work that redeems also teaches us, and whence we obtain our power we obtain our pattern likewise. Much that Christ did we cannot do—much that He was we cannot be; but the difference affects physical not moral nature, the form not the spiritual essence of His life. He wrought on a larger scale, but not in another spirit, than that which is possible to us; and all the sentiments that are expressed in our text may find, and ought to find, their realization in those who take their name and draw their whole vitality from Him.

His object was the welfare of the "lost." What is ours? Are we sincerely aiming at the good of souls? Do we love lost men?—are we striving to save them? I do not mean, are we *supporting institutions* for this purpose. Christ's was *a personal* devotion to this work, and a personal devotion apart from all outward facilities for its expression. One of the evils attending, perhaps inseparable from, the varied organizations of our day, is that men lose sight of the claim which is upon them for individual toil. Every object, from the most spiritual to the most material, is sought by societies; and it is often forgotten that, however desirable and useful they may be, they cannot relieve from the pressure of personal obligation to do good, that we cannot fulfil our office by proxy, that the call of Christ cannot be answered by pay *or* person, but demands *both*—that the *work* of each is wanted as well as his *gift*, his *power* as well as *name*, his *voice* as well as *vote*. And if there be the right spirit it will find utterance. If the heart is really alive to God and men it will not fail of fitting modes of action. " A dispensation of the Gospel" will be felt to be upon it, and it must either speak or die. This is a point of great importance. Christ was alone—He had to work from Himself, and in opposition to surrounded agencies and influences. And what we need—a great and manifest requirement of our day—is the spontaneous and independent activity of souls doing good from the good within. Do you say, "What should we do? set us to work." I answer, Find out your work and do it. Look around you and see what is the sphere appointed you by Providence, and for which you have especial fitness. It may be that there is no society which you can join—no prepared machinery ready to your hands. *Work without it.* Who, without entering a Sunday-school, cannot gather round him a class of scholars, teach them, watch over them, and make them love him ? Who, without connection with a Christian instruction society, cannot select his own district, and provide for the instruction and impression of its people ? While you are looking out for organizations you are revealing your own want of heart-preparedness for labour. There is just as much real life and love in the Church as would speak and act, if all organizations were destroyed, and not the smallest portion more. I ask, then, what are you doing, not as a congregation, but *as souls?* Oh! it would be a great and blessed thing to know that all our people, even though without the pomp of high-sounding institutions, were all at work, quietly but earnestly, seeking to save; that they were bringing, even though without the formality of printed reports, their spiritual influence to bear on the ignorant and reprobate in their own circles and neighbourhoods; that without waiting for others, or copying them, each was " serving his generation according to the will of God" in the way marked out for him by God. Christ "sought" to save. He went in quest of the lost. And here you have a feature of true Christian zeal. It is one thing to do the work that invites its own performance, to dispense the blessing that men are waiting to receive. God "is found of them that seek Him not," and Jesus had not alone to "restore," but to *pursue,* the wandering sheep. It is not enough that we are willing to do good, we must be ready to go after and create opportunities of doing it. How many are reproved by this! Place before them all the circumstances and instrumentalities of service and they will perhaps render it; but of the making discovery, both of the objects and means of usefulness, they have no idea. They are fit only for a highly civilized Christianity ; they can live and labour where the lot is well prepared and the methods are provided for their use, but are entirely destitute of the spirit and the skill to *colonize* for Christ—to go to the waste places of humanity, break up ground as well as cultivate it, build houses as well as live in them, and, if need be, make their tools as well as use them. Once more. Christ " came" to seek and save. He had to put Himself into a condition in which He could do it—a condition of infirmity and woe. He had to take a nature as well as a state. Never was such a preparation for service—a preparation involving such humiliation, loss, and suffering. And this is a grand point for us. Full many never think of this. Their utmost zeal merely respects their using rightly what they have, and all seem aspiring after new and larger powers of blessing, never at least seeking them at personal cost. Who is not satisfied, when asked to give, if able to say, " I have it not," without " labouring," or retrenching, that he " may have to give"? Who is not content, when invited to work, if he can truly say, " I have no time," without making time by giving up some profitable or unprofitable engagements ? Who is not content, when requested to perform some special task, if he can justly plead, " I am not qualified," without acquiring the necessary qualification by patient and painstaking toil ? Oh! how little is there in the best of us of His " mind who took upon Him the form of a man and a servant, and became obedient unto death, even the death of the cross."

And yet, call we not ourselves His "followers?" What does it mean? He lived only for others. How do we trace His course—walk in His steps? Followers of the Saviour and the sacrifice are they who never *deny themselves* for others—never *seek out* objects and methods of saving them from death—never *labour* to save them at all—live in selfish ease and pomp and pleasure? Is this *a following*? It may be a forsaking, a denying, an opposing, but certainly it is no following of "the Son of Man." Call we not ourselves His "friends"? Is this our conduct to our friend, showing no practical approval of His one great object, no living sympathy with His ruling spirit, no active co-operation with His master work? Is this *friendship*? It may be indifference, disregard, enmity, but certainly it is no friendship. And yet say we not that *we* are saved— saved by *Him*, and by *His seeking* of us, without our merit or desire at first! Were we not "lost" as others, and if not lost now, is it not owing to His self-sacrifice and painful love? Should not His love inspire us, and if it do, must not the inspiration take the form of His own procedure? Shall we not be "*constrained*" by it, and if so, "constrained to live not to ourselves, but to Him;" and if to Him, to be and do as He was and did when in the world? And are we not *called to this?* Is not His religion one of love and labour for human souls? And are not we renewed and saved that we may have the will and pains to benefit our fellows? Does God ever "bless" but that we may be "made a blessing"? Oh! believe me, you are not, cannot be, the saved of Christ if you are not quickened by the principles that moved and guided Him. "If any man have not the spirit of Christ he is none of His;" and His spirit dwells in none without conforming to His image and moulding to His will.

3. *You have in our subject matter for the serious consideration of unconverted men.*

Christ came to seek and to save men—came to seek and to save *you.*

Are you conscious of your lost condition and bitterly bewailing it? Do you desire salvation and earnestly seek it? Here is consolation for you. It was Christ's errand, his life and death to secure it. Without salvation His history has no purpose, His coming no design. He is "the Son of Man" that He may be a Saviour. He is Messiah, Christ, to redeem. Take that away, and you take away the essence of His office, sufferings, and work. "This is a faithful saying, and worthy of all acceptation, that Christ came into the world to save sinners."

Are you unconscious of your lost condition? See what *it must be* from our subject. And do not expect some special interference: compare not yourselves with the "lost" whom Christ sought and saved, as Zacchæus, and others. They knew not Him, but you do. He *has* come, *has* spoken to you. In a sense you are found by Him. Yea, you are resisting Him, his counsels, admonitions, and entreaties. And this you cannot help. It will *be always true* that salvation was possible, was presented, was pressed! And this increases your doom. The presence and works and teaching of Christ made the doom of Chorazin and Bethsaida greater than that of Sodom and Gomorrah, and makes *yours* greater than theirs!

ENOCH;

OR,

THE EARTHLY WALK AND HEAVENLY HOME.

GEN. v. 21—24. "*And Enoch lived sixty and five years, and begat Methuselah: and Enoch walked with God after he begat Methuselah three hundred years, and begat sons and daughters: and all the days of Enoch were three hundred sixty and five years: and Enoch walked with God: and he was not; for God took him.*"

THIS last thing might be said of any good man at death: for God takes him, and he is not here. "The flesh returns to the dust as it was, and the spirit returns to God who gave it." But we know that though the words do not necessarily convey the idea of an unusual occurrence, they were intended to do so: as indeed the fact of their being used at all, instead of the expression employed of all the others mentioned in this chapter, "and he died," might naturally suggest. Paul tells us—Heb. xi. 5—"By faith Enoch was translated, that he should not see death; and was not found, because God had translated him: for before his translation he had this testimony, that he pleased God."

There is a whole and perfect man in heaven out of each of the great dispensations of religion. There is Enoch from the Patriarchal; Elijah from the Mosaic; and Christ from the Christian. All other good men, wherever they are, are incomplete. Even "David is not ascended into heaven." They were all eminently good and faithful, one perfect; all prophets of righteousness, all called to minister in times of great corruption and wickedness; and their supernatural exit, the perhaps secret, silent, removal of the first, the gorgeous ascent of the second, and the calm, though public translation of the third, were in part a tribute paid to their personal excellence, and honourable ministry: but they were more; they were signs and voices of another world in times that needed to be warned that another world existed; that death is not man's end, but only one mode of departure hence; that those who go away by dying might, if God willed, go away without dying. And they were more; as occasional resurrections were specimens and promises, "a kind of first-fruits" of the final quickening of all the dead: so, perhaps, these may be considered as types of the final transformation of all the living—of those who will not die, but will be changed in a moment, in the twinkling of an eye, at the last trump.

It matters little, however, whether a man dies or not, or whether he is raised or changed. The question is, how he lives. The mode of his departure hence is a trifle; but the mode of his abiding here is all-important. Translation has no glory but as it indicates and preludes a glorious course: otherwise it would be rather a mockery. But "the cloud" which received Jesus out of men's sight was only the cloud of that holy presence which had attended Him on earth; "the chariots and horses of fire" were only the meet attendants of Elijah's warrior soul; and God's taking Enoch to Himself was the fitting end of one who had had more to do with God for three hundred years than any other man of his time: for "Enoch walked with God," and "God took him."

The brief narrative is full of instruction. We might say a great deal on it which we shall *not* say—a great deal which might be said on many texts. Our object will be to keep as much as possible to the immediate suggestions of the words. And doing so, I am mistaken if we shall find any deficiency of matter subservient to the purposes of "life and godliness." May it teach us to "walk so as to please God!"

I.

He "walked with God"—a brief and simple statement of a momentous fact.

Of course the meaning is, that he was a good man, that he lived religiously. There are many expressions for a religious life in the Bible; among others there are two, very significant and often used, that fitly describe its two general aspects. "Waiting upon God," "Walking with God." "Waiting on thy God continually," "Walking humbly with thy God." The one sets forth more the heavenward, and the other more the earthward aspect of religion. In the one man is the dependent, trustful, supplicating creature, in the other the active.

We all speak of men's "ways" and "walking." We mean their conduct, the mode in which they carry themselves, and the progress they make as men, rational and moral agents, in what they do. All men have "ways." All men "walk" somehow. The difference between men morally and spiritually is not between walking and not walking, but between walking rightly and wrongly; walking to heaven and to hell. Activity, incessant activity, is impressed upon all. It is the universal law. But some walk after the spirit, and others after the flesh; some in darkness, and others in light. True religion is, walking "with God."

We are meant to walk with some one. We are *social* as well as active. Solitary journeying is sorrowful journeying. Company gives safety as well as cheer, beguiles the long hours and goads the flagging spirits. Most men have fellowships in their journey through life—companions of their moral ways, "walking with the wise," or "going with the evil." But the highest of all fellowships is with God: and "if we all walk in the light as He is in the light, we have fellowship one with another." We "walk with God." What does it include? Unquestionably *realization*. God is with us wherever we are, but we are with Him only as we recognize and feel Him to be present. God is "invisible," and only *faith* can realize; and "by faith Enoch was translated." In the dark night, a stranger perhaps might place himself by our side, or just behind us, for a time, but we should not walk with him. In the dark night of sin, "God is not far from every one of us," but only one here and there are with Him. To see God, to be aware of His solemn nearness, to act as if this thought were ever in our mind, "Thou God seest me," doing His will as that of a present Master, rejoicing in His favour as that of a present Friend, and trusting in His succour as that of a present Protector— to go on thus divinely right, and brave, and happy, is to " walk with God." It includes *intercourse*. It were a poor thing to have a companion and to exchange no remark with him, to discourse not on general topics, nor even on the fortunes and prospects of the way. "But truly our fellowship is with the Father, and with His Son Jesus Christ." Sometimes it is unconscious; and it is with us as the disciples journeying to Emmaus. Jesus draws nigh and goes with us, but we do not know Him, and yet our hearts burn within us by the way: but after the communion is honour, and "the secret of the Lord is with them that fear Him," while they "pour out their heart before Him" in the frankness of faithful souls.

This bringing of God and man together is the grand end of all divine revelation and providence. Time was, when man walked wholly with God, "rejoicing always before Him," "hearing His voice in the wind of the day;" but sin rent them asunder, made God angry and man sullen, destroyed the very conditions of communion—for "how can two walk together unless they be agreed?" To heal this schism, to restore the broken union, Christ came—Emanuel, God with us—and through His sacrifice and holy spirit, "God dwells with man again," and we "walk with God."

What a glorious life is this! Who loves not to walk with a dear friend?—and the more, if he be very wise, and pure, and good. Who that had to travel a doubtful road would not rejoice if that friend were a safe guide as well? And still more, if there were fear of evil, one of a strong and skilful arm? And further yet, if, being poor himself, that friend were well able to meet all possible charges of the way? We "walk with God," who can "supply all our need," who "guides us with His eye," encompasses us with favour as a shield: and we "joy in God."

II.

Enoch walked with God, *after the birth of Methuselah*. It was then, so far as appears, that he began to do so.

It is not said that he did so before. Until then it is said that "he lived," as it is said of the rest. I am well aware that we must not lay much stress on every word, or few words, in records so inartificial and fragmentary as these. Word criticism has been at once the blessing and bane of theology: the blessing, when it has been used as an instrument of getting at the large, natural meanings of Scripture; the bane, when pursued by narrow and technical understandings. Nowhere more than in theology have words been "the counters of wise men and the money of fools." I should lay no great stress on the mere fact that before Enoch was a father he is described as living, and afterwards as walking with God, if it were by itself; but when the other patriarchs here mentioned are spoken of in the same way before and after the births of their first-born, surely there is something in it. Does it not imply that he had *not* walked with God for 65 years? Or, supposing the expression, in his case, refers to *eminence* in religion, does it not imply that at that time his religion received a new start?

We cannot tell. But we do know that he might have been irreligious until then. He lived in an ungodly time, and might have followed "the spirit of the age." There are multitudes now alive who have spent as many years in sin; and still more who have spent, though not as many years in sin, yet as large a *proportion* of their years. And think you, is it not a sad thing for a man, for any man, to give a part of his brief life to forgetfulness of God, and alienation from Him, to be "without God in the world?" And especially when it is the earlier part, that which should be to all the rest as a foundation, and a sowing of seed? Is it a thing that any man can look back upon without regret? How will you look back upon it? If you remain irreligious, will you not repent it? If you become religious, will you not repent it? If it was thus with Enoch, did he not repent it? Though he attained to eminent godliness and eminent honour, he would ever think upon the fact with bitter sorrow, and with sorrow equal to his sanctity. Sixty-five years that might have been spent in walking with God, spent without God! No divine presence to keep and counsel, to comfort and to strengthen! Many of you are not walking with God. How old are you? Some of you have lived nearly all your lives without God, and are going to die without Him. Some have lived more than half. And oh! how many a quarter. Shall any more be *atheistical?*

But there is something more here. If Methuselah's birth was the date of Enoch's religion, or of a new stage in it, there is an interesting subject for reflection. Was it *the cause* as well as *the date*? It might have been. The like has happened many times. The formation of new connections, entrance upon married life, the birth of children, have been in innumerable instances the means of beginning or of quickening religious feeling, of rousing up the soul to a new or a more earnest life. And so generally, the sense of responsibility awakened by fresh duties, and the sense of weakness awakened by fresh dangers, and the sense of defect awakened by fresh opportunities, have often led to thoughts about a man's spiritual position and powers which have ended in his being able to say, "My sufficiency is of God;" and the new outward lot or calling has been God's means of fitting the soul for all callings and all lots, and the man has entered on the strange way in life, "walking with God." And if any events have this tendency, surely they are such as increase the power or enlarge the sphere of a man's influence over souls. If anything should wake him as to the state of his own soul, the fact of other souls being placed in his charge should. And if, though careless of his own, he ought to seek grace for the sake of others, they are the souls for whose being he is responsible, and over whose well-being he has the greatest power.

III.

Be this as it may, the fact is clear that Enoch did walk with God after the birth of Methuselah, and the births of other children.

One of the two men who have had the honours of translation in this world for "pleasing God" was a man who lived in the midst of society, and was surrounded with children; he was not a recluse or a celibate. Had the subject of such signal glory been selected from the brethren of a convent, had he been one whose meagre frame and worn visage bore witness to the severity and frequency of his fasts and vigils, the world would never have ceased to hear of this attestation to the Divinity of a single and separated life. But it was not so. This man lived in the midst of men, and that in a wicked and perverse generation. He lived in that condition in which there are natural and necessary distractions and temptations. He stood in nearest relation to several, perhaps many, of those whom good men have pronounced " certain cares, and uncertain comforts," and yet, in spite of all, he walked with God: the husband and the father, and the man, through those relations and other social ties, lived a divine life. Some leave God as they enter the world. Some who were devout and pure before have, in presence of new fellowships, withdrawn from His, and lost His counsel and help at the very season when heavier tasks required performance and harder problems craved solution. The wife of the bosom has caused a divorce of the soul from her heavenly husband; the little ones have shut out the great Father of all; and the multiplication of powers and offices in all directions has deadened instead of deepened the sense of dependence and accountability; and He "whose we are" and whom we "should serve" in all is left to expostulate, "If I am a Father, where is mine honour? and if I am a Master, where is my fear?"

It ought not so to be: and, of course, if we were renewed, it never would be so. Any man may see—it requires no learned divine, no meditative monk, to tell us, that all the relations of men, and all the scenes and situations in which they can be placed, have their moral and religious perils; and as a rule, the more we have to do in this world, and with men, the points of contact with evil are increased; and it must be left to each man to say for himself how many and what kinds of these he is required by his duty to God, to men, and to himself, to encounter. But this we maintain, that there is nothing in man's state in this world, in any of the relations which God has established for him, or the offices and works arising out of them, which absolutely necessitates an irreligious life, or a life of feeble and defective godliness. What has been done may be done again. And Enoch, in the very infancy of our race, and in a most ungodly and sinful age, "walked before God and was perfect" in the midst of all the demands and cares and dangers of social and active life.

It would be saying very little for religion if such a case were impossible. It would be queer theology which taught that man must denude himself of a portion of himself, ignore some of his capabilities and propensities, in order to know and possess much, or most, of God. It is the old heresy again, which is always cropping up in one shape or another, that the natural, not the unnatural, is the evil; that there is some innate and ineradicable enmity between matter and spirit; that the world has something wrong and dangerous about it besides what it gets from sin. Here old Manicheans and modern manufacturers, knowing gnostics and country clowns, half-starved eremites and portly gentlemen, ascetic Churchmen and well-to-do Dissenters, " meet together." But it is a heresy nevertheless, though, like all heresies, having its sources and supports in our common nature, being partly false and partly true; rather a lie covering a truth, the truth contorted, dislocated, disordered, misapplied. No. We are not to conceive so of religion, as having to shun the familiar ways of men, as like some flowers flourishing best in the shade, or as being, at least in its finer and more ethereal parts, like a corpse long dead that crumbles into dust when exposed to air; but we are to think of her as the mistress and mother of all things natural and fair and wholesome; as the friend and benefactor of every human faculty and every worldly work; as able to descend to the lowest state and cheer the saddest, as the sun of the soul, first gilding the mountain heights of reason and conscience, but "shining more and more" until the whole surface of our life reflects its light, and the most humble and hidden places receive and rejoice in its enlivening rays. For religion is not only to *live* in every state and sphere, but to *bless* them. It is that without which they will be evil: there is nothing else can make any scene one of greatest joy and profit. We *must* have it, as well as *can* have it. It is no impracticable thing, no strange and unreasonable requirement; it is one entirely feasible, in harmony with all facts and all principles, just what should be; for "what doth the Lord require of thee but to do justly, love mercy, and walk humbly with thy God ?" And Enoch is a proof that that may be done—done not only by a mind wholly given to devout exercises, but dwelling among the common haunts and engaged in the common occupations of men; done when the social influence is evil and strongly evil; done when the spiritual helps are few and weak; and done in a most eminent degree.

IV.

When it is said that Enoch walked with God, it is meant that he attained to *special religious excellence.*

I don't say that the words necessarily mean that in themselves. I have said the opposite. They describe what others have done besides him, and what we are told to do: the common practice of good men in all ages. But words of general import may sometimes be used in an emphatic way, and so words of special strength of meaning may sometimes be employed with lesser and lighter significance. And there can be little question that these words may express both a common characteristic of a class and a peculiar distinction of individuals. They are no ordinary eulogium when applied to Noah.—" Noah was a just man and perfect in his generations, and Noah walked with God." Nor is it difficult to see that they do naturally express something more than mere religion, however true and pure, though they may refer to that. They contain the ideas of nearness, intimacy, familiarity, continuance, and uninterruptedness; they exclude the distant, formal, occasional, and brief. And in all their fulness and power they must be considered as applied to Enoch. He was not the first godly man of those mentioned; but there was an habitual, universal godliness about him which distinguished him even from other saints. His religion did not merely come into contact with his secular life; his spiritual humanity did not merely touch his social humanity, but, like the prophet upon the dead child, "stretched itself upon" it, mouth on mouth, eyes on eyes, hands on hands, and made it live. His religion was life, an active life. He "walked with God."

I cannot tell whether any stress, in this connection, is to be laid on the fact to which I have already adverted, of the different expressions employed to denote the first sixty-five years and the last three hundred years of Enoch's lifetime. But it is a fact worthy of remark. Of the rest it is said in this chapter that they "lived" so many years before the birth of their first-born, and then "lived" so many years after it, and died. But of Enoch it is said that he "lived" so many years before that event, and "walked with God," not "lived" so many years after it. That is, his walking with God during one part of his days was equivalent to his living during another. I don't know that the writer intended anything by this, but the words thus used are peculiar, and they do really make it out that the religion of his last three hundred years was inclusive of his entire existence as well as the life of his first sixty-five—that, in fact, it took in the whole of his life; so that to say of him that he lived, or that he was religious, was to say the same thing. He was always and in all things walking with God. And it is a great question for us whether our religion is thus broad and abiding, whether faith and love are the mainsprings of all our being, whether "the man of God" is only another name for "the man of business," and the man of the family, the citizen, the friend, the traveller, and the guest. In other words, if all of you that is not religious were removed, how much would be left? If all the portions of your time in which no part of you was religious were omitted, how long could you be said to have lived? Alas! alas! what little people, what short lives, only would remain!

Enoch walked with God, "blameless and harmless, the son of God, in the midst of a crooked and perverse generation, shining as a light in the world, holding forth the word of life;" he attained to a specially constant and comprehensive piety. His soul and common life were, in an unwonted degree, possessed by the powers of the other world. His habit was religious. This constituted his eminence, and *aided* it. "There is nothing succeeds like success." It is true of everything in which the opinions and assistance of others are concerned; but it is also true of everything else, true of things that depend only on our own thoughts and acts. Religion has to do with both, and it is more true of it than of anything besides. He who gets to realize anything like the full meaning of walking with God, will be in the way of vast achievements in godliness. Habit gives skill and strength, makes easy and pleasant. Incessancy of action is more than occasional violence of blows. Evil is more abashed by persistency in good than by fitful, though forcible exploits of goodness. And nothing fixes thoughts and deepens impressions like giving them actual form and voice in daily doings. Would you, like Enoch, abound in godliness, and "please God," more than many? I counsel you thus, do not attempt it so much by a great many of *one kind* of religious things, or a great many of all kinds *on occasions*, but by quiet, constant, universal holiness. Do not disesteem the small, nor unduly magnify the great. Do not put prayer for labour, nor labour for prayer. "Wait on God" and "walk before Him" patiently; attending, in His fear and love, to the exercise of all your powers, and the performance of all your duties. And thus caring for all, all will advance, each better than if alone cared for, for each will help the rest, and patient perseverance will slowly, but surely, secure large results; your progress shall be that of the tide which, though the waves recede, and are uncertain and unequal, steadily mounts the beach, and like the sun, which, though without sudden or startling movements, reaches the zenith. "The path of the just is as the shining light, which shineth more and more unto the perfect day."

V.

We see Enoch's eminent godliness attaining *a strange and signal honour.* "He was not, for God took him."

It is not said how, when, or where the event took place, whether with or without attendant circumstances, alone or in the presence of others, suddenly or after notice; though the natural impression of the words is that of a quiet, solitary, and unexpected removal. But it matters very little *how* a man goes to God. The going at all is the grand thing. If the devil takes a man, though amid all the splendours of the universe, it is no mitigation of hell; and if God takes him, though with every circumstance of ignominy and pain, it detracts nothing from heaven. Paul says of Enoch, he did not "see death." Christ says of every disciple that "he does not taste death."

I know not how it strikes you, but I always feel when reading this passage as if there was a beautiful fitness in this exit, a fitness of course and end. God took him who had walked with Him, bore him away to another sphere. The very silence of the historian aids the impression: there is no breach between the earthly and the heavenly life, no defined horizon—clouds, and sky, fields, hills and wood meet together, and this world's beauty and the glory of the world above melt into each other, and one unbroken scene fills and satisfies the eye. He was with God here, he is with God there. He became more and more divine in the lower and harder conditions of life, and now he has reached a state where nothing exists to check or disappoint his God-ward aspirations. He became more and more separate from the evil which, like a serpent's trail, is over all below, and more and more akin to the good which has its perfect work and joy above; and, as was meet, he has arrived where evil is not, and good is in its perfection. He was a "man of God" for three hundred years, "a pilgrim and a stranger" with him, doing his works in God, speaking the words which God gave him to speak, and God has taken him to be with him always. He had well nigh as much to do with God as one in his circumstances could have, as one on earth could have then; and so God took him where he could have more. God was very pleased with him for his sensitive conscience and his holy life, and must have him altogether. The walking with God here indicated, prepared for, promised the divine reception and fellowship for ever. And Enoch is still with God, walking with him, but in a better way, with easier, pleasanter intercourse, and amidst all circumstances of gladness and glory—for Enoch's way was " The way everlasting." " Thou hast a few names which have not defiled their garments : and they shall walk with me in white ; for they are worthy." And if *we* spend our days with God, we shall spend our eternity with Him also ; and if we are now alienated from Him in heart and life, where He is in all His glory we can never be !

The text describes the essential oneness and modal difference between heaven and earth to the good man. God is his companion here, God is his portion for ever. Now God is with him, according to the conditions and exigencies of his earthly life ; there he will be with God according to the grandeur and blessedness of *His* heavenly state. Here God make us His temples, and " walks in us and dwells in us ;" there we dwell in His temple, or, rather, in a world so full of His presence and glory, that there needs no other temple than Himself. Here He humbles Himself to notice, and succour, and gladden our hearts ; there we are raised to the participation of His unrestricted love, of the vision of His unveiled majesty. And the greater our communion and enjoyment here, the greater will they be hereafter. All else will perish. Only the divine remain. The more of *that* we possess on earth, the fuller its reward, the richer its gratification, the ampler its scope hereafter. We may not be specially honoured in the manner of our departure, but shall be in its sequence. "The secret of the Lord is with them that fear Him, and He will show them His covenant:" and the revelations of His truth, and the proof of His confidence and love shall bear proportion to the intimacy and cordiality of our fellowship with Him below.

God honoured Enoch by translating him: and, in him, He honoured religion, and eminent religion. He honours it still, and *nothing else*. It is the only thing which is in His sight "of great price;" the only thing which secures for every man "praise of God." There is no translation now for the righteous, but there is better, transformation, the being "changed from glory to glory now," and "the bearing of the image of the heavenly" hereafter. Then get religion; get eminent religion. Unite your heart on this. "Seek the kingdom of God and His righteousness." "Choose the good part:" after the figure of our text, "Draw nigh unto God." "Be reconciled to Him." Come nearer and nearer. Commune with Him, more and more fully and frankly. "Forget the things that are behind, and reach forth to those that are before." Let your aim be high; let it be the highest, as much as is possible of divine friendship and divine fellowship, the utmost measure of the faith and the following of God. An artist once said that he was never satisfied with his work until he had forgotten what he had meant to do. Never forget your ideal, and let your ideal be high; and your record shall be, in all its greatest meanings, that of Enoch; and, if not in books or on stone, yet in the thoughts of God, and the memories of men, and the experiences of eternity, it shall be said of each, "He walked with God: and he was not; for God took him."

"Even the youths shall faint and be weary, and the young men shall utterly fall: but they that wait upon the Lord shall renew their strength: they shall mount up with wings as eagles; they shall run, and not be weary; and they shall walk, and not faint."

AFFLICTION, CONSIDERED AS PUNISHMENT.

Lam. iii. 39.—"*Wherefore doth a living man complain, a man for the punishment of his sins?*"

I WISH to treat the subject of trouble in a somewhat more plain and familiar manner than it is sometimes treated. I wish you to get a common-sense view of it, rather than a theological one; the view of the world, rather than of the study or closet; and I will speak in language that is common to all topics, rather than language of a technical and scientific nature. It were greatly to be wished that this could be done in connection with all religious subjects, as it is done more than it used to be. When talking of God and religion, Christ and salvation, providence and duty, we get used to certain fixed forms of thought and speech which are the results of ecclesiastical polemics and scholastic philosophy, and which, however true and proper in themselves, and however important once and for some purposes, often hinder the perception and check the influence of truth. Uninitiated people, though intelligent, are at a loss to understand them, and may be even offended by them; while to some they are refuges of mental indolence and weakness; and others, by familiarity with them, cease to be impressed as they should be by the thoughts they clothe, and in part conceal; and forms here, as elsewhere, beget formality.

It is so with *trouble*. There are certain doctrines about trouble which all good people have at hand, and can always quote as cases require; certain commonplaces which are supposed to express the philosophy of affliction, and perhaps do. But I fear that a great deal more is said than thought, and more thought than felt; that the representations are much too general, too unqualified, for common appreciation and application; that men get into a way of talking about the causes of trouble which they do not understand, and the benefits of trouble, which they do not realize, and the proper demeanour under trouble, which they do not exhibit. We want something more specific, more accordant with our experience of life, more respectful to patent facts, and moral possibilities, and individual infirmities, and all in a dialect that can easily convey thoughts to people, and not need that people should possess the thoughts in order to understand the dialect. It would be easy to give illustrations of these remarks. But I am anxious to come to the subject suggested by the text—" Affliction, considered as Punishment," and which presents us with almost all the general aspects in which trouble can be contemplated so as to prevent complaint.

I.

It comes from God.

The text points us to the moral Governor of the world, to Him who has made us, and made us men and who orders things with reference to our condition and character as souls and as sinners. The Bible, of course, traces all suffering to God. It teaches us that He creates evil and good; that He causes light and darkness; that He appoints the rod; that if evil is in the city He hath done it; that the crookedness of our affairs is the work of God: that is, it ascribes trouble to Him, as it ascribes everything else to Him, of whom, through whom, and to whom, all things are, who made all things for Himself, even the wicked for the day of His wrath.

Apart from questions of inspiration, such language is natural. The natural piety and scientific ignorance of men would delight, and be obliged, to use it; piety longing to make as much of God as possible, and ignorance not knowing what else to do. And thus, as you go further back, you meet with strange forms of primitive simplicity, which reverently conceived of God as making "coats" for Adam and Eve, "houses" for the Hebrew midwives, and "shutting" Noah in the ark. And as we come down to our own times, the earthly causes and natural processes of things becoming more and more known, take the place of the general ascriptions of them to Deity. What used to be strange is not now miraculous; and if we speak more seldom of God as doing what happens, it is not that we think less of Him, but that we know more of it. The prodigy is only an unusual form of the natural; the judgment is the result of laws in constant operation—and often a most merciful result too.

There is, no doubt, a sense in which God does all things. That is, since He has a plan, and accomplishes

that plan—in other words, since He is all-wise and all-powerful, He must exercise a universal superintendence and control; and what He does not, He must permit its being done, and know that it will be done. If anything could take place, much less if many things could take place, in opposition to His will, or without His knowledge, His plans might be continually thwarted, and the certainty of universal success rendered impossible.

God may be said to bring about results, even in the case of the voluntary acts of men, if He has so ordered the existing system that those results shall follow those acts. If He has established laws which provide that if men do certain things, they shall experience certain consequences, God is the author of those consequences as much as if He interposed immediately to produce them. If a parent make such arrangements in his house or garden, that a particular penalty shall be the natural fruit of a particular disobedience, and make them with that view, the penalty is as much of his infliction as if he plied the rod. We may not know—for wise men have held different doctrines on the subject—whether God acts now in the way of habitual interference or ancient impulse; whether all things are done by Him as the effect of a present act, or of a past. There are strong arguments for both views, and great difficulties in both.

For our present purpose it is enough that in any true sense what happens to us is referable to His will; that it is His pleasure that it should happen; that He knows of it, and either causes it, or intentionally allows it. Our miseries, of every kind and source, are from Him; that is, from a Being having intelligence and will; not from what we call, with or without meaning, "chance," or "fate;" a personal God, a Father, a moral Ruler, means them. It is "punishment"—shall we "complain"?

II.

We have ourselves only to blame for our troubles.

There is no such obscurity resting on the subject as many say: at least there is no such *necessary* obscurity. "Mysterious dispensations" are not so common as is thought. "Mystery" in the Bible only means something once hidden and now revealed, not things absolutely beyond our power to understand: and most mysteries are only forms of our ignorance, not God's concealment of things. If we knew all, we should see that what now perplexes us was not only reasonable, but, on the highest grounds, necessary.

It is quite true, generally, that we suffer because we sin. We should not know trouble if we were not guilty. It is because of this that we are placed in circumstances in which trouble comes to us naturally: that we are "born to trouble as the sparks fly upwards:" that we have the treasures of souls and spirits in earthen vessels, frail and soon broken; that we inhabit a world whose physical condition and action upon us cannot but afford us pain as well as pleasure, and that we are compelled to live and associate with men whose miseries, follies, and sins are passive or active. God knew that we should deserve and require suffering, and arranged accordingly. And our sorrows come from our sins, just because God puts us into a suffering body and a suffering world, and keeps us in them on account of our sinful deserts and sinful necessities. We are not to vex ourselves, as good people often do, with inquiries as to the *individual* reasons and designs of our troubles; we are not to ask, in the sense of Job, "Show me wherefore thou contendest with me;" we are not to institute a particular search into the occasions of our trials, as if each had a special meaning, and indicated a special sin, after the manner of Adonibezek's punishment. It is enough for us that we are sinful, and therefore sorrowful; that we should not be *where* we are if we were not *what* we are; that God has placed us in a world of thorns and briers as well as flowers and fruits; in bodies whose organs pain as well as please; in a system of "wicked and unreasonable men;" and many more very weak and thoughtless, intercourse with whom must often vex and distress us, because we were, in His foresight, creatures meriting chastisement, and able to profit by it.

But we may go much further than this in reference to many of our troubles. We cause them by *our own acts*. They are the direct results of our own conduct, of single deeds, or of courses of conduct. And we may know it, and ought to know it. It is not a question of "inscrutable ways" at all. There are no "clouds and darkness" about the throne; the only obscurity is in our eyes. If we like, we can discover the whole truth, and it is that we have been "kicking against the goads," "eating sour grapes," "ploughing rocks," and anything else implying folly and perverseness, the breaking of inexorable laws, the expecting impossible consequences, the attempting *what can't be done*. We may ascribe troubles thus produced to God, if we like; and if humbly and wisely, we cannot do it too much; but don't let us do it to conceal our own carelessness, or to lessen our own blame. If a man becomes weak through starving himself, and scorched by putting his hand into the fire, he has just as much right to sing, " God moves in a mysterious way," as multitudes of men in reference to multitudes of tribulations. "Wherefore should a man complain for the punishment of his sins?" The mystery would be in its *absence*.

"Sins" are of many kinds, but they are always violations of rule. "Sin is the transgression of the law." And law always has penalty, sooner or later, milder or more severe. A vast deal of our trouble is just the natural product of our disobedience, and we have no more right to be surprised at it than a boy who is flogged for neglecting his lessons, or a thief who is imprisoned for stealing property.

Take the case of *physical health*. Many of our grievances are bodily. We have "trouble in the flesh." And as Gideon "took thorns of the wilderness and briers, and with them taught the men of Succoth," so we learn from material experiences, and they are often painful ones. Indeed, many people can learn no otherwise. For while it is a proverb that " fools learn only from experience," there is more truth in the criticism that fools never, only wise men, learn from experience, and most truth in the saying that fools learn only from physical experience. But of physical laws, as of other laws, there are those which provide a sure and sudden penalty for their infraction, and these are fairly obeyed, for in all laws, there is more in certainty and immediacy than severity of infliction; and there are those which chastise for transgression after a slower and less obvious manner, and these are abundantly outraged. But the whole sphere of material things is filled with law, and our material interests are constantly dependent on its practical recognition. If we suffer then in body, the chances are that we have transgressions. There are weakly bodies, and bodies prone to particular complaints; but the greater part of our bodily miseries and ailments are from ourselves. "The messenger of Satan," is only in return for some foolish message of our own; and "the thorn in the flesh" is there a pressure we ought to have avoided. God has made necessary to full health, and an even flow of animal spirits, certain conditions of fresh air, and wholesome diet, and regular exercise; and men get ill or melancholy because they breathe bad air; and eat or drink wrong things, or too much of good ones (and gluttony is as bad as drunkenness); and lie in bed, and sit at home, and loll about, when they should be giving vigorous play to their bodily powers. The father of a family is struck down by paralysis; all the mystery of the case is in his persisting, in spite of friends and feelings, in putting two days' work and worry into one. A young woman has just died of consumption; the only marvel is that she let herself, and others let her, go out of a heated room into the cold air, or wear a dress that compressed the action of her vital organs. A young man comes home from school or university, to die; there is nothing inscrutable about it, except in the unnatural strain of brain or body by work or play. Wherefore should a man " complain for the punishment of his sins ? "

And the same remarks apply to the lowness and gloom of spirits, and a hundred evils of mind and soul, that flow from a diseased or languid action of the bodily powers. Whole systems of divinity have come, ere now, from disordered organisms. A friend of mine will have it that sluggish livers have had vitally to do with the origin of heresies, especially of some kinds. Who can say, that as the different parts of the human body were of old supposed to be the seats and organs of different affections of the mind, they might not be of different types of religious thought ? And at any rate, the way in which individuals judge and act in relation to religious things, especially as connected with themselves, is largely affected by the state of their bodily humours. Despondency, and even despair, may come from indigestion. Unstrung nerves may make any one "walk in darkness, and have no light." Many Christians go to the divine for comfort, when they should go to the doctor for cure. They think God is "hiding His face," when He is really showing Himself, showing His love for them and for all men, in upholding the order of things, in which their welfare and that of all men is concerned. Wherefore should "a man complain for the punishment of his sins ? "

I might instance further in religious matters, if they came properly within our subject; for cloudiness of views, and doubt, and want of joy, are all referable to a neglect of divine laws—" Oh that thou hadst hearkened to My commandments ! then had thy peace been as a river ";—but I pass to another department of trouble—the *social*. " Our affections are our afflictions," and "*children* are certain cares and uncertain comforts." I need not enlarge upon the fact, it is too obvious: but after making all reasonable admissions, is not much of the sorrow and anxiety they occasion you traceable to your own conduct ? The moral faults of your children, whether objects of mere dissatisfaction or total reprobation, are they not in part your own ? Can perfect children come of imperfect parents; is it not to expect grapes of thistles ? Have you done *your duty* by them; have you sought their welfare, and in wise methods ? Has your family been "a church in a house"? Has your teaching been backed by example ? Has authority not been weakened by harshness or fondness ? Have prayers and effort gone together? Have you trained up a child " in his way," as the word is; the way of a child, and of your child; having due regard to his age and his idiosyncrasies ? Perhaps, you have done nothing for their chief welfare, or done only by fits and starts, and unwisely and inconsistently : perhaps exposed them for the sake of educational or worldly advantages to evil influences. If so, you are punished only for your " sins."

Take servants. They are " plagues of life;" so is it said and printed continually. No doubt there are many bad servants immoral, lazy, and ignorant; as there are many bad masters and mistresses, and bad people in other kinds. Looking at the way in which most servants are brought up, the scenes and associations in which they pass their childhood or youth, and remembering how little training they have for positions often of difficulty and delicacy, my wonder is that there are not more bad servants. But are *you* perfect? are you reasonably good? Do you give no reason to them to complain of you, to describe you as the plagues of *their* life? Do you do unto them as you would they should do unto you? Do you show the same equity, kindness, consideration, which you exact? Perhaps you screw them in wages; abridge their comforts; make them put up with unnecessary hardships; are cold and severe in your manner, rigid in demanding their part of the agreement but lax in fulfilling your own; in one word, treat them not as human beings—beings with minds and hearts and consciences—but as mere instruments, or, if more, mere mercenaries. And you wonder if they give you " eye-service," and answer roughly, and take no pleasure to please, and leave as soon as they can get another place. It would be an "inscrutable providence" if it were otherwise. It is only the punishment of your "sins."

Many suffer sadly in the sphere of *friendship*, and in general intercourse with society. They suffer in being without friends, or in losing them, or in their behaving badly. They bewail their destitution or their disappointment. Perhaps keen in feeling themselves and of glowing fancy, they have never found the ideal friend, and are disgusted that the word so deep and full of mystic meaning to them should by others be appropriated to all objects of fellowship, from a bare acquaintance to a second self. These sufferers are not the lightest sufferers, albeit theirs are "sentimental grievances." And they wonder often why their hearts, with such yearnings for confidence and love and sympathy, should be without "a mate," should be so often "overwhelmed within them," and so often mocked with deceitful waters of false profession or fickle love. But perhaps the reason is in themselves, or greatly so. They may expect too much, or yield too little, forgetting that reciprocity is of the essence of true friendship. Or they may overdo it, not "withdrawing their foot from their neighbour's house" until he "weary of" them. Or they may annoy and even injure by bad tempers, or rude manners, or incorrigible carelessness, and

> "Evil is wrought by want of thought
> As well as want of will."

Perhaps your utter failure in quest of objects of ideal love, perhaps all or most of the mistakes and coolness that have interrupted your intimacies, perhaps all your losses in the commerce of hearts, may be ascribed to something in yourselves, something that might have been prevented by consideration and self-control. And if so, and in so far as it is so, shall you "complain for the punishment of your sins?"

Once more, there are troubles in *business*, in your daily work, in trade, in your investments of capital or monetary dealings with relatives and acquaintances. These are often beyond your utmost power to prevent; no more within the reach of your forethought and providence than were Job's calamities from wind and lightning, Sabeans and Chaldeans. You could not expect the dishonesty of your clerk, or the treachery of your partner, the scarcity of this raw material, or the failure of that popular investment. You had no power over the frauds of your trustee or the insolvency of your creditor. You could not prevent trade leaving your neighbourhood, or bad times visiting it. The rival with larger capital or smaller expenses, and better opportunities and appliances, would come in spite of you. Perhaps so; and see His hand in all, who withholds or gives the increase evermore. But see it not less in troubles and losses that might have been averted or mitigated. You may have been indolent, or rash, or easy. You may have been too proud to take wise counsel, or too reckless to profit by experience. You would be "surety for thy friend," though Solomon told you not. You would have large interest, though, as Wellington said, "high interest means bad security." You have spent more than you ought, and you went on in hope when you should have stopped in honesty. "Therefore is this distress come upon you." Your straitened means, your suspension of payment, your bankruptcy is from God, but it is through yourselves. You are reaping what you have sown in folly, obstinacy, extravagance; and wherefore should a man "complain for the punishment of his sins?"

Now, this fact is a good reason not to murmur. We think to silence others thus. We say, "You have brought it on yourselves," and wonder if they are not quiet. We say it to the child with the cut finger, and the youth with the ruined constitution, and the man with the bankrupt estate. Is it not good for us as well? True, this consideration is an aggravation of the pain. It is a bitter thing to think that *we* are, and we only are, to blame; that our troubles might have been prevented; that we had to close our eyes and ears, and perhaps hearts, to much, in order to bring them on. Take the blame; it will do you good: take all. Do not say with Adam, "The woman gave me;" nor with Eve, "The serpent tempted me." Take all, frankly. But do not take *more than your share*. In great trouble there is a possibility of forgetting that in many troubles forethought is useless, and in many impossible. "Oh," cries the sobbing sufferer, "if I had done this or had not done that!" But you could not; it would have required you to act on what at the time appeared the weakest reasons, which is folly. "I did think of it," he replies, "something suggested danger; I was very nearly not doing it." Likely enough. You only mean that you thought before you acted, as reasonable people generally do; and that there were two sides, as in matters of expediency there generally are. You were then looking forward to the unknown; you are now looking backward to the known: no wonder there is a difference. No: avoid extremes; beware of proud and perverse self-justification, and beware of weak and morbid self-condemnation. There is quite enough in the truth of our troubles to humble us; let that truth content, and let it chasten us; let it check every murmuring feeling and stop every rebellious word. And if we cannot find any particular and direct cause of our troubles in our conduct, we may well remember that in moral beings sorrow is for sin, and not complain for our punishment.

III.

Trouble, *as* and *because* punishment, *might have been worse, and may be better.*

"Wherefore should a *living* man complain?" Stress is to be laid upon this. The trouble, whatever it is, might have been greater. It has exceptions and alleviations. The darkness does not cover the whole sphere of vision. The ingredients of the cup are not all bitter. We have been "chastised with whips," it might have been with "scorpions." We have run with "footmen," it might have been with "horses." We have been "wearied in the land of peace," but not overwhelmed "in the swellings of Jordan." Our trouble is not complete or not continuous. We are "not tempted above that we are able to bear." "All God's billows and waves" are not "gone over us." "The clouds" do not "return after the rain." We are not afflicted in all kinds, and in all degrees, like Job. We can imagine worse trouble. We can find worse. We deserve worse. We cannot have the worst while "living." There are sorer sorrows after death: the sorest here might be but "the beginning of sorrows," a foretaste and an earnest of the uttermost wrath of God. While living, we are not wholly lost and damned. However poor, or pained, or bereaved, or forsaken, though every strip of "bark" is off our "fig tree," and our "last coal" is "quenched," and "the fields yield no meat," and there is no herd in the stalls, and "lover and friend" have been "put far from" us, and we have buried our "only son," *we are not damned!* And *we might have been.* "It is of the

Lord's mercies we are not consumed, because His compassions fail not." They are new every morning. We are not damned, and *we need not be!* "To him that is joined unto all the living, there is hope"—hope of living even here, and hope of living in the fulness and infinitude of life hereafter. While we have ears we may hear, and while we have eyes we may see, things of peace and glory hidden and unspoken to multitudes of men no worse than we! "Wherefore doth a *living* man complain, a man for the punishment of his sins?"

And this punishment of the living *is to prevent their ever dying, in the full import of that awful word.* This trouble, while it might have been worse, *may be better*—may be best of all. In the highest sense we may say, "This sickness is not unto death, but unto life. This loss is not unto ruin, but unto wealth. This sorrow is not unto hopeless misery, but exceeding and eternal joy." The cloud has a silver lining. "The sharp needle draws after it a silken thread." Punishment of the living is chastisement, not judicial infliction; intended to benefit the afflicted, not merely to vindicate law and right. It is against God's will to punish; it is in His heart to shorten and mitigate our woes, and in His heart to bless them. "For the Lord will not cast off for ever; for though He cause grief, yet yet will He have compassion according to the multitude of His mercies." "For He doth not afflict willingly nor grieve the children of men." "I have surely heard Ephraim bemoaning himself thus: Thou hast chastised me, and I was chastised, as a bullock unaccustomed to the yoke; turn Thou me, and I shall be turned; for Thou art the Lord my God. Surely after that I was

turned, I repented; and after that I was instructed, I smote my thigh: I was ashamed, yea, even confounded, because I did bear the reproach of my youth. Is Ephraim my dear son? is he a pleasant child? for since I spake against him I do earnestly remember him still: therefore my bowels are troubled for him; I will surely have mercy upon him, saith the Lord."
"We have had fathers of our flesh which corrected us, and we gave them reverence: shall we not much rather be in subjection unto the Father of spirits, and live? For they verily for a few days chastened us after their own pleasure; but He for our profit, that we might be partakers of His holiness." "Wherefore doth a man complain of the punishment of his sins?"

THE DIVINE REJECTED IN THE COMMON.

MATTHEW xiii. 55.—"*Is not this the carpenter's son?*"

THIS was the language of the Jews at Nazareth. And it was uttered after they had been impressed with Christ's teaching in the synagogue. "All bare Him witness, and wondered at the gracious words, and said, Is not this Joseph's Son?"—Luke iv. 22. They were astonished, and said, "Whence hath this Man this wisdom, and these mighty works? Is not this the carpenter's son? Is not His mother called Mary? and His brethren, James, and Joses, and Simon, and Judas? And His sisters, are they not all with us? Whence, then, hath this Man all these things? And they were offended in Him." It was, therefore, not the language of admiration, but of scepticism; not of wonder, but of objection. They had been moved by the grace of His speech, and if they had but yielded themselves to its influence, would doubtless have come to a happy knowledge of His person and claims; but, instead of doing that, they suffered carnal impressions to have dominion, the feeling of the divine to be quenched by the feeling of the fleshly. "True, His words are wonderful; there is a strange character about the manner and matter of His discourse; but after all it is certain that we must not make too much of it, we must not be led away by Him; He is only one of ourselves, He was brought up in our town; we knew Him as a boy; His father was a carpenter, He Himself (Mark vi. 3) learned His father's trade, and wrought at it; we are familiar with His brethren and sisters, in habits of intercourse with them; all His associations belong to our common life; there cannot be anything so extraordinary after all in Him, His pretensions are not sustained by His antecedents and circumstances." Thus the spiritual gem was dishonoured because of its earthly setting, and Christ was rejected on account of that which should have secured His cordial acceptance.

For, my brethren, the truer inference had been, that the less likely He was to get His wisdom and His grace from earth, the more likely was it that they had been obtained from heaven. There was no logic in the reasoning that made His disadvantages tell against His acquirements. They told just the other way. Whatever there was in His worldly lot and relations to prevent extraordinary qualities and powers, surely rendered them only more extraordinary. A small amount of fair thought would have sufficed to say: "Out of the soil of our common life has arisen a plant of uncommon flower and fruit; from among the men of our familiar fellowship has arisen one unlike and above all other men; with no training but that of a poor handicraftsman, He has reached a wisdom and spiritual dignity denied to richest culture and best positions. What cannot be explained by ordinary laws must be sought for in extraordinary; and that which He could not have derived from men must have been given Him by God." But this was not their mode of treating the phenomena before them. The very things that made Christ so surprising an object served only to banish the feeling of surprise; their wonder and admiration were smothered by earthly impressions. They brought Christ's history and connections to resist and destroy the emotions kindled by Christ's discourse. They would have honoured Him more if they had known Him less; they had felt more reverence for one farther off.

There were probably many feelings expressed in the words. Perhaps there was *envy*. They did not like to think that one of themselves should be so much above them. This feeling works everywhere, and strongly. He who attains to greatness of any kind is least appreciated, as a rule, at home or among his own companions. "A prophet has no honour in his own country." There is a point when, recognition being compelled, there is the opposite effect. When denial is useless, then acknowledgment is warmer from the same cause. Social pride says, as long as it can, of the rising one, "He is nothing;" when it can say it no longer, it adopts a different style; "How great he is; and, *I* know him; he came from our neighbourhood; I am familiar with his kindred." So pride first disputes, then uses the glory of another. There was probably *a prejudice against Christ because of the worldly circumstances of His family*. The Jews had not our feeling as to trade. Every child had to be brought up to one, but still *the necessity of following one* was an objection, and Christ's family were poor. Poverty, alas! has always been a sore hindrance to acceptance, even more than many follies, and not a few sins. The freedom of the world is generally presented in a gold box. "The poor man's wisdom is despised, and his words are not heard." How *can* a man have anything to say who has nothing to give? There was certainly a feeling in the Jews against Christ from *the absence of any apparent means of His attaining uncommon eminence.* "Whence hath this Man this wisdom, and these mighty works?" A very fitting question, if sincerely asked; but when asked in order to disparage His wisdom, asked not to discover its source, but to depreciate its worth, a very foolish and dishonest question. But I imagine that a still stronger feeling against Christ arose in their minds from *the commonness and familiarity of His associations.* Both Matthew and Mark intimate this. It was not only the circumstances of His family; they recount the names of its members; they mention father, mother, and brethren, and sisters; and these as known to themselves, dwelling among them. I cannot but think that this was the chief cause of His rejection. The effect of Christ's teaching, though it astonished them, was lost through the nearness of His lower life. Had He come from afar; had he been shrouded in mystery; had His history and parentage been unknown, then they might have received His claims; but they had not spirituality enough to counteract the suggestions and influences of His carnal relations; they could not detect the pure ore in so much apparent alloy; could not recognize the extraordinary in so much that was ordinary, and the divine in so much that was common. They might have worshipped the "great unknown"; they might have received a prophet with whose antecedents they were unacquainted; but to suppose that the representative of the Highest should be a Nazarene, that the special messenger of God should belong to a family of neighbours, that the revealer of the kingdom of heaven, the bringer of the great jubilee, should have been their playmate; that they should meet in their daily walks, and engage in their daily business with some members of a house, and be required to look upon another member as endowed and commissioned by the special gifts and appointment of heaven, this violated their fleshly reason, and "they were offended in Him."

Perhaps we imagine ourselves very superior to them; we see at once how grossly they erred, and have no patience with their error. It is not for me to say whether we should in like circumstances pursue the like course; though there may be some reason for thinking that many among us would be no more ready than were they to believe in a Messiah belonging to our own neighbourhood, mixed up with us in social life. But of this *I am* sure, that the feeling which actuated them is still at work, and men are still backward to recognize the divine in connection with the common. There is a prejudice against it, there is an inability and an indisposition to discern it when it comes before us in connection with what is customary and familiar. We like priests after the order of Melchisedek, without father and without mother. We associate it, for the most part, with the distant, the unusual, the unknown. The earthly genealogy disproves the heavenly descent. Familiarity destroys respect. We go staring for signs in mid-heaven, and see not the beauties beneath our feet. The natural scene to which strangers flock is little thought of by those who live close by, the production being had for nothing. God comes too near to us often for our fleshly hearts. We have a wrong notion, derived from our own hearts and habits, of what befits Deity. And the very things which should endear and enforce His manifestations and communications only extort the carnal cry, "Is not this the carpenter's son?"

I wish to give some illustrations of this fact, for therefore were the words recorded, that in different circumstances, we might guard against the same error.

My first illustration shall be taken from Christ. Now, it is very possible that we have been conscious of this feeling, Christ is "God manifest in flesh," the human image of the Divine; but we have found it hard not only to believe this, but, believing it, to realize it; and the difficulty has arisen from a latent sense that such manifestation did not become the Deity. We have felt that the great God might have chosen some other and higher mode of display. We have brought our own notions of great and little to Him, (as if all things were not little to Him in one sense, all things great in another), and we have wondered that He should so intimately associate Himself with a man, with a poor man, with a man in trial, and sorrow, and death. Leaving out now the mediatorial reasons of this, there may have crept over us the thought that if God should worthily display Himself, He would select the great scenes and elements of nature, appear in some august form, clothe Himself with light and glory, as with a garment, sit majestically upon a throne of stars, speak awfully, as with a voice of thunder. Oh! my brethren, it is well He has not done so, well even because of the moral influence of the manifestation. Apart from all strictly mediatorial effects, it is well that God has come down to us thus; that He has connected Himself with our nature, and that in its suffering and humbled condition; that He has allied Himself to our toiling, weeping souls; that we are able to look at Him through a human mirror, and feel that He sympathizes with us through human feelings. But we do not always realize this. Like the Jews, the impression of the excellence of the manifestation is destroyed by its commonness, we suppress its influence by that which should augment it; and as we see Christ, clothed in flesh, living on earth, tabernacling with men, eating and drinking, weeping and rejoicing, walking and resting, now subject to temptation, now overborne by fatigue, groaning in the garden, and dying on the Cross, we are apt to say, in the spirit of their speech, "Is not this the carpenter's son?"

And the same may be said of *Christianity*—I mean the records of the New Testament. No one who has read these has failed to notice *the thoroughly human character of these writings*. Written as they were by the help of Divine inspiration, they are yet evidently the offspring, under that inspiration, of men—breathing their thoughts and referring to their circumstances, and expressing their cares, and hopes, and fears, and joys. The epistles, the fullest expressions of Christian doctrine, frequently refer to matters strictly personal and secular. They reveal not a little of the inner life of their writers. We know more of Paul from his letters, than from all other sources—how he felt, what were his chief motives and purposes, how he was influenced by external things, what a heart he had to suffer and to rejoice. Now it has often been objected to these writings that they deal with things common and insignificant, that they are not strung to a high pitch of sustained dignity, that they make mention of trifling matters, and personal concerns and feelings, say how he had meant to make a visit, and how he regretted writing a letter; that here reference is made to a "cloak left at Troas," and there advice given to "take a little wine for the stomach's sake;" and it has been said that all this is inconsistent with the claim to Divine inspiration. It seems to me that it is a very strong confirmation of that claim, properly understood. If you look on inspiration as a mere physical action on the writers—if you think that God should have propounded His will in stiff and arbitrary declarations, then I grant you that the objection is valid and forcible; but if you feel that the human is divine, that all that concerns us concerns our Father in heaven, that He not merely designed to teach us, but to win us; then I think that all this is a commendation of the Christian writings. Oh! you might have had a very different task, a book containing not the remotest allusion to the circumstances and feelings of the writers, a book simply of oracular dicta and stately precepts, a book dry as a catechism, and stiff as a body of divinity; and some may wish that such a book had been given; but if it had, it would have wanted one great charm to human beings, living in the midst of human incidents; and the craving for it is but a fruit of the feeling of the Jews when they said, " Is not this the carpenter's son ?"

A third illustration we shall take from *the divine operation in nature.* Now we hold it as a cardinal truth that God is ever at work, upholding and regulating all the creations of His power. We believe that God is as much needed for this as He was for the bringing of the existing universe out of nothing. We can no more think of a self-sustaining universe than of a self-existent universe. The constant and immediate agency of God is required for the sustentation of things just as it was required for their origination. But who does not know and feel that the daily doings of God in keeping this vast machine in motion have not the same effect as the witnessing of His great creative act would have had? Aye, and who does not know and feel that a suspension of the laws, an infraction of the order, of the present system would produce an impression which its regular and harmonious working does not produce? I suppose that a miracle, a clear and unmistakeable miracle, which produces an effect which is not produced by all our observation of the daily wonders of creation. It is proper that miracles should have such an effect; that as indications of the approval of God of a particular prophet or a particular message they should have such an effect; but are we not conscious that they would have an impression as to *the divine operation in general,* which is not produced by the constant interposition of God in the material world? The fact is that we are prevented from recognizing the divine power by the commonness of daily operations. We do not think that the flowers that greet us in the day, and the stars that smile upon us in the night, owe their beauty and lustre to the *present* power of God. We lose the divine in the constant, the familiar. If rightly minded, we should rejoice in the thought that God is ever putting forth His power, that He has not left this world to the care of an original impulse, that we have an interest in His constant thought and care; and so that the existing order of His universe is as much a revelation of His will as when it was first created : but our poor and sensuous souls do not thus think; the wondrous economy of heaven and earth fails to impress us; the customary operations of God lose their effect; we gaze on the most surprising manifestations of divine power without being moved; and thus indicate the feeling of the Jews when they asked, " Is not this the carpenter's son ? "

A fourth illustration may be taken from *divine providence*. The heathens thought their gods were degraded by being mixed up with the common and trivial affairs of men. They would rather look upon their deities as free from all concern in the petty details of human history and experience. They ascribed to the objects of their worship an indifference to the minute particulars of individual life. Let them live in cold isolation from mundane matters; let them be content with a general superintendence of the events of earth. But we have not so learned God. We have been taught that His care extends to everything that interests us; that the hairs of our heads are all numbered, that a sparrow falls not to the ground without our Father; that He does all things for us; that nothing is too little for His thought and knowledge, nothing too low for His love, that all things work together for good to them that love God.

Now there is a great evasion of this truth. We are ready enough to recognize God's working, but then it is in the surprising and extraordinary events of His providence. We cannot feel that He is equally concerned in the common and trifling. Let some unusual dispensation befall, let something occur out of the ordinary course of things, and we are prepared to do honour to the divine interposition; but as long as we have to do with neither the magnificent nor the marvellous, we have a difficulty in detecting the interference of the Most High. That is, we lose the impression of the general providence of God, because it is general. We don't realize His presence and power in the affairs of our common and customary life, don't feel that He is equally concerned with what is small as with what is vast. The God that comes near to us, regarding our ordinary experience, is not so soon seen and so warmly welcomed as the God that deals with the grand operations of the universe. We have a secret sense that there is degradation as well as condescension in His doing much that yet is done for us, and thus indulge the sentiment of the Jews, "Is not this the carpenter's son?"

A last illustration must be taken from *our common life*. All life is divine; it is a divine institute and power, and may reveal to us divine principles. Very few of you are able to exemplify the Gospel in a public sphere, on a large scale. God has given you only a private lot, and trifling means. You have not office, wealth, public work, great powers ; and it is very natural to suppose that you are shut out from the opportunity of showing the divinity of the Gospel. But the fact is not so. There is a great craving for extraordinary positions—for positions of extraordinary prominence and influence ; and we are apt to think that without them we are forbidden the honour and privilege of glorifying Christ. We cannot think that the divine can be revealed in our lowly circumstances. Should we command more magnificent conditions, how would we display the goodness and energy of the faith ! but restricted and restrained as we are, how can we " adorn the doctrine of God our Saviour in all things ? " Now, all this proceeds upon a mistake—a total misconception of the real state of the case. We suppose that what is small and vulgar to us is so to God ; we confound the quantity with the quality of the divine manifestation—we confound the secular with the spiritual—and hence we are prepared to ask, " Is not this the carpenter's son ? "

We often talk and read about the divinity of common life. The religiousness of secular things has become quite a cant; but for that very reason, because it is a cant, is it in danger of practical denial. It is a truth that God may be seen and honoured in the duties of the lowliest life ; that we may connect Him with the pursuits of secular business, and the enjoyments of social fellowship ; that we may sanctify Him in the smallest objects and most insignificant engagements. We need not seek the grand, the extraordinary, as the occasion and instrument of either experiencing Him or serving Him ; else were the great mass of men denied the privilege; but "whatsoever we do in word or deed," we may "do it in the name of the Lord Jesus, giving thanks unto God and the Father by Him." The simple fact is that it is the divine man that makes the divine life. The tiniest flower reveals God, according to its measure, as much as the largest tree; and if we are "filled with all the fulness of God," "holiness to the Lord" will be borne engraved upon the signs and means of our humblest occupations. It is not by bringing our life up to the scale of Deity, but by bringing the spirit of Deity into our life, that we make it divine; and if we do this—if we go about our worldly works as if they were works of God, and perform them with the view of pleasing Him; though we may have a poor sphere and poor resources, yet may we be "godly men set apart by the Lord for Himself." Our work may be a worship; our intercourse with men may be a fellowship with the Father of our spirits; our common labour and common gratification may be "sanctified by the word of God and prayer;" and if it be, we shall be saved from the sensuous cravings of those who connect divinity with the scale, and not the spirit, the task and not the temper of our existence—who depreciate incidents and experiences of our common history and being, on the same principle that led the Jews to reject the Saviour, "Is not this the carpenter's son?"

Do we not depreciate common life? Do we not unduly value the unusual and peculiar? Do we not disesteem the quiet, daily virtues? Do we not pour contempt on the familiar manifestations of grace and greatness—look down on household goodness—prefer camps to cottages, and palaces to the poor man's hut? God dwells with the humble—slaves are said to be the Lord's freemen; but we cleave to the lofty and noble in circumstance and state; and thus fall into the error of rejecting Christ because He is the carpenter's Son.

Let us seek to detect the spiritual and divine, wherever they are. And let us beware, like the Jews, of quenching the feeling, when awakened. Let us rather deem its lowly form and fellowships as the stronger commendation of its excellence, and the more effective method of its power.

CHRIST LEFT SORROWFULLY.

MATTHEW xiv. 22.—"*He went away sorrowful.*"
Or, MARK. x 22.—"*He was sad at that saying, and went away grieved.*"

THERE are many affecting pictures in the Gospels, pictures of human misery and sin, pictures that have brought tears from countless eyes, and opened up the deepest fountains of human feelings, but I know of none more touching than the one before us. There are scenes of physical anguish and pain; of mental misery; of Satanic hate; sometimes of two of these, sometimes of all. What more sad than the case of the child possessed with a devil, brought by his afflicted father to the Apostles, who could not help him, and then, with struggling faith and unbelief, and sobbing speech, presented before the Lord of all; and, even then not without a final and despairing strife, delivered from the evil one? What more sad than the little group met near the city gates, tending to his last long home a youth, but a few hours deceased, and the only son of his mother, and she a widow, who has seen her last "coal" in Israel "quenched," and is a "widow indeed," bereft of all? What can be more sad than the spectacle at Lazarus's tomb, with Christ's heart overflowing with tenderness and sympathy, and the sisters weeping, and the crowd looking on, some with sorrow, some with wonder, some with malice? But I think the scene before us of the young ruler's leaving Christ with sorrow, perhaps with tears, though there was less of outward effect and impressive incident about it, is more distressing than all—is more distressing, because so quiet and so free from exciting circumstances.

If that scene were painted—I know not whether it could be; it could be only by an artist of the finest powers—I think it would have an interest above many of the greatest works of human genius. And without being painted, there are few of any spiritual sensibility, though of small imagination, who may not feel that it possesses elements of deepest interest. The Christ is there—the guide of man to life eternal; known by many to be a prophet, felt by some to be something greatly more. And He is tended by His Apostles and a great multitude, when lo! a young man, a ruler, and very rich, steps forward, with reverend mien and modest gait. The greater part, perhaps, wonder at his conduct, marvelling much at his reasons: some are glad to think that such an one should care to know Him who was not in favour with the wealthy, powerful classes; and some might, perchance, hope or fear that it betokened a likelihood of interference from the authorities to capture or to crush the popular demagogue. But he speaks, and his words are solemn in matter and respectful in style. This young man, with so much worldly goods and social honour in his possession, wishes to gain eternal life; when tried by a moral test, not slight or partial, he does not shrink or blanch. All things seem hopeful, and Jesus Himself looked on him and loved him; but Jesus, who "knew all men," and adapted His treatment as a wise moral physician, to individual characters and moods, spoke of a grievous lack in this lovely and promising youth—one great want; and made a large demand, not one He made on all; (for many of His disciples did not sell and follow Him in person; the home of Bethany was not broken up, because the dwellers there loved, and were loved by Jesus) a demand that would have involved a thorough rupture with the world. And for that he was not prepared. "He was sad at that saying." There was a sudden check and chill upon his heart. A cloud came over his bright and genial face. He stood a moment in fearful suspense—looked at Jesus, looked at the disciples, looked within—a crowd of thoughts rushed into his mind; and then he made the fearful choice, and, with downcast eyes, "he went away sorrowful."

I.

He went away from Christ, though good.

In a large sphere of things, and in a sense not unworthy—good. I take it so on the strength of what he said himself, and of Christ's not contradicting him. There is no question of his sincerity and seriousness. The whole atmosphere of the scene breathes genuineness and nature. Christ quoted the moral law

—the precepts of the second table; the ruler answered without hesitation, "All these have I observed from my youth." And we may well believe that it was so, from his own manner, and Christ's tacit admission. It was much to say—vastly more than many can say, or say to Christ. Of course we dare not say that his morality was perfect: judged by a law that looks at thoughts, and feelings, and desires, it perhaps was very defective, even as morality; but whatever lack of holy principle or inward rule there might be, to a goodly degree he had maintained a character of outward excellence and social repute; he had cherished the virtues of obedience and integrity, and purity and truth. They had been his habit always, through the season of levity and inexperience, of unchastened self-will and bursting passions. It was, I repeat, much to say. Can you say it of yourselves? Have you so filled the sphere of social virtues? Have you thus rendered to all their dues in word and act? Have you thus practically honoured those above, around, beneath you? How many of you could calmly, boldly, assert that you have injured neither man nor woman; that you have defrauded none, and deceived none; and reverenced and obeyed those who gave you birth?

And yet he left Jesus. With all this goodness and this grace, these habits and ornaments of virtue, he was without the "one thing needful:" he had not that inner, holy life which would have found its satisfaction and its strength, its service and its solace, in the fellowship and discipleship of Jesus. There is too much reason to fear that the love which, both toward God and man, is the consecrating spirit of religion and morality, was, if not wholly, yet greatly wanting in his worth—that "the leaven of the Pharisees," with whom he associated, had already fermented in his soul—and that the world, of which he possessed no small portion, had too great a hold upon his heart. Indeed, you will observe that it is *only the second table* of the law that he says that he had kept. Christ did not quote to him the first, nor did he plead its fulfilment. Most likely he might have said of this, as of the other, that he had kept it, and with equal truth—that is, had kept it in conduct and discourse, in ritual observance, and reverence of the Sabbath. We cannot tell. All that is mentioned is morality; and whatever he had or had not, he did not possess that state of spirit which recognized and received the Son of God, which heeded and sympathized with Him, and was prepared, like the earliest disciples, and the woman of Samaria, to exclaim, "I have found Him, I have found Him."

Alas! that the moral should ever be separate from the holy, the social from the spiritual, the visible man of the life from "the hidden man of the heart." And yet it is full often. When Jesus began His miracles at Cana, it was at *a feast*, where love, and relationship, and friendship, all met in glee and gladness, and Christ could look on that scene with complacency and joy, and by miracle express His feelings, and increase and heighten those of others. The next time He appeared was in *the Temple*, and there all was wrong; the holy place was profaned by common barter, and His indignant zeal was revealed by the rebuke and rod of the Prophet of the Highest. So is it often still. Man is in ruins; but, as you often see in old religious houses, the part devoted to godly deeds has gone to utter decay, while that employed in providing for the lower needs of man is yet in good repair—though the spirit is wholly lost to God, the meaner but worthy offices of life are well discharged; and while the saint cannot be found, the man of the family, the place of business, and the social circle, are all that could be wished. Christ approved this ruler in the lower relations of social morality, while He pronounced him essentially defective in the higher; and "he went away" from Him in whom all morality might find its supplement and stimulus, its truest end and source. And you, however " blameless as concerning the righteousness which is in the law," however in your "manner of life from your youth up," without offence and of good report, may yet be wanting in the "faith" by which we are "saved," and the love which is the end of the commandment. You may have the "goodly pearls of justice, purity, fidelity, and reverence," and yet not " the pearl of great price;" and may leave the Christ before whom you might assert their existence—and perish!

II.

He thought so highly of Christ, and yet went away from Him.

That is, to a great extent—and to a greater, considering the time and circumstances. It is useless to inquire what were the precise opinions entertained of Jesus at different times, and by different classes and individuals. These opinions often varied, and were often indistinct, and dependent on the occurrences of the hour; and the feelings expressed had little to do with distinct conceptions, and arose from false impressions and false expectations.

This ruler, for some reason or other, was prepared to acknowledge the excellence, authority, and qualifications of Christ as a religious guide. He addressed Him as a "good Master"—a title which Jesus deemed too much as coming from him; and he inquired of Him the way to "eternal life." Compared with *your* conceptions of the Saviour, this may seem to imply but little knowledge. But remember that *Christ was not known as now;* that His own disciples did not know Him; that He had not told, and could not tell them "many things" to be revealed anon; and His spirit had not "glorified Him" by taking of His things and revealing Him unto their hearts; that they had very insufficient views of His person, and miserably false notions of His work; that they thought His death a thing to be avoided, and Himself to blame for thinking of it. And remember that he was *one of the last to get to know* what could be known of Christ. He was not in the region in which Christ lived and worked. He was one of a class always opposed to Him. He would hear but little, and see less of Him; and what came would probably come through prejudiced and prejudicing media. Knowledge must be estimated according to the means of knowledge, and by comparison. A small amount in Judea at that time was great: a small amount in a member of the ruling class was greater. And yet, though in such a time and in such a position, he could invest Jesus with the highest function any man could discharge, and recognized in Him a character which, under the circumstances, Jesus seemed to question. And yet " he went away." He lacked that inner sympathy which is deeper and stronger than official authority and doctrinal instruction—that secret affinity and unconsious yearning which taught the "sheep" to "hear Christ's voice and follow Him," in preference to "strangers"—that " drawing of the Father," under whose gentle influence the spirits of men "come" to Jesus. He would have obeyed the new Rabbi—he would have " done" what further was required by "the Teacher sent from God"—but he knew nothing of that instinct and yearning which would lead him to cleave to and follow Jesus, in all conditions and at every cost. And so he left Him.

And you may do the same, with views of Christ far fuller and clearer than were his. You may think of Jesus in every way of orthodox belief—you may have the correctest possible opinions of everything about Him, and about His work, of His nature and His offices, His relations to God and man, His earthly history and heavenly glory, His coming and His kingdom—and yet leave Him. It is not the bond of theological opinion can bind you to Him, or you may be bound to Him thus, and yet be far away! The "good Master's" claim may be rejected, and the Guide to " eternal life " may not be followed, and you may perish !

III.

He had pure and lofty aspirations, and yet he went away.

It is an interesting thing to find one so pure, and

upright, and good, *still unsatisfied*. He was not puffed up as one who had attained—did not rest in the complacent contemplation of his own excellences. It is the inevitable fate of the best and noblest worker in every kind. Dr. Johnson expresses somewhere this thought, that every man born to excel is constantly striving after an ideal which recedes from him as he advances towards it; and an artist of our own time confessed that he was never satisfied with his work unless he had forgotten what he meant to do. For there is a vast possibility of excellence conceivable in every kind, and above all, in the sphere of spirit—and the craving for it and power to attain it is increased by every new experience and possession. He who has any inspiration of right and goodness, will never think he has "yet attained, or is already perfect," for religion is not a work, but a life, and duty is not a defined task, but a right spirit. Contentment in good is a sign of a poor aim, rather than a great achievement.

This youth had something of this unrest of soul—this sense of difference between the ideal and the real—this looking, and longing, and working for something better and greater than he had yet known. He felt—though clinging sadly to the thought of "doing;" of filling up a clear outline of obligation, of finishing a set task of duty—he felt that "eternal life" was more and greater than the life he now possessed, and that it required more too; and yet "he went away."

His ideal was "pleasant to the eyes, and to be desired;" but he might not partake, though the prohibition came from within, and not without. His aspiration was weak, though pure. He had miscalculated its strength. He was only partially prepared to do the "good thing." He had imagined performance rather than sacrifice; he had expected a prescribed rule, not another life, another fellowship, another following. He looked to receive a lesson, not to enter a school. He looked to perform a feat, not begin a course of training and discipline. He hoped for something additional to his present course, not a new way and character of life altogether. "Eternal life" might attract and move him, but the present life had a strange and fatal charm for him; and, thinking he could meet every probable demand, he shrunk from total self-abandonment and self-consecration, and was, in the presence of the tender but uncompromising "Master," and His kind but stern behests, like one who essays a work with joy, but soon relinquishes it in despair—like one who would gladly gain health and soundness at any cost, and then shrinks from the medicine and the knife—like one who feels quite strong and vigorous on the couch, and falls when he attempts to walk.

And so may you be. You may be greatly dissatisfied with your spiritual condition. You may feel that you have powers whose performances disgrace themselves, senses and solicitudes that belong to another state of being. Your daily work is a poor skeleton of duty. You have vivid realizations of "the world to come." Sometimes eternity is rather the contemporary than the successor of time; and God is very near; and you "hunger and thirst after righteousness," and you think you would do anything to be saved. There are many in such case, but it comes to naught. They cannot bear the searching test; they cannot comply with the severe demand. They come, as it were, to Christ, but only to return. Expecting approving encouragement, they find scrutinizing severity; looking for gentle admonition of duty, they find unmerciful exposure of defeat. They want counsel to go on; they receive instructions to begin anew. Instead of learning what they know not, they have to unlearn what they think they know. Instead of doing more and better, they have to cease from their own works, and enter a quite different service in a quite different spirit. Instead of being improved simply, they have to be detected and rebuked. And the souls that came, it may be, with gleeful hope, are staggered, then despair, and then retire. Oh no! it is not the refinement and exaltation of your ethical conceptions that will avail you: the finest poets may be gross livers. It is not the freshness and force of your ethical aspirations that will avail you: you may sigh, aye, and strive too, for an ideal which shall entirely elude your grasp. "Eternal life" may be in your vision and desire, and eternal death in your heart and ways; and after coming to Christ for a new rule of conduct, you may go back despairingly, and perish evermore.

IV.

He went away, *though Jesus loved him*.

"Then Jesus beholding him, loved him." There was much to love. He was a man: he was a young man: perhaps of goodly form and visage—certainly of becoming carriage and address—with the greatest of words upon his lips, and the best of feelings in his heart—"pleasant" and comely in his life, and not without some possibilities of better things to come. It was when he described his conduct, frankly declared his innocence of vice and crime, that Jesus gazed upon him with complacency. I shall not try to break the force of this expression by any doctrinal disquisition; much less try to make it out that Jesus did *not* love him. I believe He did: I believe that His eye rested on this ingenuous inquirer with delight; for Jesus always is pleased with justice and goodness, truth and honour. As far as they go, they are like Himself, and give Him joy. If a devil could feel them, he would approve the feeling. Jesus loved this man, and would fain have done him good; for if He came to save sinners, and the chief of them, can He regard with indifference one who could plead a not unworthy past, and who sought a far more worthy future?

Jesus loved him; but He loved *something more*. He could not yield His right—could not relinquish His claim, as the Teacher and the Truth, the Master and the model; He could not change or ignore the essential character of "eternal life," which is not eternal pleasure, and property, and praise, but true, high, and holy life for ever; He could not allow any compromise with old traditions and worldly lusts. The man must break with the past. Like the Paul, then to come, he must count all things but loss for Christ—his lineage, and life, and social position. This he could not do: and, not doing it, though Jesus loved him, He could not save him, and the earnest inquirer became not the faithful follower. And Jesus may love *you*, and yet you may not attain to His righteousness and blessing. For this is *fact*, whatever theologians may teach; and fact *felt*, whatever man may believe: that you are free. I know nothing of the point of contact between the will of God, and the wills of man, and am utterly unable to explain the difficulties of a subject which has puzzled all that have ever thought upon it. I am wholly unable to answer Edwards on the Freedom of the Will, and am wholly unable to believe it. The logic is irrefragable; the conclusion is, and must be wrong. Arguing against consciousness is like beating a ghost. You feel that you are free; you can't help but feel it. You will feel it for ever. And Jesus Christ deals with us as free; else there could be no salvation, for there could be no sin; and no worth in being saved, if there could be. And therefore, whatever the value and necessity of Christ's grace and inward working—and we are not of those who put any limit on them—there is a point beyond which He cannot go with sinners, and beyond which it would not be saving men, but forcing machines; and therefore He may, as here, love those He does not save, and the objects of His benevolence and complacency for some reasons, may yet retire and die.

Christ may love you thus. I do not say that He feels to you as He did to this man, but still He loves you: and yet you may not have eternal life. Did He not love Israel, whom He would have "gathered as a hen gathereth her chickens under her wings;" the city over which "He wept," and whose obduracy he so bitterly bemoaned? and yet He left it to its doom. Did

He not love "the world," when His incarnation and His death were all for its salvation; when He "came into" it, and went out of it, to redeem it; and yet multitudes believe not, and are damned. And He may now behold you and love you, and you may come short of eternal life.

V.

He went away, although he did it *sorrowfully*. "He was," says Mark, "sad at that saying, and went away grieved." It was, we may suppose, the sadness of *loss*. "And cannot I have eternal life? Is the way so hard—are the terms so difficult? Must I relinquish so great a prize, bear so heavy a cross?" The sadness of *disappointment*. "Must all I sought and thought I saw in prospect vanish thus? Must my past go for nothing, and my hope be lost? Is this all that the new prophet, the 'good master' has to say —become a pauper, and follow one who has not where to lay His head?" The sadness of *self-conviction*. "Ah! he is right. I did not know myself. It is I, not He, that is to blame. He has made no obstacle, but revealed my own. I am my own great hindrance. He has but touched a secret spring I knew not of; but opened a fountain that lay hid; but taken a slight covering from a deep corruption. My treasure is in this world, and there my heart must be." The sadness of *shame*. "And I have gone to *Him*, and *He* has seen me through! Oh! that look of gentle pity; those tender tones; that hard, but loving invitation! He said not 'Go,' but 'Come.' And I have left *Him*, declined His offer, spurned His precepts. And He knows that I love something more than Himself, more than the counsel I professed myself ready to follow, more than the blessing I professed myself anxious to obtain." But the sorrow *did not prevent his going;* did not make Christ relent; did not keep Him from saying, "How hardly shall they that have riches enter into the kingdom of heaven." He was grieved, and yet he went. Not with anger, or scorn, or bitterness, but with tears, if not of the eye, of the heart, he went away; wishing that he could have stayed—and yet he went.

And you may leave Jesus with regret; not only hard, exasperated, but with tender grief. You cannot blame Him, though you try; you cannot depreciate His blessing, though you try; you feel that He is right and you are wrong, that His gifts are priceless, that His fellowship is sweet, "His commandments not grievous," and His service freedom; and yet you leave Him. But your sorrow will not avail you. It is not sorrow unto life; it is not sorrow at being wrong, but being required to be right; the sorrow of desires too weak to be fulfilled, of a conflict ending in defeat. Tears may but baptize you for the dead. You may die, and yet think heaven worthy, and mourn its loss. You may die, and yet think Jesus true, and approve His words. It is not the tears that are shed as we leave the Saviour that have worth or meaning, but those shed as we follow Him; not the sadness of the soul that forsakes Him, but of the soul that cleaves to Him; the tears of penitence that bedew the face of faith, the sadness which present love extracts from past unworthiness, and the contest of our wishes and our weakness.

To conclude. There are *special times* when we may be said to leave Christ; when we are brought very near to Him, and have to make an election, and perhaps for ever. Such a time is that of deep *religious conviction;* when we feel the reality of spiritual things and persons, feel their infinite greatness; when we are obliged either to yield to them, or make them yield to us; and when we quench the spark of desire, and smother up earnest thoughts and feelings, and return with renewed zest, or with sullen despair into the world. Such a time is that when we are obliged by *outward circumstances* to take a stand. A *new position* in life compels us to come out afresh, and either as His servants or His foes. Some *painful enterprise* of sin forces on conscience a decision. A *companionship*, promising pleasure and advantage, requires by its rejection that we honour, or by its acceptance that we renounce, the Saviour.

It matters not what we leave Him *in spite of, if we leave Him*. The greater the difficulties in leaving Him, the more sad and fearful the forsaking. All is rendered worthless in attainment, possibility, and hope, when we turn our back on Him. The moral life goes for nothing; the high thoughts of Him go for nothing; our aspirations and our regrets go for nothing; and His love to us goes for nothing. The manner, the circumstances, the hard contest, of whatever kind, do do not affect the fact—the most fearful fact of all.

And in leaving Christ *we leave all*. To turn your back on Christ is to turn your back on heaven, and holiness, and God. To forsake Him is to forsake. "Whoso sinneth against Him wrongeth his own soul; all they that hate Him love death."

Let *those who are following Him* "cleave to Him with purpose of heart;" and "follow the Lamb whithersoever He goeth." And let those who have "fallen away" beware lest it become "impossible to renew them to repentance, seeing they crucify to themselves the Son of God afresh, and put Him to an open shame;" crucify Him in a sadder manner, with greater guilt and more awful consequences than of old; crucify the spiritual, not corporeal Christ, and destroy the Saviour!

THE LOVE OF GOD

JOHN iii. 16.—"*For God so loved the world, that He gave His only begotten Son, that whosoever believeth in Him should not perish, but have everlasting life.*"

WE cannot judge of the strange effect which these words would probably have upon the mind of Nicodemus, to whom they were first spoken. He was a Jew, a Pharisee, a ruler; and to him therefore they would appear as they cannot appear to us. They are familiar to us, and we understand, or think that we understand them well. We have heard them and read them a hundred times. They were among the first we listened to and lisped. We learnt to read in spelling them out. The facts which they express have always been articles of our creed, and anything different we have called heresy. So well wrought are they into both faith and memory, that in preaching from them the danger is lest you should think the subject stale, too well known for instruction, and too old to move the heart. But every part of this brief statement would surprise, if not shock, the visitor by night. It would involve a puzzle, if not a heresy. He had been conversant mainly with ideas of law; Christ speaks of "love." He had dealt largely with bodily services, and rites, and moralities; Christ lays mighty stress upon "believing." He had been looking to rewards of righteousness from God; Christ points to a divine gift, the gift of a divine Son, and that Son Himself. He had set his hopes on a glorious future of outward prosperity and glory in heaven, and perhaps in earth; Christ holds out the prospect of an " eternal life." He had been rejoicing in the peculiar privileges of a nation, or even a sect of a nation—had been priding himself on being a Jew and a Pharisee; Christ comprehends in the meaning and the mercy of God " the world," and " whosoever believeth." Thus, the things which are plain and easy to us would be difficult, if not insoluble problems to him, and what constitutes the very essence of our faith would, at almost every point, contradict and confuse his.

Oh! if we could but hear the words for the first time, and without prepossessions either of Pharisaic error, or logical orthodoxy, hear them with nothing but consciousness of sin and thirst for life—before the love of God had been hardened into doctrine, and the only begotten Son had become a quarrel for the schools. "Do your gods love you?" asked a missionary of some Indians. "The gods never think of loving," was the cheerless answer. The text before us was read. "Read it again," asked the arrested pagan. "That is large light, read it again." A third time the blessed words were repeated; and with this emphatic response, *"That is true, I feel it."* On one occasion a missionary was dictating to a native amanuensis the translation of the first epistle, and when he reached the passage, " Now are we the sons of God," the poor child of heathenism burst into tears, and exclaimed, " It is too much, it is too much; let me put it, Now are we permitted to kiss His feet." Who would not part with much sound divinity, and much correct terminology, to be able to listen to the words of the Lord Jesus as " thus spirit and life," as indeed " good news from a far country," with all the simplicity and the earnest interest of awakened need.

It is difficult to treat such a passage as this. The multiplicity of its thoughts, the greatness of its topics, the obviousness of its truths, which seem to make it easy, really make it hard. Nothing easier than to make out of it " a body of divinity;" few things harder than to extract out of it the soul of a sermon. It would be impossible, except by selecting one subject, and making all the rest revolve around and reflect it as planets round a central sun. I take the theme of *Love*, and ask you to behold it as here represented by its best mouth and best manifestation—in its grandest source, its purest form, its greatest strength, its loftiest purpose, and its widest sphere. And while we speak, may " the love of God be shed abroad in our hearts," giving light to our thoughts, tenderness to our feelings, and filling our whole soul and life with strength, and purity, and joy. " God so loved the world, that He gave His only begotten Son, that whosoever believeth in Him should not perish, but have everlasting life."

I.

Love in its Grandest Source.

Then God can love, does love. So the Bible states, and so must we believe. I know that in ascribing human qualities and affections to God, the Bible is to be interpreted carefully and wisely. We must beware of making God only an infinite man; we must not forget that God can only make Himself known through human media, and human media must be imperfect. Yet the Bible is a revelation, not a contradiction of truth; whatever may be the case as to the speech of men, the speech of God is not intended to conceal His thoughts; and if He describes Himself as like to us, it must be because some real resemblance exists. If the moral principles and dispositions, as truth and righteousness and love, do not answer substantially to the things so called in us, how can we get any knowledge of God from their ascription to Him? God no more than man can convey his meaning to us, except by words which we can understand.

God loves. We presume not to inquire curiously into the conditions and operations of the divine benevolence, to analyze with our rude thoughts the heart of God, to tread profanely this holiest of all of the temple of divine nature: yet we dare affirm, for He has affirmed it, that He loves. Be it that love in God in some respects is different from love in us; as what is not? Be it that it is free from all defect, and associated with all that can make it beautiful and strong, that only enhances, not denies its worth. God is not a

Being cold, still, passionless—an infinite eye or an infinite ear, an intellect without thought, a will without movement: He loves. Yea, more: "God is love." It is the strongest way of ascribing properties to God or man, to speak thus of them as not His only, but Himself. But there is more than figure here, there is fact. Love is more than an attribute of God. It is as light, of which all attributes are colours. There is no moral property of God which is not essentially included in love. If "love is the fulfilling of the law," seeing that all its precepts are expressions of benevolence, love is the nature of the Deity, seeing that all His attributes are different aspects of His charity.

How near this fact brings Him to us—to our hearts. We may admire and revere other qualities, but can love only the loving. "Scarcely for a righteous man will one die, yet peradventure for a good man some would even dare to die," and scarcely for a righteous God would one die. "We love Him, because He first loved us." His boundless understanding, His immaculate holiness, may be objects of honour and of homage, but I can love only one who can love; my heart refuses to go forth towards a being destitute of affections. Christ has revealed the heart of God.

The Scriptures always make this love of God the fountain of all Christian redemption. They greatly misrepresent the order and economy of salvation, who give not to God's love the first and chiefest place, who make it not the fount and origin of all. "God was in Christ reconciling the world unto Himself," not

Himself unto the world. "Herein is love, not that we loved God, but that He loved us, and sent His Son to be the propitiation for our sins." "God so loved the world as to give His only begotten Son." Whatever the life and death of Christ did or were, they were the effect, and not the cause of God's love; they were its fruit, and not its root. Oh, do not think of Jesus merely as the pacifier. "This man is the peace." Think not of Him as the gainer, but the gift of boundless charity.

II.

Love in its Purest Form.

I mean by this that it was benevolence which had nothing to attract in its objects but their need of its intervention, and everything to repel it. The thing loved was "the world;" the world that might "perish," and would perish except for the exercise of unmerited grace. It was, therefore, love compassionating its objects, looking at and moved by sights of danger and distress. Not love dwelling complacently on the happiness and hopes of men, passively delighting itself in beholding their peace and joy, but contemplating and concerned with the wretched and the woeful. It is one thing to help the happy and prosperous, and another to succour and relieve the needy and miserable. Many a man has charity enough for the first, who has not for the last. The priest and the Levite, in the parable, were probably hardened wretches; still they might have looked upon the "half dead" traveller, and have "passed by on the other side," without being destitute of feeling. It is not every kind or degree of "compassion" which would go to a stripped and bleeding victim. And God says of Israel, "When I passed by thee, and saw thee polluted in thine own blood, I said unto thee when thou wast in thy blood, Live; yea, I said unto thee when thou wast in thy blood, Live."

And if the world was perishing, it was more than wretched, it was *guilty* too. It was an object of moral corruption, for no otherwise could it die. To love the merely distressed is comparatively easy, but to love those who add unworthiness to distress is much harder. Moral excellence may attract compassion to the miserable, but moral vileness offends and disgusts it. How much we prefer to show kindness to those who appeal to our moral judgment and sympathy, whose innocence or goodness gives a grace to their calamities, who are the victims of some gross wrong or fraud, or who bear their sorrows with placid and heroic mind—in whom, that is, there is an element of romance, and who invoke our imagination as well as our heart: "interesting cases," as we call them; the young and lovely widow, the meek and defrauded orphan, the ruined and chivalrous patriot exile,—but who, comparatively, cares for the woes of the idle, drunken, filthy? The selfish, sullen, wasteful? The bad husband, and bad father? The wretch who accepts your kindness as if he had a right to it, or as if he did you a favour in accepting it? Now Paul lays stress on this. "When we were without strength, Christ died for the ungodly." Men, says he, respect the just, and love the good; but God commendeth His love towards us, in that while we were yet sinners, Christ died for us."

There was more than this. There may be immorality allied to woe, and love may yet find no obstruction in *personal offensiveness*. The wretched may be before me in the most saddening and sickening conditions, and associated with repellent moral qualities, but I may have no personal grievances; they may have done no evil to me, yea, they may have done good; and my pity may be assisted by approval of at least a portion of their character, by my gratitude for their kindness; and while they are generally loathed and hated by others, I may be able and bound to cherish towards them feelings of another kind. I am like one gazing on a scene of desolation and ruin, who, while others see only what is sorrowful and dreary, has found a solitary peep of picturesque interest; or like one, who contemplating a countenance generally disagreeable, has chanced to light on the one pleasing expression of features. Love appears in its utmost pureness and freeness when it passes over, not only demerit but offence, not only dispenses with merit, but rises above self, withstands provocations, blesses those that curse, and does good to those that injure its possessor. This was the case here. When the world was perishing through sin against its God, God loved it. "Christ died for the ungodly." "When we were enemies we were reconciled to God by the death of His Son."

And this includes another fact—that the world's misery and peril *were caused by itself*. Every soul of man owes his real evils now and hereafter—that is, all evils that could be converted into good—penal and permanent evils, to his sin. It is always a sore strain on mercy when it is asked to redeem and relieve men from the consequences of their own faults and folly, their criminal carelessness, or wilful misconduct. How quick and natural the reply—" It serves you right;" " It is your own fault;" " You have no one to thank for it but yourselves." God might have met all our bewailings and appeals in this way. Had He not been wronged and dishonoured, perdition had never entered the prospect, nor been possible to man. " Thou hast destroyed thyself, but in me is thy help." " After that the love and kindness of God our Saviour toward man" (the philanthropy of God) " appeared, not by works of righteousness which we have done, but according to His mercy He saved us, by the washing of regeneration and renewing of the Holy Ghost." " God so loveth the world that whosoever believeth should not perish."

III.

Love in its greatest strength.

There is a benevolence which can pity without helping; which can look on suffering, and feel for it, and yet not interpose; which can content itself with tender emotions and kind words—say, in substance, " Be ye warmed, be ye clothed," without giving " the things needful for the body;" which can retain its posture of repose, and even comfort itself with the sentiment of pity; which can court the excitement of pictured and imaginary distress, and revel in the luxury of grief, and yet carefully avoid, or stoically deny, the cries of actual and far more bitter woe. "God so loved the world, that" He did something—He gave something. "The philanthropy of God appeared," "the love of God was manifested." Love is as deeds, not words, nor desires, nor feelings.

The love of God was practical in *the most costly way*. There may be interference, and effectual interference too, without sacrifice. The required effort may need no self-denial: the pleasures of benevolence may not be at the cost of interest or inclination. The test of love is sacrifice—the only certain criterion of its strength is the measure of the sacrifice. There can be no other. Whether it take the form of labour, or gift, or endurance, it is just the amount of conflict with what we value and delight in that proves its power. It is no greater than its call for the resignations of our interests and tastes, our affections and sensations. God "gave:" God gave up. "It pleased the Lord to bruise Him, he hath put Him to grief." He sacrificed not only to Himself, but of Himself. He sacrificed, in order to sacrifice. The value of the oblation he received was exactly the value of the gift which He bestowed. The cross was the self-denial of God!

Of all sacrifices, the chief are sacrifices of *persons*. No man worthy of the name of man can show his best love by giving things. The highest sphere of value is in persons—in beings capable of thought and feeling, beings having reason and will. Things may represent much of human trust and love, desire and delight; they may be precious and pleasant almost above utterance, as answering to, associated with, and providing for our good and gladness in a thousand ways, but they cannot stand for the loftiest of our regards. How much it costs sometimes to part with a mere material object, and of small intrinsic worth! A treasured coin, a memorial ring, a beloved portrait! Why to lose them may be like losing a portion of ourselves, and the heart may feel as one bereaved: but the worth of these things is mainly historical and typical; how much sorer grief is that of losing those for whose sake these things are valued, and have been so jealously preserved? It is in intelligent and moral natures that love has its strongest and its worthiest objects; and it is in them it makes its hardest sacrifice. God gave—gave up—a person.

And in sacrificing a person He sacrificed *the highest of all persons*—" His only begotten Son." "In this was manifested the love of God towards us, because that God sent His only begotten Son into the world, that we might live through Him." I don't know what this means. "The mystery of God, even of the Father and of Christ," is one I have not the power nor the desire to penetrate. The scholastic puzzles and polemics that have rent the Christian Church, and confused its intellect, be far from us! But still the Bible is a revelation, and Jesus is the word of God; and when He is called God's Son, and only Son, and the stress is laid upon the fact that in giving Him God gave His Son, and only Son, I am either being taught or trifled with; God is instructing my intelligence or mocking my heart. This is meant, or nothing is meant—that as a man's parting with his son, and his only son, would be a dreadful trial of affection to him, and an amazing proof of his affection for others, so, in giving Christ, God gave the greatest gift that the affluence of Deity could furnish. I inquire not curiously into the modes of divine being, nor ask how Jesus is a Son, but I cleave to this —that in speaking to us through our tenderest relationships, and the feelings that accompany them, God means to express a fact, and not a fiction. Just as in speaking of "love" at all, He means love essentially as I know it; so in speaking of sonship, He means sonship as I know it; and He evidently designs to make the impression, that He could give no being whose sacrifice would be more costly. If to "weep for an only son" is the Scripture type of the bitterest of sorrow, to give an only son must be the resistless evidence of the greatest love. The gift of Jesus was above all gifts, and inclusive of all. It transcended all, and implied all. "If God spared not His own Son, but delivered Him up for us all, how shall He not with Him also freely give us all things?"

IV.

Love in its loftiest purpose.

"That whoever believeth in Him should not perish, but have everlasting life." Is there any purpose greater in *kind?* We know the worth of "life." It is the chiefest of earthly good, and the most prized. "All that a man hath will he give for his life." The greatest salvation is that of the life; and, whatever some pretend, the greatest loss is that of the life. It is the condition of all else that is prized. As money is valuable not for what it is, but for what it represents and renders possible, so is life valuable. As money is not merely hard coin, or conventional paper, but whatever money can obtain—house, and food, and raiment, and every gratification of sense and taste, and much of social position, and not a little of power to do good; so life is all this, and much besides, as it is the condition and the means of the enjoyment and use of all. To be, is necessary to everything else. And thus, when we would assign the utmost value to any object, when we would express our supremest dependence and love, we call it our "life." Salvation is life; it is the first and greatest of blessings. But not only in figure; it is life in fact. "I am come that they might have life." Salvation and heaven are many things, but they are life more than all; and would be nothing, if not life. They are glory, and riches, and joy; but they are these because they are life, and these in being life. The word is used to express the present and future blessings of redemption many times more than any other word—more times than all other words put together. And there is no word, no condition, or power, or property of man, that so truly, so variously, and with such fulness of significance, represents the principles and privileges of the kingdom of heaven here and hereafter. The gift of God is life; it takes in all His gifts; it comprehends all the processes and prospects of godliness. It covers the whole career of grace. We "live by faith" through our whole course; we are "born again" when we become Christians; we "enter into life" when we are glorified. "Our life is hid with Christ in God" here, and "when Christ, who is our life, shall appear, we shall appear with Him in glory." Man has many kinds of life: composed as he is of many parts, and possessed as he is of many powers, his life is manifold. There is a life of different departments, and a life of different portions in each department: a life of the flesh, and of each fleshly member; a life of the soul, and of each of its powers and passions; and a life of the spirit, and of each of its faculties and sensibilities. Now this life, all this life, and in all its perfection, is the end of God. Beginning first in the foremost and finest portions of our nature, it will spread and strengthen until it pervades and possesses the whole of it. Man redeemed and renewed is to live, in all senses and in all respects, and to the utmost of his capacity of life. Every power raised and refined to its highest state, filled with all possible power, and freely exercised by objects suited to its nature, and of the most excellent kind; " the life of God" itself animating and ruling all the lower forms and forces of existence, perfect health, vigour, freedom, and happiness, this is the end for which God loves us, and for which Christ saves us; and this is heaven. "This is the record, that God hath given to us eternal life, and this life is in His Son."

And this life of the highest kind will be of the most lasting duration. It is "everlasting life." There is no dispute about the meaning of the word here. "The righteous shall go away into eternal life" gives rise to no controversy. No one doubts that the expression has its natural and fullest sense. It is accepted with a child-like faith by the most sceptical, with gladness by those most difficult to please. No natural dread calls into requisition the critical apparatus, no instinctive horror gives sharpness to the critical judgment. There are none who have any interest in shortening eternal life, and none who deem it wrong for God to give it to them. "Eternal life!"—life running on for ever; life followed by no death, partaking of the energy and immortality of God! We cannot estimate it. This quality of endlessness attached to a small boon would immeasurably extend it. The very thought of it gives intensity and calmness to all our joys. It makes provision for indefinite growth and expansion. And, every way, "the immortality of bliss is bliss." Everything is deathless and without decay in the "place prepared for man by Christ." The inheritance is incorruptible. The crown fadeth not away. The habitations are everlasting. The glory is eternal. The substance is enduring. The city continues, for the life is for ever. "He that doeth the will of God abideth for ever." "He that overcometh shall not be hurt of the second death." "He that believeth hath everlasting life." Sin brought death, and separated from the tree of life; Christ restored access to it, and "Blessed are they that do His commandments, that they may have right to the tree of life."

V.

Love in its widest sphere.

"The world." The word is used sometimes in a restricted sense, but there is no reason to suppose it is so here. It would be difficult to believe, did not facts prove it, that any could be so far blinded and perverted by system as to make "the world" signify the Church; but this is only one of the ingenious performances of uninspired theologians, one example of the fate which befalls any poor wayfaring thought or term that gets put by a Procrustean divinity on its merciless bed, to be shortened or extended according to the exigencies of an arbitrary rule. Partisans of theories may make the world mean the Church, but however worldly the Church may be, that is never its Scripture name. Indeed, when ever "world" is applied to a portion of mankind in a moral sense, it always means the wicked. It is "the world that lieth in wickedness," to which we are to be "not conformed," and which we are to "overcome." Wherever there is a man in the way to "perish," there is the world God loved, and Christ was given to save. God has sworn by His life that He doth not "desire the death of a sinner;" He is "longsuffering to us-ward, not willing that any should perish, but that all should come to repentance." He "will have all men to be saved, and to come unto the knowledge of the truth." And "the man Christ Jesus gave Himself a ransom for all;" and "He is the propitiation for our sins, and not for ours only, but also for the sins of the whole world."

There is nothing in the love of the Father or of the Son, nothing in the sacrifice of the Father or of the Son, to prevent the world being saved. I am not going to remove difficulties, or answer objections. Surely we may dwell upon and apply statements of Scripture, sun-like in their strength and clearness, without doing that; as if nothing was sure and safe—as if, with a slight change of terms,

> "Religion was intended
> For nothing but to be defended."

God loved the world, without limit of nation. "There

is no difference between the Jew and the Greek, for the same Lord over all is rich unto all that call upon Him." God loved the world, without limit of *condition;* for "Blessed are the poor, for theirs is the kingdom of heaven." God loved the world, without limit of character; for He was "rich in mercy," and "loved us with His great love when we were dead in sins." There is but one thing can prevent those to whom the tidings of it come being saved, and that is its rejection. "Whosoever believeth hath everlasting life." "For God sent not His Son into the world to condemn the world, but that the world through Him might be saved."

The subject has many practical bearings. Let me mention some.

You have here *a pattern and spring of love,* model and motive. "Be imitators of God, as dear children, and walk in love." "If God so loved us, we ought also to love one another." We cannot give so great a gift, nor pity objects so offensive to us as we were to God, nor confer blessings of such priceless worth. But love in us must follow love in God: follow it in caring for the vilest and most guilty, follow it in making sacrifices, follow it in seeking most the greatest ends. To make man live for ever must be our aim; to think none beneath or above the boon; and to help in giving Christ to them, to be their "life," and "hope," and righteousness and resurrection. And in doing this our purpose and power must be derived from "the love of God in Christ Jesus." Nothing but that love received into our own souls, by faith, will melt its frozen forces and unlock its secret strength. In other words, if we believe God's love ourselves, we shall dispense it; if we accept His "only begotten Son," we shall proclaim Him; if we possess the eternal life," we shall diffuse it. We shall have both the desire and the ability to do it. And if we do not, we shall have neither. And this is partly God's design in loving and saving us, to inspire us with love and constitute us saviours. This is His salvation. Love is life, eternal love is eternal life. "This is life eternal, to know Thee, the only true God" (and "every one that loveth knoweth God," and "he that loveth not knoweth not God, for God is love"), "and Jesus Christ whom Thou hast sent."

What *a Gospel*, what a good news, is here! I know no Gospel anywhere else. The moment you abridge, restrict, condition, you "destroy the hope of man." Behold the generosity, free, full, strong; like an overflowing river, like the all-pervading light and air. Its attributes are spontaneity, infinite eternity, self-caused, self-sacrificing, self-imparting. The "mercy" is "tender." The "redemption" is "plenteous." The "love passeth knowledge." The "gift" is "unspeakable." Oh! "believe the love which God hath" toward you! You have not to merit it, or move it. It is to-day fresh, living, sincere, and mighty. God loves you now. In spite of all your sins and follies and weaknesses, though to Him unloving, and in His sight unutterably unloving: whatever you are or have been, are doing or have done. The only title to this love is to be "perishing," the only condition of all its blessings is to "believe." It is not modesty to doubt it, but rankest pride; it is not humility to misgive it, but reckless presumption. Believe it, though your "sins" are "mighty," and your heart is hard. Believe it, though you have exhausted the love of others, and your own. God loves you, though a father's pride has turned to loathing, and a mother's tenderness is buried in despair; though if you sought the house of the first he would not welcome you, and though if you appealed to the pity of the other, she would not hear you. He who made the hearts of fathers and mothers "is greater than their hearts," "will have mercy on you," "and abundantly pardon you," "will rejoice over you with singing," and you will "rest in His love."

The subject, light as it is, *casts a shadow*, and by its very brightness, casts the shadow of your unbelief upon your soul and state and prospects. "This is the condemnation," "that light"—the light of love—"is come into the world, and men loved darkness rather than light." "He that believeth not is condemned already, because he hath not believed on the name of the only begotten Son of God." There is no hate like love turned to hate. There is no anger like the anger of incensed patience and mildness. There is no wrath like "the wrath of the Lamb." But I appeal to you otherwise than thus. God loves you; why should you perish? Why should you compel Him to destroy you? Why should you force Him to inflict death, when He would give life? Why not "fear His goodness"? Suppose *you* don't care about perishing, why constrain God to punish? Have you no heed for one who has given His only Son? who would give eternal life? If you can brave His fury, should you not think upon His grace? He loves you; oh! for His sake, if not your own, let His love have free course and be glorified. He would have mercy on you; oh! have mercy upon God!

REST AND PROSPERITY OF CHURCHES.

Acts ix. 31.—"*Then had the churches rest throughout all Judæa, and Galilee, and Samaria, and were edified; and walking in the fear of the Lord, and in the comfort of the Holy Ghost, were multiplied.*"

Our religion is pre-eminently historical. Its dogmas are revealed in connection with history; its principles are developed in the events of Providence and the lives of men. We have no creeds or catechisms, no symbols or platforms, in the Bible. They are the works of men; far other are the modes of God. His revelation is free, full, and spiritual; designed and adapted to stimulate thought, not to stifle it; to fill the mind with living realities, not to impress upon it lifeless forms. The providence of God is illustrated by the history of the world, and especially of the Jews; the character and spirit of God are expressed in the history of Jesus Christ; and the word and will of God, as to the internal principles and external organization of Christian churches, are to be found in the history of the societies that "first trusted in Christ."

The Acts of the Apostles, therefore, possess great claims upon our attention. We have there a record of the proceedings and experiences of the first "churches in Christ Jesus," of what they did, and of what was done unto them; and this is interesting and valuable many ways. It is so on *their* account, as illustration of the nature and treatment of their principles: the professors of a new system, or a new edition of an old system, and a system of singular character and pretensions; and it is so on *our* account, as presenting us with an example which we should copy, and this, for the most part, in circumstances of trial and trouble, in which, if we *are*, we may learn to be quiet; and if we are *not*, we may learn to be thankful.

We have chosen, for present consideration, a most pleasant and instructive account of some of the earliest churches—and one, the contemplation of which, suitable at all times, is peculiarly so on the occasion on which we have assembled to-day. We shall first briefly illustrate the description which the text contains, and then endeavour to impress upon you the principles which it suggests.

I.

It describes the churches of the Holy Land.

A preliminary remark on the *nature* of these churches cannot well be omitted. They were "congregations," or "assemblies," as the word signifies, of *good people*. They were people, or they could not have been good; and they were good, or they could not have "walked in the fear of God, and in the comfort of the Holy Ghost." And they are described as plural; as being more than one in the same country. It is clear, therefore, that they were not *material edifices;* although I, for one, do not object to, but prefer, that application of the word church; they were composed of *men*. As clearly they were not *promiscuous associations*, constituted by chance, nominal profession, outward and involuntary rites; they were real Christians, spiritual, reverential, intelligent, holy ones. They were not *national communities*, for we read not of *a Church*, but "churches," in Palestine. There were *many* in the Holy Land. Now these are all important facts. I need scarcely say to you, that in all these respects, the churches mentioned in our text were not unlike, but like, to all the churches mentioned in the New Testament. There are points of universal similarity, not dissimilarity, to the apostolical churches. They were always *men*—always *good men*—always *single congregations of good men*. Concerning these societies, several interesting particulars are given us. These relate to their *quiet*, to their *experience and conduct*, and to their *increase*.

1. *Their quiet*. "Then had the churches rest."

This denotes the commencement, not the continuance, of a state of peace. *Then*, not before, had they rest. In the beginning of the preceding chapter it is said—"And at that time there was a great persecution against the Church which was at Jerusalem; and they were all scattered abroad throughout the regions of Judæa and Samaria." Rest was, therefore, new. It was as scarce and as refreshing as the oasis in the desert, the spring in the wilderness, the shadow of a great rock in a weary land. It was the more precious for the previous opposition and distress. It was the calm after the storm, the joy coming in the morning, after the weeping that endured through the night. It may, however, be more interesting for us to consider the *causes* than the *fact* of this return of quiet. Perhaps two may have combined their influences to bring it about, although the chronology of the Acts prevents our speaking with much certainty. *One was the conversion of Saul.* He had been an active and energetic opposer of the saints—a " persecutor, blasphemer, and injurious." He describes himself as having been " exceedingly mad" against them. His cruelty was based on conscience, for he "thought he ought to do many things contrary to Jesus of Nazareth;" and of all persecutors, the worst are those who are so from conviction. But the "grace of God was exceeding abundant towards him with faith and love, which are by Jesus Christ." His opposition was destroyed, not by his ruin, but his regeneration—not by his punishment as a foe, but by his transformation into a friend. Mercy, not judgment, put an end to his enraged proceedings. The "rest" of the churches came not from the slaughter of the lion that had torn and tortured them, but from his amazing metamorphosis into a lamb. Is there no encouragement to *us* in this? He that could convert Saul could convert any sinner; and, indeed, his conversion is set forth by himself, not only as a fact, but a "pattern," an illustration at once of the power and the mercy of the Gospel. Then let Christians pray. Doubtless the objects of his fury had often entreated *his* salvation—at all events, when "the blood of the martyr Stephen was shed," and that holy man poured out his soul in an expiring supplication that his enemies might be forgiven, "*he* was standing by, and consenting unto his death, and kept the raiment of them that slew him"— and who shall say that, having shared in the sin of his destruction, he did not also share in the blessing of his intercession? We may well be comforted. Whatever malignity, and prejudice, and spiritual ignorance may characterize our enemies, as individuals or churches, Jesus Christ can still substitute the purity, peacefulness, and mercy of the wisdom from above. *Another cause was the solicitude and alarm of the Jews.* However great the effect of Saul's conversion in the restoration of quiet, we cannot suppose that it alone was sufficient for that effect. He was but a *young man;* to some extent the instrument rather than the author of the afflictions of the saints. His own danger proves that the persecution continued after his conversion; nor does the text occur in connection with the record of his conversion; so that we are prepared to look for some other reason of the state of things described. And there was one. The chronology of Paul's history is very doubtful. We, therefore, do not dogmatize. About that time the Jews were thrown into the greatest excitement and alarm. At Alexandria the Jews suffered dreadfully from the Egyptians, and in Judæa and elsewhere were in imminent peril of ruin. An attempt was made to bring the statue of Caligula unto the Holy of Holies, in consequence of some offence he had taken at the conduct of the Jews. Nothing could produce greater distress and consternation. It aroused their most vehement and sacred indignation. It was at once a national and religious insult; a dishonour to the symbol of all that was precious to them as a people and a church. One good came out of this evil. Their attention was diverted from Christians to themselves. Another direction was given to their thoughts and feelings. They were too concerned about their own affairs, to meddle with those of others. The anxieties of self-interest took the place of spite and vengeance against the saints. This is a method of divine providence. God can "restrain the wrath of man," as well as make it "praise Him." He can control the circumstances as well as change the character of our foes. He can so situate them as to make all their care and effort necessary for their own defence. He can draw them off by internal divisions, or by the creation of a common danger, and a common fear. "Saul returned from pursuing after David" when the "Philistines invaded the land." "The king's heart" (and likewise every heart) "is in the hand of the Lord; He turneth it as rivers of water whithersoever it pleaseth Him." He can regulate depraved souls that He does not purify, give a new current to the stream which retains its old filth, divert the powers he does not convert. Let this cheer us too. In such hands, the friends of Him who in such ways can preserve and deliver, we may boldly say, "We will not fear." The hearts of enemies are under the eye and the power of God. He sees their every thought and wish, and according to His pleasure, can change or confound them; cause them to take another character, or another course; make them friends to us, or nothing.

2. *Their experience and conduct.* "And were edified, and walked in the fear of God, and in the comfort of the Holy Ghost."

"They were edified." The expression is architectural. It is used figuratively of men. They were *built up* "as lively stones, a spiritual house." When the storm ceased, they set earnestly about the completing of their moral temple. When the war terminated, they looked to the promoting of their home prosperity. Not that this was neglected till then, but it was not so well and so effectively attended to. Persecution is unfavourable to the religious commerce of a Church, as war is to the secular commerce of a country. It dispirits; it diverts attention; it employs resources; it intercepts communication. External peace is favourable to internal progress. It permits the full and unfettered employment of the Church's gifts and graces for their appropriate and appointed purposes, their own edification and increase. The churches before us were edified when they had rest. It bespeaks a general advancement. They acquired a clearer vision and a deeper experience of the truth. Their principles became broader in their base, and more perfect in their symmetry. Their faith in the Gospel increased in intelligence and earnestness. As a natural result of this, "they walked in the fear of God, and in the comfort," or, rather, admonition, "of the Holy Ghost." They cherished and expressed that filial reverence for God which is called for by His greatness and goodness, His majesty and mercy; and they sought and submitted to all the intimations and the influences of the Spirit of Christ. His will, whether written in the Bible, or breathed upon the heart, received a cheerful and prompt regard. They implicitly obeyed this heavenly oracle. They bowed in lowliness beneath this sacred influence, as the trees of the wood are moved by the wind. This was their *course*. They "*walked*" according to this rule. It was not an occasional, but a constant thing. They did it everywhere, and did it always. It described them in their ecclesiastical and secular relations, as men of the Church and as men of the world, in their intercourse with heaven and their intercourse with earth. It was the principle and spirit of their conduct, sanctifying and ennobling it. This was the fruit and sign of their edification. The sanctity and spirituality of their procedure proved the light of their judgments and the vigour of their principles. Their holy life was the full and natural form required by the enlargement and maturity of their inward faith. And what was the result?

3. *Their increase.* " Were multiplied."

They received large accessions from the world. "Many were added to the Church." Better themselves, they became more in number. There was more Christianity, and there were more Christians. Saints were sanctified, and sinners became saints. The living stones became more lively, and the insensible ones had life infused into them. The pure gold increased in thickness, and covered a wider surface. There was a lengthening of the cords, as well as a strengthening of the stakes. These are the two elements of Church prosperity. These are the two ends of Church association. Christians are thus connected that, by mutual support and sympathy and friction, they may promote each other's spirituality, and that by the union of their graces and the combination of their energies they may be as light to a dark, and salt to a corrupt world. And these two things are inseparably connected. The Church cannot grow in grace without diffusing grace. Its influence is a moral one. It is the influence of *truth:* and the more that is loved and realized, the more will be done and the better for its spread; it is the influence of *holiness:* and whatever increases the purity increases the power of Christians; it is the influence of the *Spirit of God:* and the more He is supplicated and submitted to, the more signal will be His blessing upon words and deeds. The holy walking, and the increase of these churches, were, therefore, *cause and effect.* Doing the one, they experienced the other.

II.

I need not say that to describe these churches is the least part of my design, yea, is only a means of my design. I wish to set them before you for *imitation.* The record of the text was written for our use. The first churches, in their goodness and greatness, were meant to be copied. We lose the object of the record, if we attain not to the character and privileges which they possessed.

We proceed, therefore, to endeavour to promote the imitation contemplated; and, in so doing, we are encouraged by the fact, that you are in constitution and general moral condition such churches as those referred to in the text. They were apostolical churches, and you have been formed after the apostolical model. It matters nothing to us how other churches are constituted, the only question we care about is, how the first churches were constituted, and the only authority we acknowledge upon that point is the New Testament.

You may safely take the text as a specimen of its

testimony, and a proof of the Scriptural character of your societies. The churches in the text were composed of intelligent beings—so are yours; they were composed, to outward seeming, of good beings—so are yours; they existed several in a country—so do yours; and I add, they increased and prospered—so may, and should, yours. They were the first, that they might be the last. Whatever entered into their constitution had a spiritual design and tendency. And we shall greatly err if we boast of our resemblance to them in nature, and order, and offices, and do not consider all these as but a means to an end, the earthly residence of an ethereal essence; the bodily form of a living spirit; the material temple of a glory most divine. It is not in having pastors chosen, ordained, and qualified like the first bishops; it is not in having members characterized, received and disciplined like the first members; it is not in having symbolical and social services of the same simplicity and significance as the first ordinances, that we can afford to glory, if those pastors do not "so speak that many believe," if those members "adorn not the doctrine of God their Saviour in all things," if those services are not the means of fostering and furthering the faith and purity of the saints of God. Apostolical propriety is a poor thing without apostolical prosperity; yea, it is a bad thing, for it increases our guilt by augmenting our responsibility.

1. I ask you, therefore, to consider two important things brought before us in the text. *The first is the connection between the rest and the edification of these churches.* "They had rest, and were edified."

They made spiritual advancement while they enjoyed civil repose. They did not spend the season of calm in luxury and sinfulness. They did not slumber in their safety. Their activity continued and increased after their trouble ceased. This is worthy of admiration. It is frequently the case that external quiet injures and deteriorates the Church of Christ. Her time of greatest moral suffering has been her time of greatest earthly ease and safety. The favour of the world has been often far more injurious to her than its hatred and opposition. She has flourished in its wrath, and sickened in its love. Like a fresh and fragrant flower, the friendly hand of its admirer has withered her beauty and despoiled her grace. When the civil sword has been turned against the Church, she has often "lived more abundantly;" when that sword has been turned against the enemies of the Church, she has often as miserably died. The wounds that she has suffered most from *as a Church*—a spiritual thing—have been, not those she has received, but those she has inflicted. And, indeed, so almost constantly are we called to contemplate the inward peace, and purity, and power of the Church as greatest when in most outward trouble, and conflict, and disgrace: so loudly does the voice of History echo the voice of Scripture, "I did know thee in the wilderness, in the land of drought," that we get to connect together, as if inseparable, her woe and her weal, and to imagine that what is *good* is not good *for* her. Our text, however, says that rest is not ruin, of necessity. These churches lost none of their holiness or diligence when comparatively exempt from the rage of their enemies. It is a pleasant and refreshing scene, the more so from its infrequency. But it should not be infrequent. All churches in this condition may have this character. It is quite a mistake to regard affliction and persecution as indispensable to spirituality; and yet the mistake is common. You will hear individuals sometimes say, "I am sure something dreadful is coming upon me, I am in such a backsliding state." Then avert it. We need not wait for sorrow, in order to sanctity. It is wicked not to set about our reformation and return to God till we are punished; to place our dependence for the good of our souls on the dispensations of a physical force. And so, as to the Church; how familiar is the language among pious people, and the use of it passes for a great attainment of piety, "The Church is got into a bad state. It is so worldly, so divided, so selfish; it wants the fire of persecution to purge it from its dross. It has had too long a course of ease and prosperity, and it must pass through great tribulation in order to get refinement, unity, and glory." Now so far as all this supposes the *necessity* of persecution, it is bad; and if an expression of piety, it is one of a very morbid piety. If persecution would bring the Church into a good and glorious state, and if nothing but that could, we should say, "Let it come, and the sooner the better." But it may be done without. Christians should act from principle within, not from opposition without; they should not be dependent on the malice of their enemies for the welfare of their souls; nor can it be imagined that the wicked are the "salt" of the Church, without which it would speedily go into utter corruption.

On the contrary, the "rest" of the Churches is both

a motive and *a means* of their prosperity. We should, beyond all doubt, be stimulated by gratitude to a devout and diligent employment of the privileges so peacefully possessed. Rest is pleasant; no one can like pains and penalties, fines and imprisonments, the feeling or the fear of torture or martyrdom for their own sake; and the absence of them is a reason, therefore, for earnest thankfulness. When we contrast the state of persecution with the state of peace in their real nature and entire features, it is impossible not to be grateful if "the lines have fallen unto us in pleasant places." Surely we should seek to please Him who has dealt so gently with us; to attain the end of all *His* dispensations who has fixed upon such light and easy ones for us. And as we should esteem our rest as *a reason* for devotedness, we may employ it as *a means*. It affords the occasion, whether we so use it or not. The attention is not diverted by danger from the prosecution of spiritual good. There is the power of a regular and undistracted attendance on all the institutions, social and public, of Christianity. The weapon need not be in one hand while the tool is in the other; nor the watching of enemies go on with the plying at our work. The mind is left free from a dispiriting anxiety to study "the great things of God's law," and the machinery of means can play away without injury or interruption.

See you not how all this applies to *us?* We have rest in a fuller measure than the Churches of Palestine. We have been free, for a long time and to a great extent, from legal injustice and civil oppression. We sit under our own vines and fig-trees, none daring to make us afraid. Our persons, property, and sanctuaries are *protected*—all we wish they should be—by law. What is, what ought to be, the effect? Alas! they are not the same thing. We have suffered ourselves to be injured by our circumstances. We are worldly, and secular, and at ease. We have not the oneness, and devoutness, and simplicity, and zeal that we should have, that others have had. We are not as good as many who have been without our privileges, whereas we ought to be better. We are even in danger of losing them through abusing them; for the way to preserve, is to profit by, them. Let us seek a revival of godliness, and regard our "rest" as itself the argument. If we are not grateful for it, we virtually deny the Providence that has secured it for us; we treat God's kindness as a thing of naught; we practically obliterate the distinction between the state in which men have to worship the Father with sighs and tears; to deny their natural instincts, in order to cherish their spiritual principles; to lose all earthly things in gaining heavenly ones; and the state in which religion promotes, rather than hinders, our temporal welfare; the "promise of the life that now is" being enjoyed as well as "that of the life to come." And if we are thankful, can we show our thankfulness without devotedness? Is not "obedience better than sacrifices"? Let us awake, then, to a just estimate of our circumstances, to an energetic application of our powers, nor permit it to be said that mercy has less effect than misery; that the "gentleness" of God has failed to "make us great."

2. The second thing to which I wish to draw your

attention is *the connection between the edification of these churches and their increase.* "Walking in the fear of God, and in the comfort of the Holy Ghost, they were multiplied."

There is a close connection here; and, with exceptions, to which all rules are liable, a connection always observed. It is well that so it is. The piety of a people is necessary to the safe and profitable enjoyment of their increase. A Church, not eminently holy, may suffer from great multiplication. Enlargement will tend to vanity and self-sufficiency. Grace is needful to bear it well. Perhaps we may find in this the reason why some Churches remain so stationary. It would hurt them to be otherwise. They "have not" the success they "ask," because they would "consume it on their lusts." They are not religious enough to sustain prosperity. If they were more godly, they would be more numerous, because not in danger of being injured by their extension. And it is for the benefit of those who are added to a Church, that it should be greatly good. Who can think, without concern and pity, of a multitude of souls being joined to a worldly Church, placed in the midst, and under the care of, those who are selfish, earthly, and ignorant? It would be a great evil for some churches to be increased without being bettered. Allow me to ask, Are *you* prepared for enlargement thus? Would it not hurt you? Would it not hurt others? What good would they get from associating with you? Would they be refined, elevated, enlightened, purified? Is your character such as might be safely copied? Is your spirit such as might be safely drunk into?

The godliness of a Church is *a prime means of its increase*. God blesses an eminently spiritual Church. For it will abound in prayer and effort. It will "pray without ceasing;" and its prayers will not be "hindered." They will be consistent as well as earnest and persevering prayers. They will be prayers with labours, not instead of them, the only prayers that God will hear. And those labours will possess a character of earnestness and uniformity—a natural fervour and kindliness every way adapted to produce impression. They will be constant, not occasional; free, not formal; personal, not official. The spirit of self-denying love and zeal will pervade the entire body; "he that heareth will say, Come;" each individual, like his Master, will "seek" in order to "save;" none will be accounted lost that are treading Christ's earth, and breathing Christ's air; while the retort will have no ground or force, "Physician, heal thyself!" Nor is this all. The holy character of a Church in itself has no mean influence in "winning souls." The New Testament assigns to it an amazing power. As strong expressions are used about it as a means of conversion as about anything. "If any obey not the word, they also may without the word be won by the conversation of the wives." The exhibition of holiness is calculated to arrest attention by its singularity, and to produce impression by its force. It is the best manifestation of the Gospel, which is a moral system; the best appeal to men, who are moral beings; the best condition of personal influence, which, in its highest form, is a moral power. Who can think of the history of Christianity without intense regret that in its practical exhibition, whether by individuals, churches, or nations, there has been so little of its genuine spirit, that the lives of its professors have so often been a contradiction of its law of love and purity? Had Christians been as anxious to illustrate the character of the Gospel as they have been ready to battle about its doctrines, had their zeal for good works been as earnest as their care for sound words, the world would not have had to be converted now. But the religion of Christ has suffered more from the inconsistencies of its friends than the opposition of its foes; its professors have created more objections than they have answered; and the proof of its divinity may be drawn from its preservation in spite of its adherents. Had all Christians been like Jesus Christ, or anything like Him, the world would have become Christian. And let it be remembered that if in every age the holiness of Christians has been a matter of great importance, it must be especially so in an age so practical as our own. The question is being asked of everything, "For what good?"—the demand is for utility. Christianity must stand the test— it has always claimed to be tried by it. "The kingdom of God is not in word, but in power." It depends on Christians, however, what shall be the actual and immediate results of such a trial. The appeal must be made to what is, not what has been; and it will not do to quote passages when men are crying out for power, nor to cite ancient miracles when they are sighing for present mercy.

For all these reasons, the sanctification of churches is necessary to their extension. I mean, of course, their proper, spiritual extension. There is an extension which Christ does not approve, and which men do not profit by—an increase of dimensions which resembles that premature growth which issues in consumption, if not rather that extension of the body which takes place at death. But the legitimate enlargement of churches must come of their internal prosperity. Would you, as churches, be increased ? You must be quickened. A revival of religion must commence with the religious. God always begins with the godly. They become more penitent, prayerful, zealous, and active, and are then employed in bringing to a knowledge of the truth "those that are without." Be not deceived, therefore. If you are not willing to be more sanctified, you either do not desire the extension of Christ's churches, or desire it from wrong motives. This is the order of God's procedure, and must be of our prayers—"God be merciful unto *us*, and bless *us*, that Thy way may be known upon earth, Thy saving health among all nations." And remember that for this churches have been ordained. They are intended to be useful—useful to the world. If they fail of that, they fail of their end.

Then, brethren, let your attention be ever turned to the *spirituality* of your churches. Churches are spiritual institutions—entirely and exclusively so. Beware how you substitute any criterion of their state for that of holiness. Holiness is their condition, means, and end. It is not in respectability, wealth, or power, that they can glory ; or rather, their only respectability, as churches, is their unworldliness, their only riches those of "faith," their only power "the power of godliness." There is no small danger of injury to this spirituality, in the times in which we live. There are many controversies that I do not say you should shun, for they cannot be shunned; there are social questions that I do not say you should decline, for they cannot but be entertained; there are public movements that I do not say you should resist, for, willing or unwilling, they will bear you with them; but these things you must take heed do not damage your godliness. We need not shut ourselves up, as Christians, in our several small enclosures, looking with disdain or indifference on the great scenes that are being enacted and the great processes that are being wrought out in the world without. On the contrary, we cannot afford to do that. The spirit of Christianity is eminently a social and public spirit, and to say that it is necessary to avoid social and public things in order to preserve our Christianity, is one of the weakest doctrines of sickly piety, or one of the boldest pleas of cunning and cowardice. At the same time, the conflicts and controversies, the agitations and alarms, the frailties and fervour of the days through which we are passing may be made an evil as well as a good. Our thoughts may be drawn away by them from the exercise of our peculiar function, our spirit may be soured and spoiled. Beware; you can get nothing that will compensate for the loss of deep and vigorous faith, of tenderness of conscience, of eager aspirations after personal holiness, and melting pity for the unconverted. "Look well to yourselves that you love not those things that have been wrought, but that ye receive a full reward." "And *grow* in grace and in the knowledge of our Lord Jesus Christ."

"Arise from the dust and put on your beautiful garments, and your strength, O Zion." "Search Jerusalem with candles and put away every evil thing." Let your *rest* help your *religion,* and let your religion be *relative.* And may this be your record in earth and heaven—" Then were the churches established in the faith, and increased in number daily." " Then had the churches rest, and were edified, and walking in the fear of God and in the comfort of the Holy Ghost, were multiplied." Amen.

CHRISTIANITY, A VOICE TO THE PEOPLE.

ACTS v. 19, 20.—"*But the angel of the Lord by night opened the prison doors, and brought them forth, and said, Go, stand and speak in the temple to the people all the words of this life.*"

THE text belongs to one of those extraordinary events which occurred at "the beginning of the Gospel of Christ." It was a time of supernatural interpositions. Apart from the external evidence that the narrative is true, there is everything in the narrative itself to prove it so. It is simple, natural, calm. Marvels are recorded as if they were common. Miracles are described as if natural occurrences. There is no surprise, no effort to effect astonishment, nor to excite it. The visit of an angel is narrated in the same style as the visit of a man, a deliverance from prison by superhuman might is set forth in like mode with the putting into prison through Sadducean malice.

The high priest and his friends were of the sect of the Sadducees. "During our Lord's abode on earth (says Dr. Bennett) the Pharisees, with their superstition and self-righteousness, were the bitterest foes to Him who was called 'the friend of publicans and sinners;' but when He had risen from the dead, the

Sadducees, who had been more indifferent, became fierce opponents of the Apostles' testimony to the resurrection, while the Pharisees were somewhat softened by the triumphs of a doctrine which was their own. As the Jewish state hastened to destruction, the worst party seized the reins of power, and these desperate priests would suffer none to stand in their way." They, therefore, made a bold attack upon the leaders of the new faith, "laid their hands on the Apostles, and put them in the common prison," their deliverance from which is described in the text.

The record is instructive. Why not send the angel to "the people?" Why this circuitous mode? An angel *could not be imprisoned*. This opens up a large field of interesting thought. The divine system of operation is not one of mere power, but of fitnesses, and proprieties, and adaptations. God's end is not only to get certain things done, but done in a certain way, or rather *His end* cannot be accomplished except in that way. He does not go out of the common course of things, unless it is absolutely necessary. He honours His laws and arrangements. He has established by using them as much as possible. In using men in the promotion of Christianity, in making human nature the chief agent in blessing human nature, He best advances its process of education, discipline, and development. Human thought, human sympathy, human affection, are awakened and matured both in the dispensers and recipients of the Gospel, and thus this ordinance is, like mercy, twice blessed, " it blesses him who gives and him who receives." Even the impossibility of an angel's imprisonment would be no recommendation. Imprisonment is a part of the glorious scheme. Suffering, trial, death, are conditions of spiritual training, elements of spiritual power. "Except a corn of wheat fall into the ground and die, it abideth alone : but if it die, it bringeth forth much fruit." If angels are not employed to preach the Gospel, then, it it is because they would not be the best preachers. To angels they might be, but not to men. They have therefore been commissioned to bring about human proclamations of the Gospel, but, except in the first announcement, they have not been commissioned directly to proclaim it. Their office is represented in the text—"they brought them forth, and said, Go, stand and speak in the temple to the people all the words of this life."

In this comprehensive charge, we have abundant matter of the greatest interest for present consideration. My object will be to take the words as typical, and dwell not only on what they immediately express, but also on what they may suggest. The *Proclamation*, the *Place*, and the *People*, are the heads under which we shall arrange our remarks.

I.

The Proclamation. "*The words of this life.*"

The reference is to Sadducean unbelief. This sect rejected the doctrine of a future life. Their enmity to the Apostles was exasperated by their exhibition and establishment of it. Instead of ceasing their general testimony to Christian truth, and their particular testimony to this Christian truth, in consequence of opposition and of danger, they were to persevere in its bold and faithful presentation. Unbelief, looked at in relation to convenience, is a reason for silence; looked at in relation to duty and charity, a reason for louder speech. A truth is most needed when it is least liked, and the age that rejects it should have it kept, with martyr constancy, before its eye. And where the truth is inseparable from the people's everlasting good, no words can utter the strength of obligation to speak which arises from their infidelity or unconcern. The less they ask for admonition, the stronger is God's charge to give it to them; the smaller their claim upon our justice, the larger their claim upon our love. There is no policy compared with the policy of saving men's souls; there is no hazard of final failure in working for the dispensation of Almighty grace.

"Life" is the burden of the message. This, in its lowest state, is prized above all temporal blessings. "Skin for skin," said Satan; "yea, all that a man hath will he give for his life." There is a school that contradicts this doctrine, affirming that the love of life is not the strongest passion, and therefore the loss of it is not the greatest punishment. But history, observation, and consciousness, confirm the saying of the wise though wicked enemy of Job. Under a law of death, Christianity assures us of the continuance and perpetuity of our existence. It is its glory to bring eternal being to light. It thus gives an infinite multiplication of the present life of man. It makes this the common portion of humanity. It affords an unambiguous promise, and a title not to be disputed. It does not reason it out, but asserts it; appeals not to argument, but to facts. It thus supplies the defects, and fulfils the suggestions, of providence and experience. The inferences drawn from inequalities of lot, undeveloped powers, apprehensions, aspirations, it completes and establishes; making dreams into doctrines, doubtful guesses into assured faith, vague anticipations into certain prospects. What was a probability in the minds of wisest philosophers, became a proclamation in the mouths of Jewish rustics.

The *existence* of man hereafter is not, however, the only, nor the chief, prospect of blessing afforded by the Gospel. That is the *condition and sphere* of good, rather than a good itself. Existence is necessary to all things; it is the basis, the ground-work, the term of all things; but it is not in itself an essential boon. A man may be, and yet not, in any deep sense, *live*. Existence may be the bier of souls. Life, in its fulness, consists in the healthful and unfettered activity of the whole man. When all the powers are exercised in the right way, and on the right object, when they are exercised so as to assist, not thwart each other, when they are all under the strongest stimulus, and all have free scope in outward expression; when thus universality, harmony, freedom, and utmost force, mark the actions of *the man*, then, and not till then, can he be said to have the perfection of life. It implies that there is nothing within him to weaken, or depress, or divide; nothing without to let and hinder the manifestation and indulgence of every true thought, and every holy feeling. It includes, therefore, a perfect *nature*, and a perfect *state*. So that life, thus largely understood, is not *a* blessing of the Gospel, but *the* blessing; it comprehends all the powers and privileges of the kingdom of heaven. Hence it is so frequently put for the whole of Gospel goodness, and "he shall have everlasting life," is *the entire promise* made to faith.

Man is a moral being. This supposes two things, that he has moral powers and moral responsibilities. He can be a holy being, and he ought to be a holy being. Sin is a violation of his nature, and it subjects him to punishment. As sinful, he is evil within, and he is exposed to evil as an infliction. Both these are called "death." Carnality is "death." Punishment is "death." The want of holiness is death, the loss of privilege is death. They both involve and affect the condition and exercise of his powers. Cherishing the evil of sin, suffering the evil of condemnation, he cannot live according to the true and full idea of life. There is not the free and healthful action of his nature. There is restraint, confusion, weakness, woe. His capacities are not rightly filled, his proper destiny is not attained. He *is* not what he might be; he enjoys not what he might enjoy; he occupies not his assigned sphere; he accomplishes not his appointed service. The design of the Gospel is to remove and prevent this death; to renew our nature, and then put us into a scene and sphere in which all its dispositions and principles may have free course and be glorified; to make us right, and surround us with a right lot; to secure inward and universal power of spirituality, and the full and facile expression and gratification of it.

To do this it pretends and promises. The whole work of Christ, His life and death, His character and merit, the influence of His truth, the dispensations of His mediatorial providence, the operations of His Holy Spirit, all are designed to quicken the soul, to bring out, unite, and purify its powers, and prepare it for a state in which there shall be no hindrance to, but every facility for, its love, and joy, and work : in one word, that it may "have life, and have it more abundantly." Through Christ we are restored to God, His law, His likeness, His love, His service ; and no otherwise can we find our true place, and rule, and end. We are reconciled to His nature and to His providence. We are at one with Him in all that He is, and all that He does. There is the *spirit* and the *scope* of life. " He that hath the Son hath life," &c.

It would be most pleasant to dwell upon this comprehensive subject. Sufficient importance has not been assigned to it. The characteristic promise of the Gospel, its favourite and familiar expressions, are " life," " everlasting life." You know it is so. These expressions cannot be intended, it would be absurd to suppose they are intended, to denote mere existence. It would, on that interpretation, be the habit of the sacred writers to dwell chiefly upon that part of the Gospel prospect which is the smallest of all (not to say that it would follow that future existence was the portion of the saved only, and that the not-saved were annihilated), yea, to dwell chiefly upon that which is not necessarily a blessing at all. And other difficulties would occur : for instance, where it is said, " to them who seek for glory, honour, and immortality, *eternal life*," we should have *the attainment* mentioned infinitely less than *the object pursued*. We conclude that the expressions take in the whole of our prospect. But why is it "life"? Is it not taught that all the good is connected with *what we are*—that the outward blessings are related to our spiritual being, and derive all their importance from it? The Gospel turns attention to ourselves, seeks to make *us* what we should be, and its other arrangements are all adapted to the free and holy condition of our souls. Its great design is to make us live, and whatever else it does is good and great, as it cultivates and manifests our life. You cannot get its blessings but *through life*; they are no blessings without it.

And what a beautiful light is the Gospel thus presented in! How accordant is it with the deepest and most advanced thought! How *natural* is its mercy: How *agreeable* its provision! And how *indispensable* its blessing! How it lays hold of the essences of things! How every other method and object would fail—miserably fail! All ornaments, instruments, advantages—what are they apart from life? "Wisdom is a defence, and money is a defence, but the excellency of knowledge is that *wisdom giveth life* to them that have it."

II.

The Place. "*The Temple.*"

This was the best place, the most convenient, and where the people were most likely to be found. But how instructive is this simple circumstance!

1. *Do we not see in this publicity the truthfulness of the Gospel?* The first preachers of the Gospel did not secrete themselves, did not choose select audiences, did not confine their teachings to a few. They did not go to strange people, did not seek foreign lands, nor wait until the matters of which they spake had been forgotten, or could not so well be sifted. But while the facts were recent, were topics of familiar conversation, could be examined into, while the active parties in the transactions to which they referred could expose or confirm their testimony, and in the very heart of the people, before promiscuous crowds, they lifted up their voices and declared the guilty crucifixion and glorious resurrection of the Messiah. Their message, intended for the people's benefit, was committed to the people's scrutiny. Based on history, they proclaimed it to those who had the fullest opportunities and means of trying its historical integrity. They sought not, like impostors, a safe distance of time or place. Among those who witnessed the death of their Master, they asserted that He rose again, and on the spot on which He delivered His last discourses, they declared His ascension to the skies. This fact is incompatible with any supposition but that of the truth of their discourse. They *knew* that they spoke the truth, and knew that others knew it too.

And what a change in these men, for them to take their place in this courageous attitude before the people! It is vain to say that they were disciples and friends of Christ. So they were when "all forsook Him and fled." But how did they *become* the disciples and friends, not of a temporal, but a spiritual Messiah?

They were no more adherents to Him, than were the Jews in general, *in this character*, until after His death. And what could convince them but His resurrection and ascension? Supposing Him not to have risen, and supposing them to know that He had not risen (and they must have known if He had not), it is impossible to account for their course. Nothing but the truth of what they affirmed can explain it.

I need not say that the Gospel is the same to-day. It is open to the inspection of all. It comes before the people in its full utterances and evidences. It never has courted secresy, never forbidden inquiry. Read it, and you will find that it commits its credentials to the examination of whosoever chooses to examine them. Nor is this all. It especially challenges investigation. It provides for the putting its records into the hands of all. It allows of no means of bringing men to its adoption but their conviction of its truth. And it promotes, as all reason and history go to show, a spirit of intelligence, dangerous to any system that cannot stand the test.

2. Do we not see in this fact the *indifference*, if we may so call it, of Christianity. The whole state of the Jewish Church was corrupt. Never has any Church been more entirely destitute of the true spirit of religion. Its rulers were sceptical or immoral, its teachings were obscured and perverted by human glosses, its services were substitutes for, not expressions of, real religion. And the time had come when the gorgeous ceremonial ceased to be obligatory, and realism took the place of ritualism. It is true, they did not use the Temple as did others, and as it was originally intended

to be used. But I can imagine some who would not have used it at all. There have been reformers, if there are not any now, who would have shunned the place altogether, or only have frequented it to warn men of the sin and folly of making use of it. So did not they. And this is but one instance of what may be termed the moderation of the first preachers of Christianity. There was no ultraism about them. Jesus Christ, though He is to be regarded rather as a reformer than a conformist, did not shrink with sensitive disdain from contact even with doubtful things around Him. He could use them. The water-pots employed for purification He filled with wine; He accepted the invitation of a Pharisee on a Sabbath. And His servants, after Him, employed to the utmost all the occasions and facilities afforded by the circumstances and customs, even to the religious and misused ones, of the people. They visited them in their usual places of resort, they addressed them through their familiar ideas, they conciliated them by conformity to their habits. The synagogue and Temple were the chief scenes of their preaching. We find one now prudently circumcising a disciple, and now as prudently joining some who had a vow.

I confess not only that these things are to me interesting, but that they bear marks of the surprisingly healthy character of apostolical religion, not to say proofs of apostolical inspiration. The tendency of all new and great ideas, filling men with enthusiastic earnestness, is to attach inordinate importance to what may appear to sanction and support contrary and inconsistent ones. Human nature easily runs into extremes. Men always work fresh theories to death. And when I find the first preachers of the Gospel as calm as they were earnest; making no account of secondary matters, but every account of matters of first importance; equally zealous for the vital principles of Christianity, and ready to listen to the suggestions of prudence, I cannot but admire the reasonableness of their faith, and am disposed to admit that, in this, they were "taught of God."

3. There is still a higher suggestion. The Temple was the great symbol of the Jewish religion. It was the type and scene of the most sacred sentiments and experiences of a people blessed with a revelation of God's will. It had been, for many generations, the solemn resort of a nation placed under a system of special instruction. Its function had, however, ceased. The dispensation to which it belonged had virtually passed away, and it becomes the scene of the preaching of the Cross. Nor was this really inconsistent with its original design. It was part of a ceremonial economy. That economy pointed to the events and blessings of the Gospel. In declaring the Gospel in its porch, the Apostles declared the fulfilment of all it was designed to signify and adumbrate. It was the substitution of the substance for the shadow, the reality for the type. Though the strongest opposition to the Gospel, in Judæa, was derived from Judaism, it was really the end of which Judaism was the beginning, the fruit of which Judaism was the seed. When the Temple became a church, it was in the natural order of Divine Providence. What more meet than that the spot which had witnessed the pre-monitions of the Gospel,

should be the scene of its complete announcements? It had helped many to hope for "the consolation of Israel," it had directed many to the promised redemption of the woman's seed; it had suggested to many the vague idea of a great sacrifice for sin; and now it is the spot on which that hope is declared to be fulfilled, that redemption is declared to be effected, that sacrifice is declared to be offered and accepted.

Nor must we stop at Judaism. There have been other great religions among men. Men have never been, to any considerable extent, without religion. But the different systems that have prevailed, and gained an influence among them, have been marked by peculiar ideas. They have been the embodiment and utterance of some special conception and conviction. Alike in some respects, they have been different in others. And where there has been no system, there have been feelings, and cravings, and wants, all indicative of the religious nature of man, all expressive of his spiritual powers and purposes. In Christianity you have all these met and satisfied, and in it alone. It realizes, reconciles, and completes, whatever entered, or enters, into the defunct and living systems of men. It gives substance and perfection to all the images and longings of our race. It stands in the porch of humanity, and "speaks all the words of this life."

III.

The People. "*Speak to the people.*"

The word bears not a technical and special sense. It simply signifies, "preach to men where men are most numerously to be found." Still we have here a specimen of the genius and design of the Gospel. It knows nothing, as the Gospel, of the artificial distinctions of men; it regards man as man. "There is neither Greek nor Jew, Barbarian, Scythian, bond nor free, but Christ is all and in all." In reference to religion, it acknowledges and creates no privileged class—no class having peculiar spiritual rights or blessings. It sees the image of God, broken though it be and marred, in all; sees in all capacities awfully great and glorious; beholds all in need, wretchedness, and sin; and presents to all the means and promise of life, holiness, and hope. "The common salvation" differs widely in the universality of its aspects from many false religions, and philosophic systems of religion. The individual importance and spiritual equality of men are the plain and unmistakable doctrines of Christianity. The separate worth of each, and the infinite worth of all, are truths assumed in all its principles, and proper modes of action. Christ addressed himself not to a class exalted above the rest, but to the people generally, calling a man from a tree to receive "salvation into his house," teaching a woman at a well, and finding His "meat" in thus "doing the will" of God. He did not refuse to instruct and associate with others. He took meat, as we have seen, with a Pharisee on a Sabbath; He received Nicodemus, a ruler, who came to Him by night. But He clearly showed that "He came to the lost tribes of the house of Israel." So did the apostles. No anxiety to reach and win the learned and mighty class prompted them. They preached to the Sanhedrim when brought before them, but their mission was not to classes but to the "people." It could not be otherwise. Starting with the great truths that every man is alike in the powers and possibilities of being, in his relation to God, in his capacity for holiness, in his destination to eternal existence, partiality in their message would have been treason to their faith. They looked at human souls as having an intrinsic worth, apart from wealth, and wisdom, and power; and they esteemed their claims as great in proportion to their spiritual poverty, folly, and weakness. And in speaking to the "people," they not only recognized their *right* to the Gospel, but their *power* to understand and to profit by it. Their Gospel was not a problem to be solved only by faculties specially trained, an argument to be mastered only by wits most logical, a thing of hard words demanding the culture of the schools, a conclusion derived from facts lying deep in science and philosophy; but a truth to be apprehended by undisciplined understandings, to be tested by common sense and common honesty, to be felt and appreciated by hearts untutored save by the Spirit of divine love. It needs not the interpretation of scholarship; it thrives without the sanction of authority. It reveals itself to multitudes who are not endowed with human knowledge; it demonstrates itself to multitudes who are unblessed with the forms of reasoning. "Never man spake like this Man" is the language of many who know but little how men have spoken, but know full well that His speech is all divine; and many "have the witness in themselves" who are but poorly gifted to meet the cavils and the arguments of others. While skill has often served only to perplex, and learning to encumber, and worldly pomp to corrupt, the Gospel, the simple and the unlettered have "received the kingdom of God as little children," and felt it to be "in power, and not in word." While "these things have been hidden from the wise and prudent, they have been revealed unto babes." While the first have been making elaborate comments on the architecture of the Temple, the last have been humbly worshipping before the glory; while the first have been cleverly criticising the wording of the invitation, the last have been feasting joyously at the table of the Lord. We do not deny that Christianity has been so treated as to seem to be the peculiar property of classes, and some forms of it could not well become the property of any others. But the Gospel of the kingdom must be perverted or corrupted to lose its popular aspect. As men have sometimes altered it, it has been adapted only for the few; as God has given it, it is designed and fitted for all.

We say, "for all." For it is possible to err in two directions. We may leave out the great and wealthy as well as the poor and mean. We may treat the first, as well as the last, as if excluded from its mercies. We may depreciate humanity in high places as well as in low places. The schism of classes is not fostered exclusively by some. There is an aristocracy of poverty as well as of rank and riches. Pride may look up as easily as look down. The haughtiness of supposed unrequited merit may be a severer, bitterer thing than that of satiated self-esteem. "Our order" may mean as much, and as much that is unpleasant, in the mouths of the sons of toil, as in the mouths of men who can trace their genealogy to the times of the conqueror, and count their acres by thousands. The people may be flattered as well as nobles. And I am not sure that this danger has no existence now. At least I think it sometimes appears as if, in their innocent desire to reduce the value of artificial distinctions, some make a distinction of the want of them, and forget that if wisdom is not necessarily connected with learning, it is also not necessarily connected with ignorance, and if money does not certify virtue, the absence of it does not certify it either. And certainly there is often a most exaggerated estimate of *mere manual labour*, and " the working class," as a title of honour, is so applied as to exclude some of the hardest and most efficient workers of our race, as if only bodies worked, and minds never.

Christianity does not justify any error that leaves *man* in any condition and estate out of the sphere of its beneficent action. There were two disciples in the Sanhedrim, as large a proportion probably as there were among the people. There were "saints in Cæsar's household." If "not many mighty and noble and wise are called," it must be remembered that there are not many, speaking comparatively, to be called. But if the Gospel do not exclude them, it includes others. Though men may mistranslate it, its language is of impartial love. For its design is to bless with " life," and the need and power of life is in the man, in every man. Might does not create it, weakness does not destroy it; riches do not buy it, poverty does not lose it. The blessed child of God may be clothed in rags ; the heir of heaven may lie at the rich man's gate, covered with sores; "the woman that was a sinner" may be the loved and commended of Christ. The poor widow may be the most honoured contributor to God's cause; and the crucified robber the first of His converts to be with Christ in paradise.

Let us obey the angel's charge. Addressed to the Apostles, it is binding upon all. "Speak to the people." There are temptations to restriction. This mission may be harder, and, in some respects, less profitable, than that of others. But remember also, that, in others, it will be most fruitful. And "the people"—the great body of the people—are in special need of these "words of life." Though we believe, not greater than they have been, in one sense, they have always been in great need. The proportion of those to whom the term is conventionally applied that believe in, and profit by, Christianity is less, much less, than that of the other sections of the community. It is a good and blessed sign that the interest in them is awakened in a new degree, and that their welfare is sought in unwonted methods. It comes from the Gospel; and it is according to the mind of God. Let us aid every wise effort to do them good, to gain "entrance into them of the words that give light;" to give them the "faith by which the just live;" to win them to that "godliness which has the promise" of the noblest experiences and possessions here, and of all that is joyous and glorious in the world to come.

Christianity, by the influence of its truths and principles, has raised the people, and will yet raise them, to a higher social position. Its action, direct and indirect, cannot be separated from the assertion of a more prominent place in the world's affairs, and a more powerful influence over them, than they have been wont to possess. The views it gives of man's nature and relations must excite a desire for a position which the masses have not yet attained. It is impossible to mark the tendencies of our own day, without seeing that power is being wonderfully diffused. Whatever our views, whatever our apprehensions, be it desired or be it dreaded, persons and classes will be of less importance than they have been, and men in general will be of more. We may forbid the tide, but it will come in. It is not given us to say whether or not it shall be so. We cannot prevent, if we would, the realization of the prospect. With this destiny before the people, what is our duty ? To seek to *prepare them for their inheritance*. Believing that the Gospel alone can guide, and develop, and sanctify all our powers : fit for the enjoyment and exercise of every right and privilege : give "life" to nations as well as individuals; let us endeavour to diffuse Christianity, that the people may be faithful stewards in their solemn trust, beneficent holders of their rich possession. And do not mistake me. I do not mean, do this from *policy*, but from *principle*. There is something mean and almost dishonest in using the Gospel simply as a means of keeping people in order, making it a muzzle for mastiffs. It has a nobler office than to be the preserver of the peace, the protector of property. It is as a "word of life," life in all its channels—social, political, moral, religious life—that I implore you to proclaim it ; to proclaim it to "the people." Proclaim it not from fear, but love.

And let me add that nothing should divert us from the Gospel as intending to bless man *by and through his soul*. We live in a day when a just attention is directed to material and social things. It is a day of impartial benevolence more than many have been. The condition of the people, their condition in respect to health and comfort and education, occupies a place of new interest in the breasts of men. And well it is. The Gospel looks benignly on all attempts at reform and advancement in these directions. It never forgets, though its professors have forgotten, that men have bodies, and through their bodies are to be reached, and by their bodies are affected. Its miracles were corporeal cures; its symbolic services employ material signs; it addresses us through our senses; the resurrection of the body is part of its future prospect; the supply and comfort of the body one of its marked charities. But let us not forget that the condition of men may be elevated without their hearts being sanctified; that ungodliness may dwell in circumstances of plenty, cleanliness, and health; that good wages may be associated with bad conduct, and healthy neighbourhoods with diseased souls. All fashions are apt to go into extremes—the fashion of humanity among others. And to hear some people talk, you might suppose that a new Gospel had been found, and one to supply the defects of the old Gospel. "The kingdom of heaven" is nothing to sanitary reform, there are no sanctuaries like improved dwelling-houses, there is no baptism like that of baths and wash-houses, no Lord's Supper to be compared to soup-kitchens, no means of sanctification like a plentiful supply of pure water, no method of quickening men in towns like that of having cemeteries out of town. We say not a word against these things. We rejoice in them. We wish them Godspeed. They are good *in themselves*, and good *in their influence*. But let us not estimate too highly the *religious* influence of these things. They may be, and be to the greatest possible extent, and leave men without spiritual joy and purity and hope. Men may live in the full possession of them, and be " dead while they live." They may have these advantages and " consume them upon their lusts." They are no substitutes for the Gospel. They are not necessarily connected with moral and religious blessing. And while distress and disease and discomfort may lead to some sin, sin produces a great deal more of distress and disease and discomfort. Then be not diverted from the great mission on which you are sent, and while ye attend to these things, attend also, and supremely, to the greater things of spiritual salvation. " Go and speak to the people all the words of this life."

In seeking the Christianization of the people, it is important that we should exactly understand, and be well assured of, the nature and necessity of our own spiritual agency. We should guard against the precipitance of *mere' zeal and fear*. It is said of a modern statesman (Lord Melbourne) that he was never alarmed except when he heard people say, " *Something must be done*." We must avoid the idea that there is *mystery or miracle* in the question. There is no great discovery to be made. We must not be *impatient*, supposing any sudden and surprising change is probable. That is not God's method. We must beware of attaching too much value to *institutional* and *instrumental* changes, as if the great cause of popular alienation from the Gospel lay in ecclesiastical buildings, ecclesiastical offices, or ecclesiastical economies. Above all must we not substitute the conversion of the Church to the world for the conversion of the world to the Church ; not fall into the terrific blunder of trying to remove unbelief and sin by denuding Christianity of its peculiar truths and peculiar sanctities. The work of the Gospel is not to change the wine into water, but the water into wine. The "earth" suffers dreadful loss when the "salt" no longer retains its "savour." What then must we do ? *Live, speak, act*—the words of life. Let each one do *his own work* in *his own sphere.* Let each one do it *quietly, earnestly, patiently ;* not vainly imagining or hoping for other powers and opportunities. *Your* part is to do what *you can,* little or much, and doing *that,* you will help, and must help, the great cause of the kingdom of God.

THE DEVIL IN CHURCH.

MARK i. 23—26 : *or*, LUKE iv. 33—36.—"*And there was in their synagogue a man with an unclean spirit; and he cried out, saying, Let us alone; what have we to do with Thee, Thou Jesus of Nazareth? art Thou come to destroy us? I know Thee, who Thou art, the Holy One of God. And Jesus rebuked him, saying, Hold thy peace, and come out of him. And when the unclean spirit had torn him, and cried with a loud voice, he came out of him.*"

IT is important, on some accounts, that the reader of the New Testament should know that the devils of whom we read as possessing men's bodies are not to be confounded with *the* Devil of whom we read as tempting men's souls. The terms applied to him are never used in the plural number of spiritual beings. It is a pity that the word "demons" is not employed in the Gospels to distinguish from him the wicked beings that were permitted to have such strange and hurtful power over men. It has been a great question among those who believe in the reality of these possessions, who these demons were? I shall not attempt to answer it. It is enough for my purpose that they were so Satanic in character and work, that to cast them out was to "cast out Satan;" that they are spoken of as spirits, as wicked spirits, as only seeking to injure and destroy those in whom they dwelt, and as dreading and deprecating the power of Christ; as doing the work and obeying the rule of the Devil proper. One of the most striking cases of demoniacal possession is in the text.

The New Testament gives us a fearful picture of the operations of demoniacal agency. Reading the Gospels, it almost seems as if the unseen, evil world had been let loose; as if the imprisoned demons had been let out for a holiday. A great, if not the greatest part of Christ's miracles consisted in the expulsion of demons. We find them in all kinds of subjects, modes, effects, and places. All things and beings seem perfectly indifferent to them. They were careless in whom they acted; good and bad, men and women, boys and girls, and even pigs, were their embodiments and victims. They were careless as to number; sometimes appearing alone, sometimes in company; now it is "a devil," now "devils;" now "seven," and now "a legion." All evils were alike to them, inflicting evil indiscriminately on mind and body; weakening, confusing, infuriating the one, and destroying or injuring the organs and functions of the other. And we find them in all kinds of places, sacred and profane, solitary and public, on the shore and on the plain, in streets and houses, and, in the text, *in a synagogue*. I think we may find the last scene exceedingly instructive and impressive, although Olshausen, the best of expositors, in his commentary, says of it, " a narrative we pass over as containing nothing remarkable."

I.

A Devil in Church.

For "synagogue" means *church*. Both words signify "assembly;" though both came, in course of time, by natural causes, to be applied to the buildings in which they met. In the New Testament, therefore, "synagogue" always designates the building. These assemblies, originating we know not when, and for which no formal provision was made under the law, representing the natural and moral, as distinguished from the arbitrary and ceremonial, were the real models of Christian Churches. Not the Temple and its services, but the synagogue and its general constitution and conduct and objects, were the types of the congregations established by the Apostles; a fact which, better than any, lays the axe to the root of ritualism and sacerdotalism. A synagogue was essentially, and for the time, a Church.

And this synagogue was *a Christian Church;* for the occasion, it was a Church. What is the essence of a Church? The teaching, the truth dispensed in it. Not the truth professed, much less the error; not the doctrines, however sound, that lie hid, or as good as hid, in Articles, and Homilies, and decisions of Courts; but the things constituting the matter and basis of the actual and regular teaching of the people, set before them as the material of their religious nourishment, their light, and strength, and comfort, as beings made to live the life and share the immortality of God; not the Prayer-book, even, if there be one, for that is a form, and a form of expression rather than instruction: but the living ministry, that which comes day after day from the lips, and souls, and lives of men, and which, to a great extent, forms the religious views, and guides the hearts and consciences of congregations. The clergy have often called themselves, and acted as, the Church. In a high and solemn sense, as having power over the mind to mould it, and as, when true, the organs and embodiments of the truth, they are the Church, much more importantly than in any way of official power or grace. "Like people, like priest." In this synagogue, and on this Sabbath, *Christ was the Preacher;* for "He entered into the synagogue and taught; and they were astonished at His doctrine."

In this synagogue was *a devil.* We find devils in strange places in the Bible. It is commonly believed that the "old serpent, the devil," was in the garden of of Eden, that the "murderer from the beginning," who "abode not in the truth," there plied his bloody trade of falsehood. Yes, even in Paradise he appeared upon the scene; perhaps abashed at first at the innocence of our first parents, and, as Milton says, looking "stupidly good," but succeeding, by deceiving Eve, in laying the foundation of his kingdom of darkness, and gaining "the power of death." We find Satan "among the sons of God, when they came to present themselves before the Lord," in the Book of Job. We find, in the vision of Micaiah, a "spirit" coming forth and standing before the Lord, and offering to persuade Ahab to go up to Ramoth-Gilead to be killed. And in the text a demon attends a lunatic to church.

The narrative suggests one thought, one which all

the other references I have made suggest; and one indeed which all that is said in the Bible of "the devil and his messengers" suggest,—their *infinite impudence*. Place and presence, scene and service, are nothing to them. Before the saints and the Saviour they are unabashed. If the arch-fiend tempted Christ, no wonder that his subordinates rebuked Him; if he attacked the Son of God directly to seduce Him, no wonder they attacked men in His presence to destroy them.

Devils go *where men are*, and wherever they are. They love to fish where fish are plentiful, though not regardless of private opportunities of work. As thieves love a crowd because there are most purses, devils love a crowd because there are most souls; and thieves would as soon have the crowd in the church as in the theatre.

It is hard to say whether this man *took the devil to church*, or *the devil took him*. Many have found one there, but this man was possessed before he went thither. I have no doubt there are more devils in churches than anywhere else, than on race-courses and in theatres. The devil is needed most there. He leaves men alone who are doing his work for him, tempting themselves, destroying themselves; and sends his finest forces where their pursuits and works are most opposed to his. He would keep men from churches if he could, except such as are "the synagogues of Satan," where he himself prescribes the ritual and dictates the doctrine, and inspires the preacher; but he accommodates men. He has no objection to accompany his subjects to church, if they wish to go. He can act the religious devil as well as the "unclean," and both together, the "angel of light" as well as of darkness.

But wherever he is, *he has but one purpose*. He is true to his character of "murderer," enemy of God and man. This poor man he maddened, and polluted, and, even when exorcised, he convulsed him; and though perhaps (but perhaps *not*) that work of his is stopped, he worketh still in the churches of the living God; he is there ever vigilant and active to inflict a greater madness, and to seek a far worse death; to cloud man's spirit, if not his mind; "to catch away that which is sown in his heart;" to make him a fool indeed, a fool to the heavenly wisdom which says, "Whoso findeth me findeth life, and shall obtain favour of the Lord; but he that sinneth against me wrongeth his own soul; all they that hate me love death."

In this view, how melancholy it is to think of the multitudes who every Sunday go to church (I include all places of worship), if not at the instigation, yet under the influence of evil spirits, all more or less mad. A *self-righteous* devil accompanies to "puff them up with pride," that they may "fall into his condemnation;" and they flatter themselves unctuously with the thought that God is somewhat to be congratulated for having worshippers so extremely proper. A *critical* devil attends others, whose object is not to receive good, but to detect evil; to quarrel with the faults of the doctrine, or the folly of the preacher. Some go, with satanic encouragement, to exhibit themselves, and some to observe others. These to spend a lazy hour, and those to meditate their worldly schemes, to "buy and sell in the temple;" while others, "having an unclean spirit," go to feed their lusts, "almost in all evil in the midst of the congregation." Thus "the lusts of the flesh and of the mind," "the lust of the eye and the pride of life," may all find scope and stimulus, under the ministry of "the god of this world," in "the church of the living God."

II.

The Devil's Creed.

"Jesus of Nazareth, art Thou come to destroy us? I know Thee who Thou art, the Holy One of God." No small or poor creed that. It takes in very exalted conceptions of the person, and mission, and destiny of Christ, the sanctity and speciality of His character and coming. It is very questionable whether at any time before Christ's death any of His followers advanced beyond them, and pretty certain that at that time none had advanced so far. This was not the only occasion on which demons acknowledged Christ as the Messiah, the Son and Servant of the Most High, the vindicator of His claims, and the destroyer of His enemies, and with a readiness and frankness peculiar to themselves. "Unclean spirits, when they saw Him, fell down before Him, and cried, saying, 'Thou art the Son of God.'" The evil spirits were the first to recognize His dignity.

This demon was *orthodox*. He was, as far as he went, "sound in the faith." According to the then opportunities of knowledge, he had clear and full conceptions of Jesus of Nazareth, and His work. The devils believe and tremble. We talk much of heresy, but there is not a devil in hell that is not orthodox. "The devils believe and tremble." That is more than many a man does who believes all the creed of Pope

Pius, or all the Thirty-Nine Articles (nicknamed the "forty stripes, save one"), or the whole of the Assembly's Catechism, or the Declaration of Faith and Order of the Congregational Union of England and Wales. The question, *what* we believe, important as it is, is much less important than how, why, and with what results we believe. A faith, though an exact copy of the thoughts of God, that is ours without our choice, without our spiritual sympathy, without any regulating and purifying power over our hearts and ways, is nothing. Such indeed is not a faith, but a creed, which may exist apart from faith, and may be a grievous obstacle to it, which may attend and encourage any amount of doing of lies, and "error" of the "ways." And yet there are cathedral properties where brothels may be founded, but not chapels; and yet there are clergymen who unblushingly avow that they prefer immoral men to dissenters; and yet in all sects there are those who would think less of a sinner than a misbeliever, and shrink more from a new theological opinion than an old atheistical vice. Orthodox devils!

Don't lay any stress on your having correct notions. I don't inquire what you have, but I repeat, it matters nothing if you are without "the faith which worketh by love." Wherever you got them, they have no more virtue *in you* than the accurate impressions of your bodily senses. Devils excelled apostles in Christ's days on earth, and I doubt not that now the miserable children of perdition could beat pastor or presbyter, priest or pope, in any theological examination.

And what this demon believed, this demon *confessed*. It was no secret creed, no hidden knowledge. He avowed Christ when Christ was little known. He made what we should call *a public profession* of his faith. Many of you are not doing it. You have a better faith than his, but you are silent. He confessed Christ, though a foe; you do not, though a friend. He confessed Christ, from fear; you do not, from love. He confessed Christ, though expecting only His wrath; you do not, though hoping in His mercy. How will you stand before Him who hath declared that He will, in the day of doom, be ashamed of all who are now ashamed of Him and His words?

His confession *was rejected.* "Jesus rebuked him, saying, Hold thy peace, and come out of him." Christ often commanded both men and devils not to proclaim Him. Luke iv. 41 :—" He suffered the devils not to speak, for they knew that He was Christ." It was a prudential course. But we can imagine a feeling of horror and loathing at the words of this "unclean spirit," this filthy fiend proclaiming Him as "the Holy One of God." At any rate, He forbade his speech, and ordered his departure. "Keep thy faith, and loose thy victim." Submission, not profession. And to how many might He say to-day, "Hold your peace, and loose your sins. I want not your fine words, give up your lusts; cease from evil: and while you are maddening yourselves and others, your orthodoxy is the worst of lies, your confession the worst of blasphemies."

III.

The Devil's Prayer in Church.

"And he cried out, saying, Let us alone; what have we to do with Thee, thou Jesus of Nazareth?" There were two properties of this prayer that should belong to all prayer, must to all real and effectual prayer. It was *earnest and social.* "He *cried out*, let *us* alone." It is possible to pray fervently and yet pray in vain. It is *what* we wish and *why*, not *how much;* not the *strength*, but the *character* of our desires, that determines the goodness of our prayers. It is the "fervent" prayer that "availeth much," but only "if we ask anything according to His will, He heareth us." And we may ask for others as well as for ourselves, and not acceptably. Christ describes the rich man "in torment" praying for his "father's house" and his five brethren. Benevolence is not religion; and we may pity others' miseries, especially if shared by ourselves, without loving God.

It was a devilish prayer, one suited to the offerer. "Let us alone, what have we to do with Thee?" There might be *fear* in this. On another occasion, demons said to him, "Art Thou come to torment us before the time?" "And they besought Him, that He would not command them to go out into the deep—the abyss." They knew that He was to "cast out the prince of this world," and to "destroy the works of the devil." They recognized in Him their future Judge. The "unclean spirit" felt abashed and afraid in presence of the Holy One. Men have prayed this prayer under the influence of fear. When Peter beheld the miraculous draught of fishes, he prayed, "*Depart from me, for I am a sinful man, O Lord.*" I say it is a devilish prayer. The devil has no objection to it. He inspires it. To separate the sinner from the Saviour, to breed distrust and dread of Christ in the sinner's heart, is his object. Let it be gained, and you are lost! "Woe be unto them when I depart from them!" The prayer which the Spirit of God breathes into us, is—" Leave me *not* alone; draw near to me, help me to come unto Thee, cast me not away from Thy presence, and take not thy Holy Spirit from me."

Not only fear, but *wickedness*, prompted this prayer. The demon wished not to be dislodged, wished to be allowed to go on tormenting and ruining this wretch. And so in the case of the Legion, they besought Him that He would not send them away out of the country, and that "He would suffer them to enter into the swine." They wished to do more mischief there. This *is* wickedness, pure wickedness, devilish wickedness, to ask Christ to permit a continuance of malicious mischief, to find "torment" in not being allowed to continue it. You may not be equal to this, but you may wish Christ to let you alone that you may sin, and not torment you by making you give up sins. The Gadarenes, whose unlawful property in swine He had destroyed, "prayed Him to depart out of their coasts;" and we read of wicked men who "say unto God, Depart from us, for we desire not the knowledge of thy ways." That is, not that they *say* it, but *do* it. Prayer is *desire*, and desire in deeds is as good prayer as desire in words, and, if actions speak louder than words, better. Men say to Christ, *so that He can hear*, "Leave us alone to sin," when they *do* sin, when they go into scenes of sin, when they quench thoughts and feelings that are against sin, when they avoid or oppose those who warn them of sin. This is prayer without the form of prayer; and it is *a devil's prayer;* a prayer the devil likes, and quickens; loves to listen to, and to see answered.

IV.

The Devil's Excommunication.

The Saviour rebuked him, and commanded him to come out of his victim; "and when the devil had thrown him in the midst, he came out of him, and hurt him not;" convulsed him even in leaving him, and doing as much harm as possible in his last momentary opportunity: as an evil-disposed outgoing tenant damages a house as much as may be, or as a defeated city or garrison fires the place before quitting it. But depart he must, however loth to do it; and he may not "hurt" him more, however he may convulse him.

What an expulsion! Before all the people—like a detected spiritual burglar, who has broken into a man! If a devil could blush, that poor maniac would have been well-nigh transfigured with shame. And by *a word* only. Well might the people be amazed and whisper to each other, "What a word is this! for with authority and power He commandeth the unclean spirits, and they come out." This is the most wonderful and comforting of all Christ's miracles; no wonder the belief in this power lasted longest in the Church. The obedience of devils. Oh! it was much to work by words in the lower sphere of matter, to disturb the order of nature, and heal the sick, and raise the dead; it was more by words to awe and abash evil men, to expel the Jewish trafficker from His "Father's house," and prostrate the Roman soldiers sent to seize Him; but oh! it was far more: more in Him and more to us, to command the spirits thus. The Apostles sometimes failed: even when Christ was returning from the Mount of Transfiguration, they were being humbled at its base. They could not cast out the dumb and deaf spirit; the "kind" that "goeth not out but by prayer and fasting;" but Jesus "charged" him, and he withdrew. Let us rejoice in the Lord of spirits, and yet be afraid. It is true of Christ as God, and of power as knowledge: "Hell and destruction are before the Lord; how much more the hearts of the children of men!" But this expulsion was in vain. The demon "trembled," but did not repent. His presence there was malice; and he vented malice even in departing, sinned further while obeying Christ. No wonder. There is nothing more hardening than despair; and no place more hardening than a church. And so he went to his former haunts and former companions, perhaps to "spirits more wicked than himself," "seeking rest, and finding none," to "remain in the congregation of the dead."

And this came of his *orthodoxy*; for it was without fruit, and "faith without works is dead, being alone." And this came of his *prayer*, for it was without faith.

He "asked and had not, because he asked amiss, that he might consume it upon his lusts. And so will *your* faith fail, if it be allied with impurity, and disobedience, and malice, hateful passions, and hurtful lusts. And your prayer, if of selfishness or fear, will come to naught. Think not that you shall obtain anything of God. If He answer, it will be in His wrath.

Brethren. This expulsion was not alone. It was only a token and an act of that great separation of evil and good which is always going on, and will be perfected and perpetuated in the Day of Judgment. Then shall we "discern between the righteous and the wicked," who will be divided as tares and wheat, as sheep and goats, and go away into everlasting punishment or everlasting life. For the Son of Man "shall send forth His angels, and they shall gather out of His kingdom all things that offend, and them which do iniquity, and shall cast them into a furnace of fire," that fire "prepared for the devil and his angels." But there are separations *here*, when "men of corrupt minds" are "made manifest," are, in the name of the Lord Jesus Christ, "delivered unto Satan;" or when good men "withdraw from," and "have no fellowship with," the evil, and leave them to "their own company," to the congenial and assimilating intercourses of those "like-minded" with themselves. And there will be a separation at *death*, when the body returns to the earth, and the spirit unto God who gave it. The same graveyard, perhaps the same grave, contains the dust alike of the saint and the sinner; but how different the conditions, thoughts, and expectations of their souls in the unseen world, looking forward with exultant hope because their "redemption draweth nigh," or anticipating, with quivering terror, the coming of "the Holy One" to "torment" them. "And so I saw the wicked buried, who had come and gone from the place of the holy, and they were forgotten in the city where they had so done: this is also vanity." His life a crime; his religion a fraud; his death a doom. Well may his epitaph be, "Vanity."

www.ingramcontent.com/pod-product-compliance
Lightning Source LLC
Chambersburg PA
CBHW051732300426
44115CB00007B/527